Trader Vic
on
Commodities

Founded in 1807, John Wiley & Sons is the oldest independent publishing company in the United States. With offices in North America, Europe, Australia, and Asia, Wiley is globally committed to developing and marketing print and electronic products and services for our customers' professional and personal knowledge and understanding.

The Wiley Trading series features books by traders who have survived the market's ever changing temperament and have prospered—some by reinventing systems, others by getting back to basics. Whether a novice trader, professional, or somewhere in-between, these books will provide the advice and strategies needed to prosper today and well into the future.

For a list of available titles, visit our Web site at www.WileyFinance.com.

Trader Vic on Commodities

What's Unknown, Misunderstood, and Too Good to Be True

VICTOR SPERANDEO

John Wiley & Sons, Inc.

Published by John Wiley & Sons, Inc., Hoboken, New Jersey.
Published simultaneously in Canada.

For general information on our other products and services or for technical support, please contact our Customer Care Department within the United States at (800) 762-2974, outside the United States at (317) 572-3993 or fax (317) 572-4002.

Wiley also publishes its books in a variety of electronic formats. Some content that appears in print may not be available in electronic formats. For more information about Wiley products, visit our Web site at www.wiley.com.

Library of Congress Cataloging-in-Publication Data:

Sperandeo, Victor.
    Trader Vic on commodities : what's unknown, misunderstood, and too good to be true / Victor Sperandeo.
        p.   cm.
    Includes index.
    ISBN 978-0-470-10212-1 (cloth)
    1. Commodity exchanges.   2. Commodity futures.   3. Speculation.   I. Title.
    HG6046.S636 2008
    332.64′4–dc22

                                                                                    2007029957

Printed in the United States of America.

10 9 8 7 6 5 4 3 2 1

Here, as in *Trader Vic II: Principles of Professional Speculation*, I must thank Douglas Kent. If not for Doug, you would not be reading this book.

Doug's father Dick Kent and I started trading options for Filer Schmidt and Co. on the same day, back on January 2, 1968. We were good friends, and through him I met Doug, who has been working with me on and off since he was 16 years old.

Dick died in 2005. He and the late Norm Tandy were my best friends, partners, and associates through the 1970s, 1980s, and early 1990s.

I owe Doug in many ways, and he is truly one of the smartest people I have known (for pure IQ anyway; he likes to say he makes up for that with a lack of common sense). Maybe I've known him for too long, but "thanks" is not really enough.

Contents

Preface

W hen I was first approached to write a book on commodities, I was hesitant to sign on to the project. At the time, there was a lot of focus on the commodities markets by the media and the investment community. This was mainly due to skyrocketing demand for energy products and metals, particularly by India and China, while on the supply side the Environmental Protection Agency had restricted domestic drilling and mining. The war in Iraq, strikes in Nigeria, political upheaval in Venezuela, nuclear aspirations in Iran and North Korea, supply fears, and the constant threat of further terrorist activity had all combined to drive more and more money into the precious or industrial metals and energy sectors. Some of it was institutionally directed, but much of it was speculative in nature and driven by the public's fascinating habit of being the last one to jump in the pool, or in this case the final sucker to get into the pyramid scheme.

As is common during such periods, historical perspective was all but ignored. Newsletters and so-called experts who had for 20 years been predicting the upcoming bull market in gold or oil were suddenly crowing with their I-told-you-so attitudes. Meanwhile, their disciples and followers seemed oblivious to the fact that when it comes to commodities markets, if you make the same predictions over and over again you will eventually be correct—like a broken clock that shows the correct time twice a day. Unfortunately, those who had been foolish enough to follow their advice over the long-term were now only making back a fraction of the money and potential returns they had given up in the preceding decades, if they had any investment funds left at all.

Although potentially the commodities markets could sustain their gains for a long period of time, it seemed inevitable to me that when it came to the general public, more money would be lost on the way down than could possibly be made on the way up. This might seem to fly in the face of the fact that the commodity futures markets are by rule a cyclical business, but when you separate out the producers and large-size professional speculators, over time the public gets burned time and time again. Like the dot-com boom and bust, preceded by the biotech boom and bust, and the countless bubbles before that—all the way back to tulip bulbs—the pyramid scheme of commodities speculation would in the end leave a bitter taste in the mouths of many of those who got suckered in.

The more I thought about the idea of this book, however, the more it began to appeal to me. First of all, this book would give me the opportunity to explain in rather simple terms how these markets operated, in order to remove some of the *unknown* mystique and misunderstood uncertainty involved. The more educated the investment community can become, especially the small investors, the less likely it is that they will be taken in by less-than-reputable advisors peddling their newsletters or "win big" strategies. Second, I would be able to debunk some common myths about commodities and various trading programs. It never ceases to amaze me how the same ideas return time and time again, gaining favor for a short period until the losses pile up and "experts" burn through one list of clients, preparing to build a new one. If understood thoroughly, futures trading is not really that complicated—no more than Texas Hold'em. And it should be played in a similar fashion—bet on the hands statistically likely to win, or fold your losing hand as soon as possible. In fact, in almost every category commodities are actually easier to comprehend than options trading. Aside from the dangers of losing much more than the amount "invested" because of the margin rules and the incredible leverage commodity futures provide, they are quite simple to trade. For example:

- Short sales can be made without the necessity of borrowing that stock entails.
- Many markets can be traded 24 hours a day to some degree, due to common markets throughout the world and through the use of electronic marketplaces such as Globex.
- There is always a cash market to compare the futures price to, so unlike many equities, the market price must in most respects be tied to realistic forces and factors.
- From an individual's perspective, futures should be easy to comprehend. The price of a pound of sugar or a gallon of gasoline is something every person can relate to, while the compounded annual growth rate of a multinational corporation, or the year-over-year same-store sales for a chain of jewelry stores might be more difficult for average investors to wrap their minds around.
- Perhaps most importantly, futures trades are marked-to-the-market on a daily basis. When a position moves in your favor, you've made the money, whether you choose to close out the trade at that point or not. Likewise, losses are incurred immediately. This forces an investor in the futures market to constantly reevaluate positions and the rationale behind each of them. This eliminates the "I'll wait for it to come

back" mentality, which results in people winding up with accounts full of worthless penny stocks, good only for tax-loss sales at the end of the year.

- Commodities don't go bankrupt like some companies do. But because they are cyclical, you must adopt a long and short strategy to generate returns above T-bills. For example, corn was $0.80 a bushel in 1930, and as I write this is $3.68 a bushel. That's only a 2.0 percent compounded return in 77 years. In the last 37 years, corn has traded almost exclusively between $1.50 a bushel and $5.50 a bushel (except for a spot price spike in the mid-1900s), passing $2.50 75 percent of the time (see Figure P.1). Perhaps that is *fair value?*

Countless books could be written solely exploring the reasons *why* investors continue to return to strategies that fail time and time again, but I imagine the best works on that topic were first published long ago, in Charles Mackay's 1841 classic *Extraordinary Popular Delusions and the Madness of Crowds.* Anyone who intends to make a living (or simply to profit on a consistent basis) from the financial markets should make it a point to read, absorb, and understand that book.

For readers who have had enough of such trading strategies, I believe the second part of the book you are holding in your hands will be a true revelation. I have developed the Standard & Poor's Diversified Trends

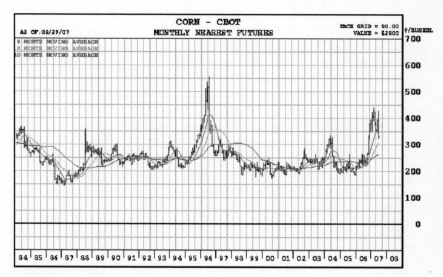

Figure P.1 CBOT corn 1980 to 2007.
Source: Used with permission of Barchart.com.

Indicator (S&P DTI) as a tool to capture price movement, premiums, and discounts in the commodity futures markets. It is a systematic rules-based approach to building a portfolio of commodities, rather than speculation in a single market. Moreover, it is designed to be complementary to other investments, with a negative correlation, or completely noncorrelated to other investment classes, producing alpha consistency (93 percent in 12 months) with low volatility (6 percent) and small drawdowns, rather than to produce outsized returns with higher volatility. "Too good to be true?" As I said, commodities are cyclical in nature, so my experience has taught me that the best goal is to capture as much of the major trends of each market as possible, while balancing that goal with a minimum of risk. Finding ways to remove the emotion and personal judgment from an investment strategy is also a crucial factor in long-term market profitability. The S&P Diversified Trends Indicator has accomplished these goals, in my view, more successfully than any other strategy I have ever encountered.

Whether you try to incorporate the S&P DTI into your investment strategy, or use it to develop your own trading ideas or programs, I believe you will find an understanding of the methods and philosophy behind it to be enlightening and educational. Armed with knowledge of what doesn't work, and introduced to a methodology that does, you will be better prepared to survive and thrive in the world of commodities.

Let me say with full disclosure that I don't sell the S&P DTI, but S&P will license it to anyone with enough capital to buy the exposure, in which case I do personally benefit. However, as all my former readers know, I *share* my observations that work, so that you may benefit also—a trading altruism of sorts, if you will. I try to provide what works, and if you don't want to use it directly, you can certainly use my example to construct your own (perhaps better) version. You take it from here.

I have been in this business for a long time, a lifetime. After 40 years of trading, I see things that others don't. Time and experience are excellent teachers.

I'll meet you electronically in the trading pits. Good luck!

Victor H. Sperandeo
Dallas, Texas

Acknowledgments

Work assumes the great part of a 24-hour period. My current business is not only about trading, but about working with people to accomplish a goal. In part, that goal focuses on introducing unique financial instruments that add alpha to the marketplace. In that side of the industry, the people *are* the business, and who you work with determines whether or not you are enjoying what you are doing.

Trading is about you—just yourself and a machine. It is much different than what I am doing now. There are no personalities, no outside emotions, no external character flaws, no problems that others create or bring with them. In that respect, trading is actually much simpler and clean-cut.

My personality is such that in interpersonal and business relationships, I weigh loyalty very heavily. Loyalty, honesty, and respect make up a powerful trinity. It might be the Italian in me—similar ideals can be found in the *Godfather* movies.

In addition, I look at the good and the bad in combination. I don't forget the good, ever. Many people who would look at me today alone, without combining the good and the bad, might tell you that I can be a problem. Just ask some of my venture capital partners. I can be seen as a bad administrator by some. Perhaps—we all have our own style, and mine is rather subtle. I believe that people who are dedicated to you are the primary cause of success for yourself and the company as a whole.

My conscious model for that opinion is Queen Elizabeth I.

King Henry VIII was nicknamed "Bluff King Hal." From a taxation point of view, he was called "Heister Hal" because he pulled off one of the biggest heists of all time: taking assets from the Catholic Church throughout England. However, stealing and high taxes did not get him the results he desired. When he died in 1547, Edward VI took the throne. Then in 1558, Henry's daughter Elizabeth took sole power, and ruled to 1603.

Elizabeth I defeated anyone who dared to attack England, and under her reign it became a world superpower. How did she do it? In the same way government accomplishes things today—with money. But she did it with *voluntary taxes!* As Charles Adams describes in his invaluable book *Fight, Flight, Fraud: The Story of Taxation* (Euro Dutch, 1982), the nation Elizabeth the Great helped build would dominate the world for 400 years. She chose intensely loyal and capable men as her assistants. Her tax policy was unprecedented—never before or since has a monarch behaved that way toward taxation. Not only were many taxes voluntary, but she made little effort to strictly enforce the tax laws and grants given to her. She decided she would simply be loved by her subjects, and accept whatever revenue they were willing to give her. She said, "To tax and to be loved is not given to man" (Adams, 1982).

When the all-mighty Spanish Armada challenged England, Liz turned to Parliament for funds, but none were available. She then turned to her people, as "her chiefest strength and safeguard was the loyal hearts and goodwill of her subjects." With the issue of writs—for ships, sailors, guns, and money—the needs were filled beyond expectation. The resulting defeat of the Armada ended Spanish world domination.

Incidentally, I have a significant interest in taxes and their effect on a nation. After all, I did co-author a 1,573-page book called *Crashmaker: A Federal Affaire*, in part to help show how important taxes are.

When I wrote my second book, *Trader Vic II: The Principles of Professional Speculation*, I dedicated it to the greatest male and female world leaders in history—Thomas Jefferson and Queen Elizabeth I. It was from Elizabeth that I learned the most about human nature, loyalty, and success. The United States Democrats, world socialists, communists, and dictators should think about this and try to learn something from her the way I have.

Therefore, in the spirit of all I have learned from Queen Elizabeth I, please allow me to properly thank and show my appreciation for some of my associates who work with me directly and indirectly within my companies. To keep things simple, I will list them in the order of how long I have known them.

Kelley Price and Rick Meadows are good friends, and they serve as the administrators to our funds. Their firm, Price Meadows Inc., was voted in the top five Hedge Fund Administrators in the United States last year. I have known them since the early 1980s. They are a unique team, as they have been partners since 1982 and I believe still operate on a handshake—my kind of men.

Doug Kent knows more of what I do than anyone else, and started with me in the mid-1980s. I have already spoken of him elsewhere in this book.

Adam Watts wrote me a letter in 1992 wanting to become a trading trainee. I was getting hundreds of such letters each month at the time. Adam FedExed his letter to me, saying that his father told him I would never respond. Fast forward to present day, and Adam is a partner in our companies and very critical to our current success. He has worked in varying roles but currently writes all of the firm's computer programs, along with his father (who is a true NASA rocket scientist). No one who deals with Adam, including some of the biggest firms in Wall Street, does not think highly of him. A portfolio-testing program he wrote is world class, and can mix assets in such a way that you can get portfolio mixes of the data bank back to 1961 instantly, and in any time frame. This is better than any other I have known. Adam was 19 when he wrote me, and has worked with me since 1994. He is an all-around asset and does much more than I have space to mention.

Cal Donsky is our outside counsel and a limited partner in multiple firms. We met when I moved to Dallas and lived in the Stoneleigh Hotel— also known as Heartbreak Hotel, as most of the people living there were going through divorces. I met some of my best friends there in August 1994. Cal is very conservative and careful. I thank him for all of the help and advice he has given me and the firm.

Brad White and I have known each other since the mid-1990s. He is a partner and has been responsible for sales of our products. He is a good friend, and aside from his loyalty and friendship he also brought in the connection with Standard & Poor's. On his own initiative, he called Standard & Poor's and suggested they look at our DTI concept. To my knowledge, this was the first time that company went into a joint venture on a product it did not develop. Brad is unique in many ways. If he targets a goal, he will get it done—he is the best in sales I have ever met, and he knows what I do *cold*.

Fred Magnamini is our director of derivative products and was trained by Brad in sales. He is a very good relationship builder, extremely professional, and someone I think highly of. Derivatives are a tough business to learn, and he has learned it very well. To his credit, he got to service Nomura International PLC's Ingo Heinen, who is one of the smartest derivatives men in the business and their director of equity and fund derivatives. Ingo is someone who is really a math professor, but who looks like a professional athlete. I would be hard-pressed to not mention him in the world of derivative all-stars. It says a lot that Fred has become so skilled in the derivatives world in only three years, and finds himself on a level to do business with Ingo.

Jason Schmidt is our chief in-house counsel. I never knew how important a lawyer could be until I met Jason. Let me say, I could not be without him! His turnaround time is amazing. I am lucky to have Jason as part of my family.

Nilson Lopes joined forces under Brad, as a future Fred, and he is on his way. Nilson is a very hard worker and a gentleman. Originally from Brazil, he is fluent in Portuguese and will cover South America to spread the ideas we offer.

Ashley Lane recently started with us and is working under Jason Schmidt. She has expressed a deep interest in learning all there is to know, including derivatives.

I also want to thank all of my limited partners, my venture capital partners like Steven Chrust and Ron Schreiber, and all my friends for their trust and patience in this adventure. I promise never to bother you again!

Last, but not least, let me mention Marian Petrie. Marian has worked as my chief assistant for more than three years. All I can say is I simply cannot live without her. Of all the women I have had in this capacity—trading, computers, accuracy, talent, brains, (not to mention beauty)—she is the best of the best all-around. Louise Gunn, Dena Mahoney, Desire LaCharite were my past right hands and they all had great talents in some areas—they are remembered fondly by me. But Marian is the cream of the crop.

I could go on and on in this section of the book, but if I go outside the companies, we might need to make this book a two-volume set! So please forgive me in advance if you are not mentioned here, as I had to put some guidelines and limits on how long to make these acknowledgments. Many other people have contributed to help present my firm in a positive light.

V.H.S.

Trader Vic
on
Commodities

CHAPTER 1

The Basics

S ometimes something that seems convoluted and meaningless will actually hold within it some very deep or profound meaning. Take, as an example, a personal favorite of mine—a quote from Donald Rumsfeld, former U.S. secretary of defense. At a Department of Defense news briefing on February 12, 2002, he said: "As we know, there are known knowns. There are things we know we know. We also know there are known unknowns. That is to say, we know there are some things we do not know. There are also unknown knowns, the ones we did not know we know."

If that sounds confusing to you, go back and read it again, for it is worth taking the time to understand the grand design of what he said. We also added a final category: unknown unknowns, which are the things we did not know that we do not know. Those classifications are not just valid as the keys to military victory, they are also the keys to trading successfully! And as Satyajit Das wrote in *Traders Guns and Money* (Prentice Hall, 2006)—a highly recommended book—these are also the keys to the derivatives world. I imagine they are equally applicable in almost any complex intellectual or financial universe!

More than anything, the most important aspect of translating Rumsfeld's categories into successful trading is to realize the truth inherent in his statements, especially that there are unknown unknowns. It is impossible to know everything, to have all the information in the universe. Doing all you can to minimize the effect of those unknown unknowns—partially by simply acknowledging that they exist—can be the difference between a winning trade and a losing one.

BREAKING IT DOWN

You drink coffee each morning, eat your cornflakes and enjoy a glass of orange juice, take a shower with water running through copper pipes, put gas in your car, and head off to work. Each one of those actions involves a specific commodity, all of which happen to be traded as commodity futures on one of the major U.S. commodity exchanges. But the reason those commodity futures exist is not because you use the physical item (not directly anyway). Perhaps the best way to understand the commodities markets is to know why they exist in the first place: *Commodity futures were created not to make you rich, nor for you to trade them, but rather to allow the producers of the commodity to hedge their risk.*

Now please understand this next important point, as for almost everyone it is an unknown unknown: *They* pay you *to take this risk!* That is correct: The producers and hedgers pay you! That may sound like some late-night television infomercial sales line (usually followed by "But wait, there's more!"), but it happens to be true. The premiums and discounts of commodity futures are, in effect, payments to speculators to entice them to buy and sell the contracts, generally speaking. This is similar to the way you ask insurance companies to take on the risk of you having an accident—by paying them insurance premiums.

Really, the concept should not be all that surprising, when you consider that commodity futures are simply another major investment vehicle. Many stocks offer dividends, and bonds have their coupon. So why would commodity futures be any different?

The similarities don't stop there. Just as a portfolio of bonds and notes will have an overall yield, a portfolio of long and short futures creates a yield, as long as you follow the trends. This is explained in detail in later chapters, but it can be proven. The primary key is to follow the trends properly and to build a balanced portfolio of commodities. I can think of no better way than using the S&P Diversified Trends Indicator (DTI) as a method for both.

The S&P DTI is deterministic, not stochastic. That is, it is fundamentally driven. It has a better 12-month win ratio than the Lehman Agg, when combined with T-bills (i.e., total return). It is not a magic formula and it was not optimized, curve-fitted, or data mined. Any system or method based on optimization will fail in the long run. This is because markets change and evolve, they do not remain constant. So if you structure a system based solely on the past, it cannot survive the future.

The second important basic to understand about commodity futures is that no cash capital is required to buy or sell futures. Only collateral is needed. This concept is mostly misunderstood. Therefore, you can use stocks, bonds, T-bills, or many other liquid assets to own a position in futures. It is the ability to overlay your futures portfolio over the other assets that creates additional alpha and increased returns.

As the word implies, *futures* settle at a future date for cash or via delivery. However, the stories of people having a boxcar full of corn delivered to their front yard are nothing but fantasy these days. Unless you *want* to take delivery of a particular commodity, because you are an industrial or commercial purchaser or have some other legitimate need, the delivery process can be stopped far in advance (although there is a cost involved). Still, all of that can be avoided simply by rolling out of a futures contract into a later one before first notice day.

The reason for the collateral requirement is simply because your bank or broker cannot take you at your word that you will pay up if you lose. Think of placing a bet on a football game with a bookie. You only need call him up, place a bet, and it is done. If you lose, you *have* to pay. Otherwise, instead of the SEC or CFTC knocking on your door, you'll find a big man named Buster asking you for the cash. You'll soon learn he is far more of a problem than the government, bank, or broker you would owe the money to if you were trading commodity futures.

Futures contracts are created if enough volume and open interest in what is being hedged can be generated, and if a ready supply of the specific commodity in a consistent condition can be assured. A diamond contract would be problematic, for example, as diamonds are of such individual quality and value. The underlying commodity must also be *fungible*, and settled for cash.

Futures are contracts that discuss the terms of maturity, in addition to the specifics of what you are buying and selling, while forwards are futures without a standard maturity date. For the purposes of this book and the S&P DTI in general, we will be discussing futures contracts, but I think it is important to understand that forwards are a similar investment vehicle and can be used in some of the same ways.

Futures contracts are made to fix a certain value. A Comex gold futures contract in the United States is based on 100 ounces of 99.9 percent pure gold. Therefore, if gold were trading at $650 per ounce, the total contract value is $65,000 (although the margin or collateral one needs to put up to trade that contract is a small percentage of that). If the contract were for 1,000 ounces of gold, it would be worth $650,000, and would be too large to attract as much public interest as a $65,000 contract, for obvious reasons. It is for the same reasons that stocks go through stock splits—to keep values at a manageable and attractive level for investors, so the minimum investment does not grow to a size that causes people to consider other investment choices merely on that basis.

EVERYBODY WANTS SOME

Recently, there has been a tremendous resurgence in interest in commodities. This seems perfectly natural, considering the rise in prices seen in the energy, precious metals, and industrial metals sectors. Commodities as a whole are experiencing a new up cycle. An examination of the major factors contributing to these price increases suggests they are not short-lived.

The first, and most acknowledged, cause behind the commodity price increases is strengthening global demand. World populations continue to expand, in some cases at a rapid pace. The industrialization in China and India has greatly increased the need for energy and industrial products, while the supply remains limited. The formation of the European Union to a lesser extent has also caused increased demand, as a stronger economic force leads to more growth, as opposed to a number of weaker, less-efficient countries.

Growth is not limited to China and India, of course. Throughout the world, demand for physical commodities is growing. Thailand, Indonesia, Brazil, Argentina, and all around the globe, a growing number of people in increasingly modern economies outbid each other for the limited supply of materials. By definition, increasing demand, combined with supply that is either static or increasing at a slower rate, equals higher prices.

This leads us into the second reason for the new surge in commodity prices, from the supply side: the environmental movement. This is very misunderstood, and rarely talked about in this context. A theme I have suggested at times is, "Buy what you have to dig, sell what you have to grow," although lately it seems more like the answer is simply to buy everything, as long as your timing is right.

Digging has become virtually impossible during the current global fascination with environmentalism. The environmental impact of any new mining or drilling operation is more scrutinized than ever before. Even when new supplies of oil or other natural resources are located, the political and environmental hoops that industry must jump through in order to get permission to access those supplies are not only timely and complicated, but also expensive. This increases the cost of any such operation, which means those supplies cannot be profitably utilized until process have increased to higher levels. This has a tendency to become a self-fulfilling prophecy, as without those new reserves, supplies dry up and drive those prices higher.

At the same time, the land that would normally be used to grow edible crops is allocated more and more to government-sponsored biofuel projects of questionable scientific value, which only makes food supplies even more scarce. Ethanol is a perfect example—any increase in the fuel supply by the use of ethanol in motor fuels is arguably offset by lowered fuel efficiency, so we wind up with higher fuel costs and higher grain costs. This, combined with changing weather patterns, leaves the global food supply in occasionally precarious situations. The markets remain jittery, as they never know what could happen next. Often, the threats to the food supply are unexpected, such as the recent problems with pollinating fruits and vegetables caused by a sudden drop in the honeybee population.

Global instability keeps all the commodities markets on edge. A sudden storm, a plague of insects, a weather-related disaster, or a large terrorist attack could have lasting ramifications on the supply side of the equation. This isn't limited to the threat of a strike on the Saudi oil fields or other energy infrastructure. The global food supplies remain attractive terrorist targets, and in many cases they are relatively unprotected. Whether in the form of a biological, chemical, or radioactive event, or simply a strike at processing or distribution systems, the fact remains that in today's global environment market nervousness in all commodities sectors means increased volatility, which also means generally higher prices. These fears also create the desire for larger government stockpiles, which draws supply away from the open market. At the same time, those larger stockpiles are often no source of comfort to the markets, because they themselves appear to be attractive targets to sabotage, and because the timing and quantity of any release from the stockpiles is an unknown—in this case a known unknown.

Another cause of rising prices is global aging of the world's population. The older the population becomes, the more money needs to be committed to health care, pensions, or programs like Social Security. The only way for younger workers to pay for the older generations is for the government to inflate the world into more revenue. This "solves" many problems, including the deficit. Did you ever wonder why the market seems not to care about budget deficits? If the United States has a real $10 trillion debt (taking a conservative accounting of contingent liabilities), and it has a $300 billion annual budget deficit with a 3 percent annual inflation rate, it comes out to a wash; 3 percent of $10 trillion is $300 billion. Too good to be true!

The situation is the same with the trade deficit. Look at the whole, not the incremental monthly increases. You also need to consider capital outflows, which is a very misunderstood concept. If the United States is investing in India and China, then money is flowing out. If foreign countries are receiving dollars, they use that money to buy U.S. assets or U.S. Treasuries. This finances our deficits.

What could potentially cause all of this to change? Lower interest rates, a weaker U.S. government, and lower energy prices (which would result in less inflation). These situations would have to remain in place for a long period of time, without additional economic growth from the stimulus of lower interest rates and lower energy prices. This seems highly unlikely. If you are investing in the stocks of emerging nations, in effect you are investing with the big users of commodities. The net result is that you need to own commodities. The question that you are left with is not *if* you should, but *how* you should!

BUY AND SELL, OR BUY AND HOLD?

With the increased volatility in the commodities markets, the surge in interest, and the generally higher prices in everything from crude oil to copper to cocoa, it seems clear that you should desire at least some exposure to commodities. But there is a major difference between owning commodities, trading commodities, or profitably investing in commodities. And they do not have to be mutually exclusive.

The first option is simply to *own commodities*. There would be various ways of accomplishing this, depending on how you wanted to go about it and how diversified you wanted the commodities exposure to be. The most direct method would be to purchase physical stores of commodities, from gold coins to bales of copper wire. This method has major drawbacks. It allows little or no leverage, requires sizable movement and storage costs if you buy in bulk, and—most importantly—there is the aging process to contend with. If you purchase freight-loads of grain or herds of livestock, those assets can only be held for so long before they either spoil or have to be slaughtered.

The next option would be to purchase futures contracts on any number of commodities, in the hope that they increase in cost. Even with large capital behind you, this seems to be a cumbersome and dangerous method. Exactly how many contracts do you purchase, and of what commodity and what delivery date? What if your timing is off, and the markets sustain a sharp correction for a month or two? With the leverage futures that contracts provide, can you afford such a price decline without allowing it to swallow all of your investment funds? What if you don't buy the market that experiences the greatest price increase, but do purchase the biggest loser?

This leaves a third option for owning commodities: the purchase of a long-only commodities index such as the S&P GSCI. Whether accomplished by purchasing the futures on the index with trade on the Chicago

Mercantile Exchange, or an ETF or fund developed to track the index, at least this option allows the investor some diversification regardless of the amount of funds invested. However, by the nature of its design the S&P GSCI is heavily weighted toward the energies, so if that sector experiences a decline in prices you could still see a negative return even if other sectors experience robust price increases. More troubling, with the increased volatility in the commodities markets at the present time, the danger of a sharp price decline in any given market in the form of a correction in a bull market still looms. Despite the diversification, the S&P GSCI and other long-only commodity indexes are meant to profit only when markets continue upward price movement.

The second commodities strategy is *trading commodities*. This is the method that most likely offers the greatest potential return, but also a good deal of risk. It also requires an investment of time, energy, study, and emotional discipline, in addition to the monetary aspect. However, there are a number of strategies that can give the commodities trader an edge over the general market, maximizing return while limiting losses. I have attempted to discuss some of those ideas in Chapters 2 through 4. Chapter 2 explains my theories on how to limit your losses in commodities. Chapter 3 discusses some of the more common indicators used on commodity trading, and potential pitfalls they may carry. Chapter 4 gives a refresher course in the 2B rule, which I first introduced in my book *Methods of a Wall Street Master*. It remains a powerful tool to identifying potential changes in trend, combining limited losses with the possibility of large profits. Direct trading and speculating in commodities is not for everyone, but if you develop the necessary skills, it can be a rewarding endeavor. In addition, please realize that regardless of how deeply you become involved with trading commodities, your overall portfolio will be just as enhanced by investing in commodities as people who do not trade the markets directly.

That is the last of the three strategies: *investing in commodities*. Without question, in my opinion the most attractive way to do so is through the use of the Standard & Poor's Diversified Trends Indicator (S&P DTI). This vehicle not only offers you a fully diversified portfolio of futures that is equally weighted between financials and commodities, but by its design as a long-short index-like strategy it allows you to profit from both sides of the market, and often obtain hedged interrelated positions. As a supplemental vehicle, the Standard & Poor's Commodity Trends Indicator (S&P CTI), offers investors the same methodology but without the exposure to the financial futures. Either way, the S&P DTI and S&P CTI can become an additional asset class within a typical investment portfolio, whether or not you speculate in commodities as an overlay. They offer the ability to lower your overall portfolio volatility without sacrificing return, whether used in combination with stocks, bonds, or both.

All strategies have risks large and small, and nobody should invest in any program or product without a complete understanding of the risks involved.

So let us move on to the main focus points of this book, and study them one at a time: first, *trading* commodities (especially losing properly); and then, *investing* in commodities through the S&P DTI.

CHAPTER 2

You Can't Win Them All

L osses are part of the trading business. Even if you do everything right every time, there will be occasions when the market moves against you for an unforeseen reason. More importantly, if you are trading properly, you should find yourself able to lose more often than win and still remain profitable overall. Learning to accept, deal with, and minimize losses is the most important factor in determining your success as a trader.

WHY MOST TRADERS LOSE

Individual losses can happen for any number of reasons, but my years of experience have taught me there are three major causes a trader loses on a consistent basis. Please read my first book, *Methods of a Wall Street Master*, if you want a more detailed and useful list of hard and fast trading rules that you need to apply to your trading style. Of course, everyone is an individual and has his or her own strengths and weaknesses, but all traders share similar patterns and experience the same potential pitfalls.

In the commodity futures markets, there are three main causes of traders losing:

1. *Leverage.* Minimum margin on a commodity futures contract is about 5 percent of the total contract value in most instances. What inexperienced traders will do is divide their bank book by the margin and buy the most contracts they can. About 5 percent later, they are borrowing

money from their relatives to eat. You have to be sufficiently capital-
ized to trade successfully. Even if everything is lined up in your favor,
both the fundamentals and the technicals, all it takes is a single unforeseen event to change everything.

2. *Gambling* (or swinging for the fences). This is a corollary to the first
   reason. Gamblers try to get rich on one single trade, instead of planning
   to achieve more consistent but reasonable returns. Balanced diversification is as important in the commodity futures markets as in any other
   type of investment. We all hope to see a trade turn into a home run, but
   not many do, and basing your decisions on hope is a quick ride to the
   poorhouse—or worse.

3. *Cutting losses.* One of the first rules I mention when it comes to trading
   is to cut your losses and let your profits run. Like Kenny Rogers sang in
   "The Gambler": "You've got to know when to hold 'em, and know when
   to fold 'em." Have a specific stop loss on any trade before you enter into
   it, so you know how much you are willing to risk. When the reasons for
   the trade no longer hold true, get out. And if you are not profitable in
   the trade on the first day, close the position. You can always get back
   in the next day if you determine a new trade is desirable.

If you can learn to avoid the pitfalls these three mistakes will cause
you, you are well on your way to joining the ranks of successful commodity
futures traders and investors.

HOW TO LOSE PROPERLY

Since I live in Texas, and have played poker since I was 15, allow me to
draw an analogy between trading commodity futures and playing Texas
Hold'em. In both instances, the key to success is not how you win, but how
you lose. You win by losing—a lot of times, but in very small amounts.

Although it has gained wide popularity in the last five years, I suppose
some readers have not yet learned how to play Texas Hold'em, so I will
briefly describe the way the cards are dealt. Initially, two cards are dealt
face-down to each player. Those are the only cards you receive—the rest of
the cards in the hand are dealt as community cards. There are also antes—
called *blinds*—which are forced bets on each hand. These will become
losses on any hand you fold on, but they are small and limited. The *big
blind* and *small blind* are generally 1 percent and 0.5 percent respectively
per pot, with the dealer betting 1 percent and the first bettor 0.5 percent.

After you receive your two cards, there is a round of betting. Then
three cards are dealt face up. These are known as *the flop*, and they are

universal to all players. A round of betting follows, and then another card is dealt face up next to the three up cards (*the turn*). Another round of betting takes place before the fifth and final up card is dealt (*the river*). A final round of betting takes place before the cards are exposed and a winner takes the pot. Your hand is the best possible hand you can make using five of the seven cards (your two and five up cards).

The best way to win in Texas Hold'em is to only bet on good cards. If you're dealt two high cards (9s to aces), or two cards of the same suit from which you can possibly build a flush, you can play the hand out unless the betting gets too active, or unless the cards facing up do not fit well with your down cards. Obviously, a pair is a very strong hand to start with, as well. If you have anything else, fold immediately and be patient. Don't try to make something out of nothing. Cut your losses and wait for the next hand, unless you intend to bluff.

Now here is the rub: When you begin to play, you will find yourself focused solely on *your cards* and what you have, not what the others have. Thereby, you will not think about the whole picture of what is going on; you will be ignoring both the *known unknowns* and the *unknown unknowns*.

For example, you're at the table with a $10,000 bankroll. Let's say you are dealt two kings, which is the second-highest hand you can start with (the highest being two aces). You go ahead and bet 10 percent of your money ($1,000), driving out a few weak hands immediately. The flop is dealt, revealing a king of clubs, 3 of hearts, and 6 of spades. Now you've got three of a kind, which is even better. You go ahead and bet another 15 percent ($1,350).

When 8 of hearts is dealt as the turn, you are focused on your *trip kings* (poker lingo for three kings—a sure winner in your mind at this point) and bet 20 percent (another $1,530). No one else is betting or raising (they don't have to, because you are doing it for them), but to your delight, two players are calling your sizable bets; you don't think to ask yourself why. Then the river is dealt as the 2 of hearts. On the table we now have:

king of clubs   3 of hearts   6 of spades   8 of hearts   2 of hearts

You now go *all in* with the rest of your cash (or $6,120) and are very excited, as you can't wait to collect—until one player turns up a four of clubs and a five of spades—a straight. You lose! To top it off, the other player turns up a jack of hearts and a ten of hearts—a flush. You both lose!

How could this happen? You had three of a kind, a powerful hand considering the cards on the table. Yet you lost, and lost BIG, because you did not know what someone else had. You did not notice the three supposedly unimportant hearts, you did not notice the potential straight—you cared only about your strong hand.

This is what all novices do in both the markets and poker. They take a long position in soybeans and the market goes up slightly. But they don't notice corn and wheat starting to decline, or the fact that soybeans are closing in the lower half of the range two days in a row. Instead, they add to their winner, until somewhere in the world a government has decided to subsidize farmer's crops for the grains. Countless additional acres will be planted. When it's announced, soybeans are down the limit. The novice investors lose.

The key is focusing on what is going on elsewhere, not only on your position.

Then, of course, the sister trade is that you buy gold and it goes down. Instead of selling your position when you reach your predetermined mental stop price, you buy more. You keep buying because you know it's going up again. Eventually, the trade blows you away as gold keeps going down, and you're busted. So you lose because something changed—an unknown—and you had too much emotional desire built into a win. You were unable to adapt, or to stick to the trading disciplines you knew could help ensure your long-term success. In effect, your lack of emotional discipline was itself an unknown unknown. (For a thorough discussion of emotional discipline in trading and investing, see Part II of my first book, *Trader Vic—Methods of a Wall Street Master*, published by John Wiley & Sons, 1991.)

THROW IN YOUR HAND

The key to successful losing, if you'll allow for the slight contradiction in terms, is to be willing to take a loss whenever necessary, instead of trying to figure out how to turn a loser into a winner. The idea is to lose, but lose small; fold your bad hands. To be a superior poker player in Texas Hold'em you must figure out what the other players have and play your cards according to that deduction. Do not go *all in* unless you are willing to go bust based on the first two cards. My suggestion: You can consider going all in with two aces or two kings or ace and king, depending on the circumstances—nothing else! This way if you lose you will still have some chips. After all, you can't win unless you stay in the game. If you want to roll the dice on a bad hand, you may as well put your money on the craps table or the roulette wheel.

The way you deduce what the players have is by the size of their bet. Yes, bullying is part of the game too, but two things should be remembered in that regard:

1. Bluffing is rare, and only occurs about 5 percent of the time.
2. You can input the fact that a particular player has a tendency to bluff into your deduction, and look for "tells" that help you determine when this is the case.

In general, you can deduce the strength of the players' hands solely by how they bet. In a $5,000 table stakes game, if a player bets $1,000 on the deal, he has high cards or a high pair. If he then bets $2,000 on the flop, he has three of a kind—*trips*.

Similarly, if the markets go up in a strong way, it is the players (or in this case, the traders) telling you that the market has strong reasons! "The bet is big." This is especially true if the market is rallying on good news. The market or future is talking to you—listen! Don't look at your position as a wish or hope, base the trade on what is happening. Your position has nothing to do with the future. Play like a pro in poker—fold 'em on nothing, or sell if you reach a predetermined small loss. You can't enjoy a winner if you've been knocked out of the game.

The markets are strong or weak for a reason, but you may not know why—a known unknown. Either way, the market is giving you information, it is your job to pay attention to everything it is saying, and to notice what it isn't saying.

TRADES APPEAR EVERYWHERE IN LIFE

Having lived in the northeast for most of my life, you might wonder why I chose to move to Texas in the first place. The reasons are simple: First and foremost, Texas has no state income taxes! That would be reason enough in some cases, but there are other attractions here, as wellw. For example, the people are polite and friendly, especially the southern women. But one must be careful; Texas has the best of everything, and that includes gold diggers. They are among the best in the world in Texas. There is even a popular novel out now entitled *The Dallas Women's Guide to Gold-Digging with Pride* (J.C. Conklin, Random House, 2007).

At one time, one of my favorite restaurants in the Uptown Dallas area was Star Canyon. It has since closed, a fate that many restaurants in the city suffer as tastes and fashions change. One evening, I was sitting at the bar in Star Canyon and a woman seated nearby began to speak to me with interest. In New York, she would probably have been considered a 9, but down here in Texas the scale is a bit more difficult; she was more like a $7^{1}/_{2}$. I quickly learned her name was Mary Lou, and we started a casual conversation as she moved into the seat next to mine. After a few minutes, the maitre'd came over and discreetly whispered in my ear, "Bob would like to see you in the washroom immediately, sir." (Bob is a gentleman I know pretty well.) I excused myself and went to the men's room, where I found Bob waiting for me by the sinks. He said, "Victor, I had to warn you; you are sitting at the bar talking to the Bubonic Plague."

"Tell me what you mean," I replied.

"She's a pro. She picks men up at the bar, has sex with them, and then claims she is pregnant. She'll say she wants $50,000 or else she will sue for child support."

"How does she get away with it?" I asked.

"Well," Bob explained, "the scam is, she goes to her doctor, who is legit, and then they send out for DNA tests. She partners with a guy at the lab her doctor uses, and for a 25 percent cut he gives her the results she wants. If suspicions are ever raised or the real test results are ever discovered, he can just claim it was a lab error or a contaminated sample!"

Naturally, I thanked him and made a quick exit out of the bar. Cut your losses and let your profits run! As we've already covered multiple times in this book, only bet when you have a strong hand, and pay attention to what the other players might have. My king and queen looked strong, but it had suddenly become clear she was holding a pair of aces. Oh, by the way, as it turned out, Bob knew enough to warn me because he had lost the $50,000 on a "prior poker hand" so to speak. Fortunately, eventually word got around, the scam became public knowledge, and the temptress was out of business.

CHAPTER 3

Indicators and Tools

There are countless tools and indicators one can use when trading commodity futures, and many of them can be applied to equities or other investment vehicles—especially the technical ones. Moving averages, one of the most popular technical indicators, are a major basis of the entire S&P DTI design. As a supplement to the price charts and chart patterns, I have always found many of the common indicators to be valuable methods of confirming or overriding trades I was considering getting into (or out of). Obviously, I must believe indicators have value, since without them the S&P DTI would not exist at all! Allow me to touch on a few of the other most useful tools, and point out some of the positives and negatives in their implementation.

RELATIVE STRENGTH

Robert Rhea first wrote on relative strength in *Barron's* in 1933. Rhea was the greatest Dow theorist ever, and was one of the best advisors in the world, writing a newsletter every two weeks. In essence, the theory behind relative strength is, the stronger an object is the better, while the weaker it is, the worse. William O'Neil, in his books, proves this concept works for stocks. Next to following trends, Relative strength is the best money maker in the pits. For stocks you generally use a relative strength, which compares the stock in question either to a benchmark index or to a master group of other stocks. For commodities, you would use the relative

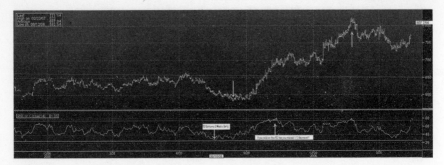

FIGURE 3.1   Two-year chart of July 2007 CBOT soybeans.
Source: © 2007 Bloomberg L.P. All rights reserved. Reprinted with permission.

strength index (RSI), which compares the magnitude of gains over a given period with the magnitude of losses. Either way, it can be a valuable measurement of the strength of an object.

If you look at Figure 3.1, a two-year chart of soybeans with an RSI chart beneath it, you'll see the relationship between the commodity price and the RSI. Take particular note of how, while the RSI can indicate a potential top or bottom, the overbought or oversold condition does not in and of itself mean a change in trend.

Like stochastics or oscillators, relative strength can be used as an indicator of overbought or oversold conditions in any given commodity market. However, overbought/oversold indicators should *never* be used as a primary tool. Certainly they are valuable, but only a secondary method to help determine if the trend is changing. Overbought/oversold is never to be viewed as an indicator first, or as a reason to initiate a position. The most violent up or down moves in markets can take place at the end of a trend, when the market is already extended and overbought or oversold. Trying to pick the top or bottom with these tools is akin to financial suicide or Russian roulette with five bullets. Believe me, the markets can remain overbought or oversold a lot longer than you can remain solvent. If the trend is turning and you have an overbought futures position—good—short it, but not until the trend has already started to turn down or not until you have a major technical reason to believe the trend has changed.

TREND FOLLOWING VERSUS MOMENTUM

Recently, several different strategies have emerged that attempt to use momentum as a basis of commodities trading. When applied to active indexes, momentum trading is a technique that relies on a comparison of prolonged or major shifts in price momentum (movements) between strong and weak commodities to indicate buy or sell signals. Simply, it is a trading technique that suggests the strongest performers over a period of time will *continue* to perform well, and the weakest performers will continue performing poorly over a given future time range. This is usually attempted through models that identify and compare extended price movements (over six to twelve months) of one commodity to another. For example, a strong positive performer would be purchased or held long while a poor performer would be sold or held short. Momentum trading is riskier than the trend-following approach because shifts in momentum can be short-lived or end suddenly, causing trading models to misread the market. Many of the momentum models that have recently emerged to trade commodities or commodity indexes will short the worst performers over the last 6 to 12 months and go long the best performers over the same time period. These positions are then held for the forthcoming six to twelve months, potentially incurring substantial losses. Basically, it assumes what is going up will continue to perform better on a relative basis, and what is falling will likewise continue to be relatively weak.

Trend following attempts to identify trends that have recently changed, with the goal being to participate in the bulk of the movement (either up or down) until a new trend is confirmed. Trend following attempts to accomplish this by utilizing indicators such as a moving average of prices over a given period for any given commodity or sector. Trend following models identify recent futures prices that have risen above or fallen below the indicator and then position the commodity long or short accordingly. The long and short positions are then readjusted based on trends that are identified month to month. The risk here is a trendless market, resulting in whipsaws, but those losses are generally small.

While neither momentum trading nor trend following are perfect, trend following is much better suited to commodities. This is because commodity price movements are based on different fundamentals than stocks. Momentum trading works quite well with stocks, but historically is not suited to commodities. Time and study have proven that the bulk of all commodities revert to the mean price when looked at in a large enough time frame; most stocks do not.

In the commodities world, supply and demand are not a function of innovation, but of substitution. If cattle prices go up due to an unforeseen factor such as mad cow disease, it is possible that people will switch to chicken or pork, until prices come back down. When one grain goes up in price, farmers switch acreage away from the other lower-priced crops, which will eventually bring the prices back in line with each other. Hence the cyclical nature of commodity prices which allows "trends" to not only exist but be identified.

Corn is a good example. In 1930 corn traded at about $0.80 a bushel, and now trades around $3.40 a bushel (a 2.0 percent compounded annual return), but obviously the value of a dollar has changed as well. From 1970 to date, corn has traded in a range between approximately $1.15 and $5.55, but in over 80 percent of those years it has traded at $2.50 a bushel at some point. Corn is now also a fuel, but commodities adjust very quickly to demand, in this case by farmers planting more corn, which increases the supply and meets the additional demand.

Stocks, on the other hand, gain momentum or relative strength by having some sustained competitive advantage over other companies. This can be due to patents on technology (such as Xerox had), being the first to develop a new idea (like Federal Express), or by continued successful expansion (Starbucks). These companies can build and market themselves differently than one another. This enables stocks to gain momentum, which in many cases persists for years not months. In commodities, gold is always gold, it cannot be wheat. Gold will go up in inflationary periods, and down in disinflationary periods. The economic cycles may be longer or shorter in length, but they always take place. So gold will never be Intel, and as such does not develop momentum in the same way as Intel.

In the short term, exceptions in commodities can and do occur. Take the recent case of the industrial metals and oil. China and India have seen continued economic expansion, combined with modernization and industrialization. Political shifts in those regions towards a form of limited economic capitalism have opened their huge populations to global markets. This has led to rapid growth in demand for industrial metals and oil. At the same time, western nations have gone green, making it more difficult (and expensive) to dig or drill for these materials. The net result is a spike in demand which has not been met by growth in supply, and therefore sharply higher prices. Over time however, this situation will resolve itself, either through increased production, or lower demand through slowed growth (caused by the higher prices) or substitution.

Trend following is different from momentum trading. Trend following suggests cycles in commodities are seasonal, and thereby commodities are better suited as short- or intermediate-term trading objects than momentum investing vehicles. A century of market data has shown this in both fundamental and technical illustrations. To suggest otherwise, or imply that commodities are now like stocks, is false on its most basic premise. Commodities age with movement as consumers shift to alternatives, and that will not change. Consumers consume; investors seek growth through investments.

So buy low, but buy when prices have already started to move up. Likewise, sell high, but sell when prices have turned and begun to go down. Ignoring the cyclical nature of commodities and concentrating solely on momentum will soon reveal that it is all a "fashionable accessory" in the commodities markets and is destined to go the way of the bow tie.

SENTIMENT

It can be very easy to be influenced by the crowd, by popular opinion, by the things you read or hear. Call it peer pressure, call it the psychological desire to fit in, call it being open-minded even. The point that needs to be remembered is that people are frequently wrong, and the fact that a particular opinion is widely held does not make it correct. You'll also find that there is rarely a correlation between how strongly an opinion is held and how true it turns out to be.

Be very careful when everyone is bullish or bearish. Changes in sentiment are important, but like anything else the sentiment can become overdone, or in this case, overbought or oversold. When sentiment is nearly universal on one side or the other, to me that is the time to play the other side, and fade the consensus. But you should only initiate the fade when good news does not move the markets up, or bad news down. Until then, just watch the markets and bide your time.

COMMITMENT OF TRADERS

The *Commitment of Traders* reports are a good way of comparing the differences between the professional traders with public sentiment. This can be very useful in determining when a trend may be coming to an end. Used during a trendless market, or one stuck in a trading channel, it can be an early indication of when a new trend is getting ready to begin. Still, you need to wait for technical confirmation before initiating a trade. Remember: Always lean to the big speculators' position, never the public. See Figure 3.2 for an example of a typical COT report. Like equities, the public is almost always the last to get in and the last to get out; inevitably they buy the top and sell the bottom.

LONG-ONLY COMMODITY INDEXES

These are not really a good asset play for traders, as commodities are cyclical and therefore go up and down. Most also tend to be overly weighted to the energy sector. However, long-only commodity indexes will add some efficiency to an investor's diversified portfolio, as they are noncorrelated to

```
WHEAT - CHICAGO BOARD OF TRADE                                           Code-001602

Commitments of Traders - Futures Only, May 8, 2007

--------------------------------------------------------------------------------------------
        :  Total   :              Reportable Positions                     :  Nonreportable
        :-------------------------------------------------------------------  Positions
        :  Open    :        Non-Commercial       :  Commercial    :    Total      :
        : Interest : Long   : Short  : Spreading: Long  : Short  : Long   : Short : Long  : Short

--------------------------------------------------------------------------------------------
        :         : (CONTRACTS OF 5,000 BUSHELS)                                   :
        :         :                                                                :
All  : 360,386:  82,235   79,798   47,740  201,917  181,295  331,892  308,833:  28,494   51,553
Old  : 331,030:  70,149   84,551   40,320  193,883  161,448  304,352  286,319:  26,678   44,711
Other:  29,356:  19,290    2,451      216    8,034   19,847   27,540   22,514:   1,816    6,842
        :         :                                                                :
        :         :      Changes in Commitments from: May 1, 2007                  :
        :  1,112:  -5,004   -5,224    5,290    1,501       68    1,787      134:    -675      978
        :         :                                                                :
        :         :    Percent of Open Interest Represented by Each Category of Trader  :
All  :  100.0:    22.8     22.1     13.2     56.0     50.3     92.1     85.7:     7.9     14.3
Old  :  100.0:    21.2     25.5     12.2     58.6     48.8     91.9     86.5:     8.1     13.5
Other:  100.0:    65.7      8.3      0.7     27.4     67.6     93.8     76.7:     6.2     23.3
        :         :                                                                :
        :# Traders :            Number of Traders in Each Category                 :
All  :     325:     81      117       96       58       97      215      252:
Old  :     322:     77      122       87       57       96      203      251:
Other:     123:     30       21        6       14       63       50       87:
        :--------------------------------------------------------------------------
        :         Percent of Open Interest Held by the Indicated Number of the Largest Traders
        :                    By Gross Position                 By Net Position
        :              4 or Less Traders   8 or Less Traders   4 or Less Traders   8 or Less Traders
        :              Long:   Short    Long    Short:    Long    Short    Long    Short
        :--------------------------------------------------------------------------
All  :              26.1    17.5     40.0     25.8     26.0     16.3     39.9     23.8
Old  :              27.9    17.6     43.0     26.1     27.8     17.5     43.0     25.0
Other:              57.0    23.7     77.1     36.7     56.2     22.4     74.1     34.2
```

FIGURE 3.2   Commitments of Traders report for CBOT wheat.

stocks and bonds. While they are not a play for traders, they're often useful for the real retail public or pension funds. It is not that the people running pension assets are not smart—they just have a huge handicap that drives them to lose, as they have to be prudent, that means last in and last out!

    Take a look at these two-year charts of the S&P GSCI (Figure 3.3) and of spot crude oil (Figure 3.4). Notice how closely they follow each other. This is because of how heavily weighted the index is to the energy sector. As a long-only index, the S&P GSCI requires rising commodity prices for it to show positive returns.

FIGURE 3.3 Two-year chart of the S&P Goldman Sachs Commodity Index (GSCI).
Source: Used with permission of Barchart.com.

FIGURE 3.4 Two-year chart of spot crude oil.
Source: Used with permission of Barchart.com.

The combination of being heavily weighted to one sector, and being unable to profit (or even unable to limit losses) during periods of declining commodity prices, is what leaves long-only indexes a generation behind a long/short strategy such as the S&P DTI. However, these long-only products serve an institutional purpose of asset allocation, and therefore do fill a need.

REBALANCING

Remember, the profit is made in commodities when you buy and sell (or short) them—that is, when you trade them, not when you eat them. Cyclical objects go up and down. Therefore, you must rebalance them. For a detailed and scientific explanation of rebalancing, I can't think of a better reference for you to devour than Erb and Harvey's "Tactical and Strategic Value of Commodity Futures" (2005). The key section is called "Turning Water into Wine." This is really all you need to read on rebalancing to understand why it is so important!

CHAPTER 4

2B or Not 2B

A Classic Rule Revisited

Since I have been concentrating on indicators and tools in the last chapter, and the concept of how to lose properly in the one before that, this seems like as good a place as any to combine those two ideas into one. Ideally, the trader mentality should always be to cut your losses and let your profits run. A corollary to that is the notion that the best trades are those that limit your risk at the outset and provide a clear exit point to determine that the position you've initiated is incorrect. If it is possible to focus on trades that fit into the latter category, and that allow you to utilize the former rule to its fullest extent, you're already on the road to success.

CHANGES IN TREND

In my first book, *Methods of a Wall Street Master*, I introduced readers to my view of how to technically determine a change in trend, using the 1-2-3 criteria. In simple form, there are three observations to watch for:

1. A trendline is broken.
2. The trend stops making higher highs in an uptrend, or lower lows in a downtrend.
3. Prices go above a previous short-term high in an existing downtrend, or below a short-term low in an existing uptrend.

When all three of these conditions are met, by definition a new trend has started, although either of the first conditions alone is enough to signal

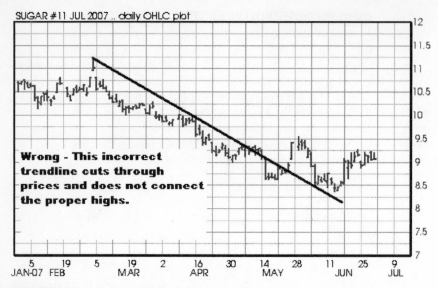

FIGURE 4.1   The wrong way to draw a trendline.
Source: Used with permission of Barchart.com.

FIGURE 4.2   The right way to draw a trendline.
Source: Used with permission of Barchart.com.

a possible (or probable) change in trend. By the way, it is imperative when utilizing this method that you draw the trendlines properly. You can see a detailed explanation in Chapter 7 of *Methods of a Wall Street Master*. But in brief, an upward trendline is drawn from the lowest low to the highest minor low point preceding the highest high—but in such a way that the trendline does *not* pass through prices in between the two low points you are connecting. Conversely, a downward trendline is drawn from the highest high to the lowest minor high preceding the lowest low, but not through the prices between those two high points. Figure 4.1 shows a chart with an incorrect trendline, and Figure 4.2 shows the correct trendline, to give you a visual example of each.

THE 2B RULE

With those skills in mind, I want to introduce (or reintroduce) a powerful rule for determining a possible change in trend. A corollary to rule number 2 above, this is the trading rule I coined the 2B. Of all of the concepts I discussed in my first book more than 15 years ago, the 2B remains one that many readers continue to mention to me as useful and memorable. Likewise, it remains a rule that I still teach to the uninitiated whenever possible, because not only does it carry a high probability of a change in trend, but it also limits losses and specifies a designated out point for a trade before a position is ever initiated.

As stated in *Methods of a Wall Street Master*, the 2B Rule is as follows:

In an uptrend, if a higher high is made but fails to carry through, and then prices drop below the previous high, then the trend is apt to reverse. The converse is true for downtrends. This observation applies in any of the three trends: short-term, intermediate-term, and long-term.

For short-term highs or lows, the new high or low should fail to follow through within a day or two. In the intermediate term, it may take three to five days. And in the long-term, with major 2B signals, it could take up to 10 days. The net effect, however, is the same: The market in question fails to follow through, and returns to below the prior high or above the prior low. It is at this point that you initiate a position based on the belief that the trend may be changing.

The most crucial part of the 2B rule is that you *lose properly*! If the market trades back above the new high, or below the new low, you need to admit defeat immediately and take the loss. You can go ahead and initiate the position again if the market once again returns to within the original range. The key is to allow yourself to be whipsawed, which keeps your losses small. Those losses, even taken two or three times, will still be smaller than the potential profit when the 2B signal *does* signal a change in trend. Sometimes that seems a bit difficult to believe, but when applied to true situations you will realize with experience how true it is.

After 15 years, the 2B rule works as well today as it did when my first book was published. Let's take a simple example to begin with. Figure 4.3 shows a daily chart of July 2007 platinum. A high of 1345.0 was set on April 23. About two weeks later on May 7, the contracts made a new high of 1,353.8. The following day it closed back in the prior range. This is the classic 2B sell signal, as a higher high is made but fails to carry through. You would go short the market and use the new high to compute your initial stop or out point at 1,353.9.

Remember that there are both minor 2Bs and more major ones, depending on the importance of the highs and lows. Examine Figure 4.4, a chart of the August 2007 feeder cattle contract. You'll see a few very short-term minor 2Bs in the latter part of April, followed by a more major buy signal on May 7. There is then the major 2B sell signal on May 22. Pay particular attention to the lack of 2B signals on the way up through February and March, and again the lack of a 2B on the way down in late

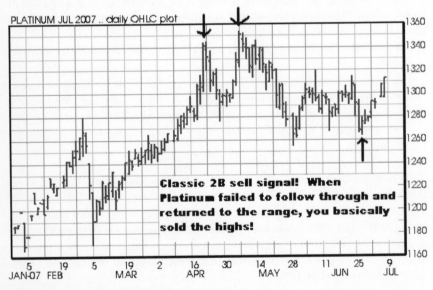

FIGURE 4.3 July 2007 platinum.
Source: Used with permission of Barchart.com.

FEEDER CATTLE AUG 2007 .. daily OHLC plot

Whether or not you followed the minor 2B signals here was up to you, but the sell signal in late May was too perfect to pass up!

FIGURE 4.4 August 2007 feeder cattle.
Source: Used with permission of Barchart.com.

May and early June. The absence of a signal can be as telling an indicator as the presence of one, although with the opposite conclusion.

One of my favorite 2B signals is where the market gaps up or down on the open, and then returns back into the range. The fact that many markets trade round the clock has altered the frequency that you see this occur, but especially in the nonfinancial futures markets the opportunities are there if you keep your eyes open. Figure 4.5 shows a major 2B sell signal in July 2007 cocoa. Note how the market opened, ran to new highs on April 18, and then immediately sold off, giving you a terrific entry point.

Another example of the gap opening signal is shows in Figure 4.6, the June 2007 five-year Treasury note chart. Again, you should also note the lack of a 2B buy signal when the market broke the lows set in early April. This confirms the trend and the overall weakness of the market.

In Figure 4.7, the July 2007 pork bellies chart, you'll see a number of 2B examples, both minor and major. Note the whipsaw in early June, where there was a typical 2B buy signal followed by a decline to new lows the following day. Whipsaws like this are part of the 2B reality, but as long as you follow the rules and immediately admit defeat in the current trade, the losses are minimized.

Figure 4.8 demonstrates how the 2B rule can still generate some positive results during the consolidation phase of a trend. The fact that the

FIGURE 4.5 July 2007 cocoa.
Source: Used with permission of Barchart.com.

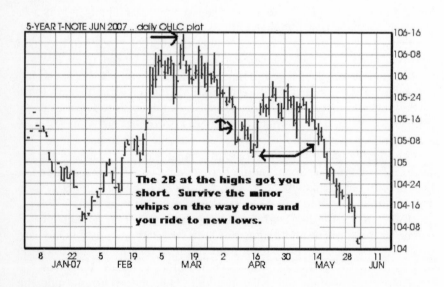

FIGURE 4.6 June 2007 five-year Treasury notes.
Source: Used with permission of Barchart.com.

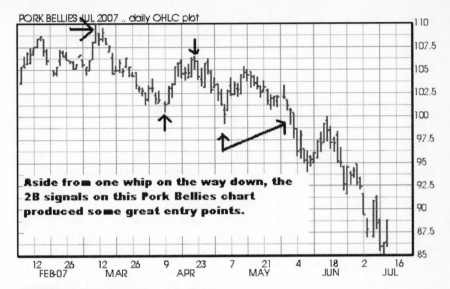

FIGURE 4.7 July 2007 pork bellies.
Source: Used with permission of Barchart.com.

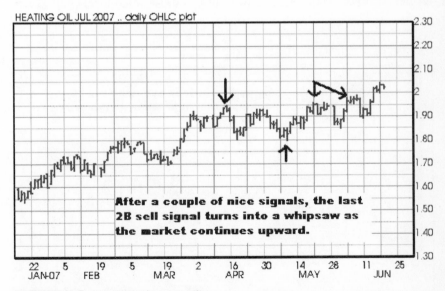

FIGURE 4.8 July 2007 heating oil.
Source: Used with permission of Barchart.com.

market failed to make lower lows after the May 9 2B buy signal, as well as the occasional whipsaw sell signals, suggest the upward trend is going to resume.

LONG-TERM 2BS

The 2B rule can be just as easily applied to longer-term charts, like weekly or monthly bar charts. In Figure 4.9, we see a long-term chart of the rough rice contract. A powerful 2B buy signal was given in May 2005, which signaled an upcoming change in trend. If you bought rough rice on that 2B, you basically bought the low of the entire move.

When markets stay within trading ranges, even long-term ones, the 2B rule can be a valuable tool. See in Figure 4.10 where the 2B got you short the feeder cattle market at the 2005 highs, only to reverse and go long at the lows months later.

Even monthly bar charts can display 2B signals. Take a look at Figure 4.11, a long-term cotton chart. Although some of the shorter-term 2Bs marked might have shown up on a daily bar chart or a weekly bar chart, the major low in 2001 would have required a monthly bar chart to illustrate its significance. Cotton has yet to return to those price levels, but if you

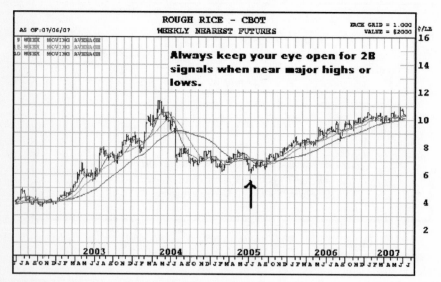

FIGURE 4.9   Rough rice weekly bar chart.
Source: Used with permission of Barchart.com.

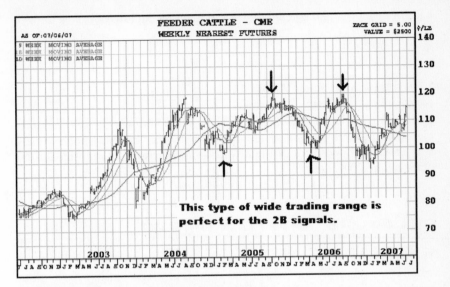

FIGURE 4.10 Feeder cattle weekly bar chart.
Source: Used with permission of Barchart.com.

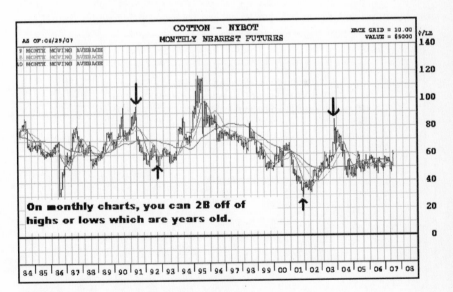

FIGURE 4.11 Cotton monthly bar chart.
Source: Used with permission of Barchart.com.

had followed the 2B, you would have bought at the lowest prices in over 20 years.

SPREADS AND THE 2B RULE

The 2B rule works with spreads, too, if the spread is a widely followed one. Figure 4.12 shows a chart of the NOB spread (U.S. Treasury notes versus U.S. Treasury bonds). Most recently, a very successful 2B buy signal took place in late 2006.

CALL OR FOLD, JUST STAY IN THE GAME

The New Zealand dollar chart shown in Figure 4.13 has a few minor 2B signals through 2005, and then an obvious 2B buy signal in June 2006. Note the 2B sell signal in 2007, which whipped you out as the trend continued upward a month later. This brings up an important point about using the 2B

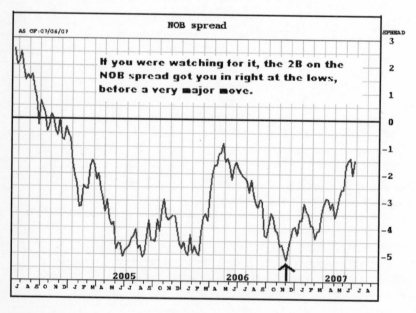

FIGURE 4.12 NOB spread weekly chart.
Source: Used with permission of Barchart.com.

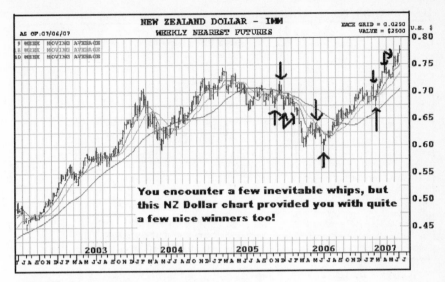

FIGURE 4.13   New Zealand dollar weekly chart.
Source: Used with permission of Barchart.com.

rule—when to take profits. The two trading rules involved here are "Never let a profit turn into a loss" and "Cut your losses and let your profits run." Often, when I trade off of a 2B signal I position myself in two ways: half the position as a quick profit, and the other half to ride the move out with. So if I had gone short the New Zealand dollar on the 2B sell signal, I would have been looking to take a profit on half of my position once I saw it approach a level of support. The other half I could let ride, and if I received a new 2B sell signal or another technical sell indication, I am free to resell the half I bought back, but at a higher level. Using this strategy, you make sure that even if the market moves against you after an initial profit, you still break even or end up with a small profit overall. At the same time, you are allowing the core position to reach a maximum profit potential. Either way, remember that it is imperative that you get out of the trade once the 2B signal has been broken through. Throw down your cards, fold, and wait for the next deal.

Although the 2B rule is highly valuable, there are periods when no signal will be seen. A good example of that can be seen in Figure 4.14, the June 2007 lean hogs chart. You see that after two 2B buy signals, and two sell signals, the market began to trade in a range. Since higher lows and lower highs continued to be formed, there never was an additional 2B signal to follow. I hope that in this case, you got a nice profit out of the last buy signal—you certainly had plenty of time to close out the trade and move on to something else.

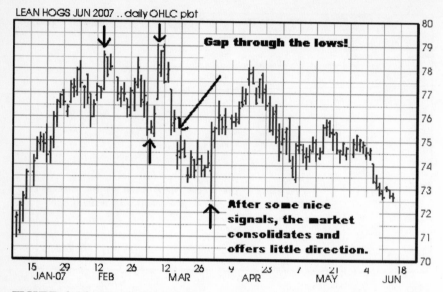

FIGURE 4.14 June 2007 lean hogs.
Source: Used with permission of Barchart.com.

If you read my first book, I hope this refresher course in the 2B rule has been helpful and enlightening for you. And if this is the first time you've been introduced to the 2B concept, I hope you will make it a part of your trading strategy. Once you are aware of the rule and how it works, you'll begin to find 2B signals all over your charts. The 2B is as powerful and profitable now as it was back in 1991!

CHAPTER 5

An Introduction to the S&P DTI

With commodities, as with any other investment vehicle, there are two different ways to allocate your money. First, as we have been discussing through this book, is trading. In that instance, you speculate on the direction of the market, determine your own entry and exit points, watch the markets the best you can, and hope to profit overall despite a number of losses. The rewards can be great when trading, especially with commodities, because of the leverage factor inherent in the futures markets (but without the constant erosion of time premium you find in the options markets). Yet trading requires constant attention, dedication, and energy, and can generate incredible stress in the process. Ask any of the people who worked with me back in the days when I day-traded S&P futures and bonds all day long; more often than not, you'd find me with a cuff wrapped around my arm, checking my blood pressure.

The more time I spent trading like that, the more I longed for an automated trading system that I could use to speculate in the markets without having to make each trading decision myself. Over the years, I developed a number of systems like that myself, including the Sperandeo System, which was designed solely to trade S&P 500 futures on the basis of the Dow Jones Industrial and S&P 500 index movement. I also purchased various commodity trading systems that were popular at the time. Although some were based on valid ideas, none of them were profitable for me over long periods. They were either too narrow in scope or they traded too short term, which meant users were eaten alive in slippage and commission costs. The ones I purchased experimentally had the added problem of, in my opinion, being too curve-fitted and data mined. The only way to keep them moderately profitable even in the short term was to constantly reoptimize them to the most recent market data.

Regardless of whether there were methods to make that work, it is simply not compatible with my personal trading style. I make my living based on understanding the past and using that knowledge to determine the likely future. The idea that the most recent past is all you need to focus on is too foreign to me. So for all intents and purposes, I felt that in order to trade successfully, even in the intermediate term, I would need to give up my dream of automated deterministic systems and focus on manual chart reading and market movements as I had always done.

Let us leave the trading aspect alone for the moment. The other major way to utilize the commodity asset class is through investment. Aside from precious metals (most notably in the form of coins, ingots, or bars), I don't think direct investment in the physical commodities space is viable. First of all, there is no leverage, and second of all, diversifying requires a mechanism for storage of the physical product. How much lumber can you fit in your garage, and how many head of cattle do you plan to stick in your backyard? So we should agree that true commodities investment is best accomplished through a diversified portfolio. The simplest way of doing that is through a commodities index such as the Standard & Poor's Goldman Sachs Commodity Index (GSCI).

THE LONG-ONLY INDEX—LEAVING TOO MUCH ON THE TABLE?

The SPGSCI gives you exposure to a broad-based portfolio of commodities through one investment. However, to me this approach was always lacking in two major ways. First, the SPGSCI is too heavily weighted in the energy sector for my taste. Although that helps secure better returns during those years when crude oil sees a rise in value, I find it minimizes the effects of the rest of the portfolio too much. If you remember, in Chapter 3, I showed you a chart of the SPGSCI and one of crude oil (Figures 3.3 and 3.4), where you could see just how closely the two track each other.

The second way I find that the SPGSCI, and other commodity indexes, do not meet my needs is they have static exposure. By that I mean they are always long every component in their universe. As someone who uses technical analysis as a basis for so many decisions, this is another strategy I cannot abide by. I would rather miss part of an increase in prices in exchange for avoiding being long in a sell-off. Take a look at Figure 5.1, a chart of July 2007 sugar #11. Pay close attention to the price action since the end of 2005. During that entire time, the sugar market has either been declining or consolidating. Technically, it has never given any serious buy

FIGURE 5.1 July 2007 sugar #11, weekly Barchart.
Source: Used with permission of Barchart.com.

signals, yet any commodity index that includes sugar would have been long the whole way down. What sense does that make to a trader like me? Isn't it possible to develop a commodity index that could avoid owning sugar in a bear market? Or, better yet, why not one that would actually profit during that period by going short?

COVERING ALL THE BASES

It was the desire to create such a long-short strategy that led to the development of the S&P Diversified Trends Indicator (S&P DTI). Not only does the S&P DTI give you the ability to be either long or short any of the component markets (except the energy sector, which due to risk factors can only be long or flat), it also uses a simple deterministic method for positioning. The S&P DTI concept, when used as leverage with other asset classes, is so innovative that it has been issued patents in the United States and Australia on its design.

To begin with, the S&P DTI is diversified. It is a composite of 24 commodity and financial futures, grouped into 14 sectors. The allocation is 50 percent to financial futures and 50 percent to commodities. By including both financials and commodities, you mitigate risk because the two asset types are usually negatively correlated. However, the position direction is determined by sector (except for the softs), not by individual item. In other words, you cannot be long corn and short wheat at the same time, but you can be long coffee and short sugar at the same time, as they are very different. The sectors are rebalanced monthly, but the individual components are rebalanced annually, which I will explain in a moment.

The S&P DTI is also balanced. Although energy remains the sector with the largest allocation, it is only 18.75 percent, much less than most long-only commodity indexes. And when energy is flat, that 18.75 percent is distributed between the remaining commodities sectors, as well as the financial sectors. Tables 5.1 and 5.2 show the weighting scheme for the S&P DTI when long the energies and flat the energies, respectively.

TABLE 5.1 S&P Diversified Trends Indicator Weighting Scheme—Long Energy

Market	Market Weight	Sector	Sector Weight	Component	Component Weight
Commodities	50%	Energy	18.75%	Heating oil	3.00%
				Light crude	8.50%
				Natural gas	4.25%
				Unleaded gasoline	3.00%
		Industrial metals	5.00%	Copper	5.00%
		Precious metals	5.25%	Gold	3.50%
				Silver	1.75%
		Livestock	5.00%	Lean hogs	2.00%
				Live cattle	3.00%
		Grains	11.50%	Corn	4.00%
				Soybeans	5.00%
				Wheat	2.50%
		Softs	4.50%	Cocoa	1.00%
				Coffee	1.50%
				Cotton	1.00%
				Sugar	1.00%
Financials	50%	Currencies	35.00%	Australian dollar	2.00%
				British pound	5.00%
				Canadian dollar	1.00%
				Euro	13.00%
				Japanese yen	12.00%
				Swiss franc	2.00%
		Treasuries	15.00%	U.S. Treasury bonds	7.50%
				U.S. Treasury notes	7.50%

TABLE 5.2 S&P Diversified Trends Indicator Weighting Scheme—Flat Energy

Market	Market Weight	Sector	Sector Weight	Component	Component Weight
Commodities	38.50%	Energy	0.00%	Heating oil	0.00%
				Light crude	0.00%
				Natural gas	0.00%
				Unleaded gasoline	0.00%
		Industrial metals	6.15%	Copper	6.15%
		Precious metals	6.46%	Gold	4.31%
				Silver	2.15%
		Livestock	6.15%	Lean hogs	2.46%
				Live cattle	3.69%
		Grains	14.15%	Corn	4.92%
				Soybeans	6.15%
				Wheat	3.08%
		Softs	5.54%	Cocoa	1.23%
				Coffee	1.85%
				Cotton	1.23%
				Sugar	1.23%
Financials	61.50%	Currencies	43.07%	Australian dollar	2.46%
				British pound	6.15%
				Canadian dollar	1.23%
				Euro	16.00%
				Japanese yen	14.77%
				Swiss franc	2.46%
		Treasuries	18.46%	U.S. Treasury bonds	9.23%
				U.S. Treasury notes	9.23%

The commodities weightings in the S&P DTI were developed partially using estimates for worldwide production (or in the case of natural gas, North American production). For the financials, weightings were based on GDP, but were not made directly proportional. Adjustments were made to account for liquidity, trading significance, and potential correlation. Political significance was also considered, which helps explain the 2 percent allocation to the Swiss franc.

Rebalancing is the key to the S&P DTI. Each month the sectors are rebalanced to their fixed weights, although the components are only rebalanced annually. This rebalancing helps to keep volatility low, since otherwise an extended move in one group or sector would overweight the S&P DTI and potentially lead to significantly higher volatility.

The position determination rule is simplicity itself. The S&P DTI uses a 1.6-weighted seven-price exponential moving average (See Appendix A for details regarding the exponential average). The second-to-last business day of each month is known as the *position determination day* (PDD). At the close of business of the PDD, we compute the percentage price change for the month, and from that compute the cumulative price change and the price input. Those monthly price input values are the numbers used to compute the exponential moving average. For those sectors other than softs with more than one component (energy, precious metals, livestock and grains), the price inputs from the respective components are aggregated to determine positions for the sector as a whole. The softs sector is the exception to this rule. Since there is no fundamental tie between its various components, the position of each is determined separately. In other words, the softs sector is the only sector where you can be long one component and short another at the same time. For the industrial metals sector, and the eight financial sectors, each component has its own price input and direction determination.

DO IT YOURSELF?

In effect, that is the simple description of the S&P DTI. There are no secret formulas, no form-fitting selections of the moving averages, nothing that you couldn't do yourself. In fact, before we move on to detailed analysis of the S&P DTI in the chapters that follow, I will run down the simple steps you would use to trade the entire S&P DTI yourself. However, the question you need to ask yourself is whether you have sufficient capital to execute the strategy on your own. If you are trading at 1 to 1 leverage, based on the actual contract values within the S&P DTI (not the margin requirements, but the actual values of the commodities each contract represents), you would need approximately $7.2 million (currently) to properly match the designated allocations. Of course, if you do not require exactly the same allocations, you could proceed with much less, or you could approximate the allocations with less capital through the use of leverage (as the margin required for the $7.2 million in commodities is only a fraction of that amount). If you do not use leverage, your allocations will not be precise, since you cannot buy or sell a partial contract. If you cut the dollars invested in half, for example, you would have to eliminate the Canadian dollar from your portfolio, because the allocation would be too small to purchase or sell a single contract.

A number of solutions to investing smaller amounts of capital in the S&P DTI (and in its subindexes, the S&P CTI, and the S&P FTI) are currently under development or consideration by various firms. These include both open-end and exchange-traded funds. Currently, however, the simplest solution is investment in one of the Rydex Managed Futures Funds, which make investments designed to track the S&P DTI. These are open-end funds. The three trading symbols are

RYMFX, Class H shares

RYMTX, Class A shares

RYMZX, Class C shares

Okay, so let's walk through a sample month of the S&P DTI, using the end of May 2007 as our blueprint. If you need additional specifics, examples, or instructions, remember to examine the material included in Appendix A. As we approach the position determination day, our positions on a hypothetical $10 million portfolio are shown in Table 5.3.

TABLE 5.3 S&P DTI Positions on $10 Million Portfolio, May 2007

Commodity	Month	Long/Short	Current Allocation	Contracts
Sugar	July	Short	1.00%	10
Cotton	July	Short	1.00%	4
Cocoa	July	Long	1.00%	5
Coffee	July	Short	1.50%	4
Euro	Jun	Long	13.00%	8
Japanese yen	Jun	Short	12.00%	11
Swiss franc	Jun	Long	2.00%	2
Aussie $	Jun	Long	2.00%	2
British pound	Jun	Long	5.00%	4
Canadian $	Jun	Long	1.00%	1
T-bond	Sep	Short	7.50%	7
10-Yr note	Sep	Short	7.50%	7
Wheat	July	Short	2.51%	10
Corn	July	Short	3.76%	20
Soybeans	July	Short	5.23%	14
Live cattle	Aug	Short	3.03%	8
Lean hogs	Aug	Short	1.97%	7
Crude light	Sep	Long	7.87%	11
RBOB blend	Sep	Long	3.26%	4
Natural gas	Sep	Long	4.57%	6
Heating oil	Sep	Long	3.06%	4
HG copper	July	Long	5.00%	6
Gold	Oct	Long	3.52%	5
Silver	July	Long	1.73%	3

Following the example shown in Appendix A (especially Table A.4 and Table A.5), after the close of the market on the PDD of May 30, 2007, we are able to determine that the following positional directions have changed:

Swiss franc from long to short

Grains from short to long

Precious metals from long to short

In addition, the S&P DTI needs to roll a number of open positions from one contract month to another, without changing the directional position. In this example, these rolls include all the softs, all the currencies, and copper. They also include the grains, silver, and the Swiss franc, all of that have new directional positions being implemented.

TABLE 5.4   S&P DTI Positions on $10 Million Portfolio, after May 2007

Commodity	Month	Long/ Short	Current Allocation	Last Price	Contract Value	Contracts
Sugar	Oct	Short	1.00%	9.33	$10,450	10
Cotton	Dec	Short	1.00%	56	$28,000	4
Cocoa	Sep	Long	1.00%	1903	$19,030	5
Coffee	Sep	Short	1.50%	114.2	$42,825	4
Euro	Sep	Long	13.00%	1.34765	$168,456	8
Japanese yen	Sep	Short	12.00%	0.8341	$104,263	11
Swiss franc	Sep	Short	2.00%	0.8234	$102,925	2
Aussie $	Sep	Long	2.00%	0.8199	$81,990	2
British pound	Sep	Long	5.00%	1.9734	$123,338	4
Canadian $	Sep	Long	1.00%	0.9341	$93,410	1
T-bond	Sep	Short	7.50%	109.125	$109,125	7
10-Yr note	Sep	Short	7.50%	106.484375	$106,484	7
Wheat	Sep	Long	2.51%	524.75	$26,238	10
Corn	Sep	Long	3.76%	384.75	$19,238	20
Soybeans	Nov	Long	5.23%	837	$41,850	14
Live cattle	Aug	Short	3.03%	221.9	$36,440	8
Lean hogs	Aug	Short	1.97%	36.35	$29,560	7
Crude light	Sep	Long	7.87%	91.1	$65,560	11
RBOB blend	Sep	Long	3.26%	2.091	$87,822	4
Natural gas	Sep	Long	4.57%	8.121	$81,210	6
Heating oil	Sep	Long	3.06%	1.9208	$80,674	4
HG copper	Sep	Long	5.00%	329.85	$82,463	6
Gold	Oct	Short	3.52%	665.4	$66,540	5
Silver	Sep	Short	1.73%	1334.9	$66,745	3

With the new computations, Table 5.4 shows the full computation used to determine how many contracts of each position the S&P DTI needs to be long or short at the end of May based on the $10 million portfolio. All you would need to do now is simply execute the appropriate trades required to match your ending positions to the ones shown in the table.

This brings us to the one part of the S&P DTI transaction that causes some difficulty. The official S&P DTI results no longer execute all these trades on the last business day of the month. Instead, in order to preserve liquidity and to prevent front-running, the trades are executed on one of the first five business days of the new month. This random-day selection is done by Standard & Poor's, and the date is not released to the general public until after the fact. In the future there will likely be a five-day roll process as well, which is similar to the way the S&P GSCI is executed.

The simplest solution to this problem would be for you to execute your trades on the last day of the month. If so, your results will differ from the actual S&P DTI results, but over time the difference should not be material. Or, you can select a specific day during the first five business days of the new month, or even determine a random date yourself through a roll of a die. The method is unimportant. What is important is that you use a consistent method, instead of trying to guess which day is the best day to execute. The last thing you'd want to do is make the decision to use an indicator like the S&P DTI and then pollute the results with personal opinions. You may as well override the buy and sell signals then!

I hope this introduction has helped to demystify the S&P DTI and how it works. Aside from a few mathematical formulas, mainly in computing the individual weightings and the price inputs for the moving averages, the indicator is simple and straightforward. Now that you have an understanding of *how* it works, we can begin to examine *why* it works, and *in what ways* it works best.

CHAPTER 6

A Challenge to the Random Walk Theory

A *theory* is a hypothesis—a subjective and general observation that lacks proof, or even the support of evidence that would verify the observation as true. In this case, that is the exact opposite of true science or math. According to the *New Shorter Oxford English Dictionary*, theory is defined as follows:

1. A mental scheme of something to be done, or of a way of doing something;

2. Mental view, contemplation;

3. General principles or methods ... (b) a system of ideas or statements explaining something;

4. A formulation of abstract knowledge or speculative thought; an unsubstantiated hypothesis; a speculative (especially fanciful) view.

Once a theory becomes widely accepted, a strong tendency exists to treat it as though it were an unassailable truth, even if conflicting evidence mounts that challenges the very basis of the theory. In the history of scientific thought, theories are often maintained—to one degree or another—simply because change is so difficult. Many times, academics and researchers who have based their entire careers and research on a specific theory are, at the very least, reluctant to admit that their theory is false. Such is the case in finance with the random walk theory.

In 1973, the theory of *random walk* was put forth by Burton G. Malkiel (a distinguished professor at Princeton University) in his best-selling book,

A Random Walk Down Wall Street. He wrote, "A random walk is one in which future steps or directions cannot be predicted on the basis of past actions. When the term is applied to the stock market, it means that short-run changes in stock prices cannot be predicted. Investment advisory services, earnings predictions, and complicated chart patterns are useless." It is also known as the *efficient market theory* and suggests that all price information is known and cannot be used to predict the future, as the price can randomly move up or down from where it is today, and trends do not and cannot exist to predict anything.

TREND FOLLOWING IS A LEGITIMATE CHALLENGE TO THE RANDOM WALK THEORY

The efficient market theory can easily be refuted by deductive logic and empirical evidence. Empirical evidence depicts facts that have occurred, can be demonstrated, and *may* act as proof of the facts being demonstrated. A long period of securing empirical evidence *may* be enough to prove a deterministic outcome. For example, the sun rises every day. The reason you can bet it will rise again tomorrow is because our mere existence has provided us with a very long experience of such empirical evidence, coupled with the proven scientific fact that Earth revolves around the sun every 24 hours.

The efficient market theory states that "all information is known" and that "past prices cannot predict the future." However, all information is not known by everyone, and even if all information were known, the interpretation of it would be different. Ultimately, this is the fallacy behind this theory. To even suggest that investors, traders, speculators, specialists, scalpers, and professors know and judge all information correctly is obviously false at its premise. In addition, it also denies the fact that many investment decisions are not based on rational analysis of information at all, but on the investor's greed or fear. Markets dominated by greed or fear tend to overreact to the information, creating trends over the short and long-term time frames.

The strategy of *trend following* assumes that fundamental events occur that cause prices to trend, until those events are offset by other events, which, in turn, cause a change in those fundamentals and therefore the trend of prices. This strategy is contrary to the random walk theory. Seventy-seven years of empirical evidence can provide a significant challenge to the random walk theory, if not disprove it altogether. A few pieces of evidence are displayed on the tables at the end of this chapter, using the

S&P 500 from 1928, the S&P Diversified Trends Indicator (DTI) from 1985, the LSM from 1929 to 1934, and the LSM from 1961 to 1984.

Trend following is a widely used strategy. It is used by the largest and most successful commodity pool operators (CPOs) and commodity trading advisors (CTAs), although they differ in exactly how they implement the use of this strategy. Although the outcome varies more or less, they are generally viewed as being profitable in the long term.

Trend following is not magic; it is based on fundamental events. For instance, when OPEC lowers oil production and demand remains the same, oil prices must rise. The concepts of supply and demand are taught in Economics 101. Another example would be when the Federal Reserve raises interest rates: Bonds generally decline, and will continue to do so until the economy, or the Fed, show signs of a change. A trend is now established. What is the mystery here? The reasons why this must occur are fundamentally obvious. Interest rates rise, bond yields adjust to the current market prices by increasing; thereby, bond prices decline in order to adjust the yield for the increase. The history of the Fed shows that it generally raises and lowers rates in small incremental steps, mostly 25 basis points. Ultimately, a trend in bond prices is sustained over time, as depicted by prices moving up or down. This is maintained until the Fed lowers rates concurrently with an economic slowdown.

Of course, the previous example of bond trends is not always exactly the model, as sometimes the bond market anticipates the Fed is moving too quickly or too slowly. It also discounts changes in Fed policy, so the exact match of Fed actions and long bond yields is not identical. But in general, this is what takes place.

Just as we can deduce that the sun will rise tomorrow from the facts and empirical evidence provided, we can deduce that the strategy of trend following will be successful over time, and it is used by many successful investors in their trading strategies because of the facts and empirical evidence provided.

HE WHO STATES A CLAIM MUST PROVE HIS STATEMENTS

The interesting psychological outcome of the random walk theory is that the theory intimidates its opponents, because they feel to win the argument they must demonstrate why the random walk theory is not true. Trend followers seem to take the position that must prove why they make money, and that their profitability will continue to occur. This is backward logic at its most obvious. It is he who states the claim (theory) that must *prove* his statements. For example, I can say, "There are vending machines on Mars." If someone objects, can I support my position simply by retorting, "Prove it's not true"? Ultimately, it is the responsibility of the person that makes the claim—in this case, "There are vending machines on Mars"—to provide the proof to substantiate the claim. It is not up to the rest of the world to show this is not the case.

Leonard Peikoff stated this idea differently in the "philosophy of objectivism" when he said, "Falsehood: True and false are assessments within the field of human cognition: They designate a relationship of correspondence or contradiction between an idea and reality. . . . The false is established as false by reference to a body of evidence and within a context, and is pronounced false because it contradicts the evidence."

The truth is that some managers outperform the market (or their specific benchmark) substantially over the long run. Supporters of random walk theory blatantly disregard those managers—dismissing them entirely or waving them away with "they don't count." Then they attempt to rationalize that no one can beat the markets using postprice movements, or earnings analysis. That isn't a theory—it is a flim-flam. Truth is the identification of a fact of reality. If it exists, there is no rational option that it is not true.

Of course, *most* managers can't outperform benchmarks over time, and for a good reason: Fees! Also, virtually all distribution bell curves have small tails. For example, in the case of large cap stocks, the long-term compounded returns are 10.74 percent, and if the average mutual fund fees are 1.55 percent (or 14.4 percent of the total return), most managers will certainly underperform. This is common sense, not a theory, but it is as sure as a casino's edge assures that it will always win in the long run. However, it does not take away from the fact that some managers do outperform the market and overcome the fees.

Even if only a small percentage of money managers can outperform the benchmark, then they must also be considered as an example of disproof of the random walk theory. In the January 9, 2006, edition of *Barron's*, an article describes 19 money managers who earned from 16.4 to 20.0 percent from 1991 through 2005, while the S&P 500 earned 11.52 percent compounded during the same period. Most of the money managers listed had standard deviation numbers similar to the S&P 500. The only random walk retorts would be, "Fifteen years is not a long enough sample," or, "So what; how can you know which money managers will be the winners?" My answer is that 15 years *is* long enough, and picking winners is not the issue, especially because the random walk crowd states that there can't be any winners anyway! The question I pose to the random market or efficient market theorists is, how do superior money managers constantly outperform their benchmark (even over and above fees) when the theory says this *can't* happen?

A CHALLENGE

The random walk theory is, at best, just an investment recommendation for indexing—because low fees are an obvious benefit to returns—not an empirically valid theory. The implications that the market has no predicative value unto itself, and that certain human beings who have the desire, emotional discipline, and intellectual capacity to outperform (even after fees) will be unable to are ludicrous, unsubstantiated statements. Not only are they based on a false premise, but they are contrary to reality.

My point is simply this: I challenge anyone to prove that the facts shown in the following attachments are *not true* and will not continue. Because of the nature of the very strong empirical evidence (77 years for stocks and 50 years for futures), we can also deduce they will reoccur, just as we can deduce the sun will rise each day. Nothing as robust as the S&P Diversified Trends Indicator can be anything but fundamentally deterministic. Therefore, if someone can disprove the results, please do so. Until then, as far as I am concerned, the efficient market theory is shown to be as accurate as the once-accepted "fact" that the world is flat.

TREND FOLLOWING STATISTICAL ANALYSIS EXPLANATION

In Table 6.1, we use an arbitrary algorithm developed in 1999 that was designed to *reflect* trends in futures, not predict the future. The algorithm is not special, magic, or a crystal ball. It is merely a means to capture movements—if they exist—in intermediate trends. *Intermediate trends* were defined by Charles Dow in the 1800s as lasting from "weeks to months."

The algorithm is a seven-month moving average (MA) that is 1.6 times weighted to give greater importance to the fact that recent prices are more critical than dated ones. However, any moving average will do, as empirical evidence will show that *if* trends exist, the concept of trend following will earn a return in virtually any market and in any environment over longer-term periods (e.g., 24 months).

The statistical information presented in Table 6.1 represents gross returns (i.e., does not account for execution costs incurred in replicating the

TABLE 6.1 Depression Analysis, 1929–1934[a]

	LSM 7 months Weighted 1.6X	S&P 500 Total Returns	Long-Term Government Bonds
1929	10.20%	<8.42%>	3.42
1930	19.62%	<24.90%>	4.66
1931	<5.28%>	<43.34%>	<5.31>
1932	15.19%	<8.19%>	16.84
1933	20.50%	53.99%	<0.07>
1934	3.79%	<1.44%>	10.07
Compounded Price Return (T-Bill interest, used as collateral, is not included)	**10.28%**	**<9.67%>**	**4.70%**

	LSM UAV	Cumulative % P & L From Inception	S&P 500 Total Return UAV	% Cumulative P & L From Inception	Long-Term Bonds UAV	Long-Term Government Bonds
12/31/1928	1000.00		1000.00		1000.00	
12/31/1929	1102.00	10.20%	915.80	<8.42%>	1034.20	3.42
12/31/1930	1318.21	31.82%	687.77	<31.22%>	1082.39	4.66
12/31/1931	1248.61	24.86%	389.69	<61.03%>	1024.91	<5.31>
12/31/1932	1438.27	43.83%	357.77	<64.22%>	1197.51	16.84
12/31/1933	1733.12	73.31%	550.93	<45.00%>	1196.67	<0.07>
12/31/1934	1798.81	79.88%	543.00	<45.70%>	1317.17	10.07
Compounded Return:	**10.28%**		**<9.67%>**		**4.70%**	

Source: Wall Street Journal. Data compiled by Enhanced Alpha Management, LP.
[a]Simulated Results, LSM Unweighted 7-month 1.6 weighted (S&P DTI Algorithm) (Listed in the Wall Street Journal 1/02/1929).
Futures on: Cocoa, Cotton, Wheat, Coffee, Corn, Sugar, and Rubber.

S&P DTI by, for example, acquiring the futures positions underlying the S&P DTI, nor the effects of position slippage, if any).

The *depression analysis* shows that the long/short methodology had a 10.28 percent simulated compounded price return over the six-year period—without T-bill interest added. Interest is always part of the total return of a stand-alone futures investment, as you should always buy futures with interest-bearing collateral such as T-bills. If T-bills were added to the return, the investment would have earned 11.88 percent compounded! The statistical information presented in Table 6.2 represents gross returns. It does not account for execution costs that might be incurred in replicating the S&P DTI (for example, by acquiring the futures positions underlying the S&P DTI), nor the effects of position *slippage*, if any.

True, the S&P DTI is complex. However, just as a complex timepiece such as the Audemurs Piquet Royal Oak Grande Complication (with 2,885 calibrated movements) may be a little more efficient than a less-complex design (like a Timex), perhaps the S&P DTI is a little more efficient than a less-complex design. In any event, what we do believe is that the S&P DTI offers a robust 6 percent gross alpha to a portfolio by using a trend-following strategy (pursuant to simulations dating back to 1929).

Table 6.2 illustrates that trends apply equally in modern times compared to the earlier part of the twentieth century. From 1961 to 1984 the *long/short methodology* (LSM) is used, and from 1985 to 2006 the Standard & Poor's Diversified Trends Indicator (S&P DTI) is used. The LSM uses the same algorithm as the S&P DTI. However, the individual components are equally weighted and are not formed into sectors, as in the S&P DTI. Also, there is a different basket of components to some degree in the LSM, as there were less futures contracts trading during that period. The hypothetical combined price return from 1961 to 2006 was 11.52 percent, and the total return would have been 17.86 percent. Again these are *not* curve-fitted, data-mined or optimized. The 88 variable algorithms tested all show similar returns, with slightly higher or lower performance. From 1985, the 88 algorithm variations show a low return of 5.33 percent and a high return of 6.95 percent, while the S&P DTI was 5.92 percent for price return only. For total return, add T-bills (that equals annual interest of 4.74 percent), and when compounded the return then comes to 11.37 percent. This is 10 percent greater than 30-year bonds over the same period with half the volatility.

In Tables 6.3 through 6.5, we test and confirm that stocks also trend. Since data is available back to 1928, we have a 78-year history of trends we can examine. We used nine simple moving average tests: three each for 150 days, 200 days, and 250 days without any weighting. The increased returns (with less risk) were dramatic!

TABLE 6.2 Simulated Gross Performance 1961–2006

Year	UAV LSM	Annual Percent Change
1961	109	9.06
1962	122	12.09
1963	129	5.12
1964	152	18.52
1965	193	26.96
1966	216	11.79
1967	222	2.55
1968	242	9.36
1969	275	13.48
1970	306	11.07
1971	315	3.14
1972	377	19.71
1973	707	87.42
1974	1006	42.29
1975	1167	16.05
1976	1471	26.01
1977	1819	23.65
1978	1726	−5.1
1979	2098	21.55
1980	2258	7.62
1981	2898	28.36
1982	3330	14.9
1983	3550	6.62
1984	3955	11.4
1985	4343 S&P DTI	9.81
1986	4545	4.65
1987	4932	8.51
1988	4857	−1.51
1989	5253	8.15
1990	6077	15.68
1991	6346	4.43
1992	6579	3.67
1993	6716	2.09
1994	6982	3.97
1995	7547	8.09
1996	8726	15.62
1997	8867	1.61
1998	9306	4.95
1999	9869	6.05
2000	10999	11.45
2001	10939	−0.55
2002	11098	1.46
2003	11479	3.43
2004	12921	12.56
2005	13514	4.59
2006	13706	1.42

Sources: LSM: Commodity Research Bureau (CRB) 1961–1984. S&P DTI:
S&P White Paper 2003, 1985–2003. S&P DTI: S&P Web site 2004–2006.
Compiled by Enhanced Alpha Management, LP.

TABLE 6.3 S&P 150-Day Moving Average Study from August 7, 1928, to December 31, 2006

	SP 500		SP MA Test #11[a]		SP MA Test #21[b]		SP MA Test #31[c]	
Compound	5. = 60%		7.27%		7.87%		7.31%	
Average	7.52%		8.15%		8.78%		8.21%	
Annualized STD	19.24%		11.57%		12.47%		11.75%	
Max Drawdown	−86.03%		−50.04%		−47.05%		−34.84%	
1928-12-31	$100.00		$100.00		$100.00		$100.00	
1929-12-31	$124.17	24.17%	$124.17	24.17%	$124.17	24.17%	$124.17	24.17%
1930-12-31	$110.06	−11.36%	$124.88	0.58%	$124.88	0.58%	$134.55	8.36%
1931-12-31	$78.71	−28.48%	$120.49	−3.52%	$108.90	−12.80%	$115.80	13.94%
1932-12-30	$41.66	−47.07%	$120.49	0.00%	$103.50	−4.96%	$110.06	−4.96%
1933-12-29	$35.51	−14.78%	$99.38	−17.52%	$105.33	1.76%	$112.00	1.76%
1934-12-31	$51.15	44.08%	$103.58	4.22%	$130.07	23.49%	$130.65	16.65%
1935-12-31	$48.59	−5.02%	$101.55	−1.96%	$124.40	−4.36%	$126.22	−3.39%
1936-12-31	$68.91	41.82%	$145.74	43.52%	$173.17	39.21%	$175.71	39.21%
1937-12-31	$88.15	27.92%	$186.43	27.92%	$221.53	27.92%	$218.64	24.44%
1938-12-30	$54.13	−38.59%	$167.87	−9.96%	$197.83	−10.70%	$204.61	−6.42%
1939-12-29	$67.42	24.55%	$205.57	22.46%	$242.27	22.46%	$250.57	22.46%
1940-12-31	$63.93	−5.18%	$188.30	−8.40%	$201.04	−17.02%	$202.29	−19.27%
1941-12-31	$54.28	−15.09%	$182.81	−2.92%	$188.15	−6.41%	$189.15	−6.50%
1942-12-31	$44.59	−17.86%	$162.52	−11.10%	$174.29	−7.37%	$181.20	−4.20%
1943-12-31	$50.13	12.43%	$180.03	10.77%	$198.69	13.99%	$206.56	13.99%
1944-12-29	$59.88	19.45%	$210.61	16.99%	$232.44	16.99%	$244.03	18.14%
	$68.14	13.80%	$229.56	9.00%	$252.25	8.52%	$262.70	7.65%
1945-12-31	$89.07	30.72%	$300.09	30.72%	$329.75	30.72%	$341.98	30.18%

(continues)

53

TABLE 6.3 *(Continued)*

Date	SP 500		SP MA Test #1[a]		SP MA Test #2[b]		SP MA Test #31[c]	
1946-12-31	$78.50	−11.87%	$308.39	2.77%	$338.86	2.76%	$349.73	2.26%
1947-12-31	$78.50	0.00%	$304.50	−1.26%	$306.31	−9.61%	$315.98	−9.65%
1948-12-31	$77.99	−0.65%	$288.95	−5.11%	$294.53	−3.85%	$305.66	−3.26%
1949-12-30	$86.15	10.46%	$320.86	11.05%	$334.13	13.45%	$346.76	13.45%
1950-12-29	$104.82	21.68%	$390.43	21.68%	$406.57	21.68%	$413.63	19.28%
1951-12-31	$121.76	16.15%	$453.49	16.15%	$472.24	16.15%	$459.16	11.01%
1952-12-31	$136.33	11.97%	$482.10	6.31%	$503.51	6.62%	$479.05	4.33%
1953-12-31	$127.30	−6.62%	$449.62	−6.74%	$476.15	−5.43%	$465.54	−2.82%
1954-12-31	$184.61	45.02%	$652.05	45.02%	$690.53	45.02%	$675.13	45.02%
1955-12-30	$233.35	26.40%	$824.21	26.40%	$872.85	26.40%	$853.39	26.40%
1956-12-31	$239.46	2.62%	$810.07	−1.72%	$844.72	−3.22%	$797.38	−6.56%
1957-12-31	$205.18	−14.31%	$798.55	−1.42%	$850.67	0.70%	$803.00	0.70%
1958-12-31	$283.28	38.06%	$1,020.08	27.74%	$1,114.20	30.98%	$1,051.76	30.98%
1959-12-31	$307.29	8.48%	$1,067.44	4.64%	$1,165.93	4.64%	$1,121.53	6.63%
1960-12-30	$298.15	−2.97%	$985.77	−7.65%	$1,120.23	−3.92%	$1,082.10	−3.52%
1961-12-29	$367.11	23.13%	$1,213.76	23.13%	$1,379.33	23.13%	$1,318.34	21.83%
1962-12-31	$323.76	−11.81%	$1,161.96	−4.27%	$1,396.48	1.24%	$1,346.13	2.11%
1963-12-31	$384.92	18.89%	$1,381.47	18.89%	$1,660.28	18.89%	$1,539.18	14.34%
1964-12-31	$434.84	12.97%	$1,560.64	12.97%	$1,875.61	12.97%	$1,738.81	12.97%
1965-12-31	$474.25	9.06%	$1,663.33	6.58%	$1,999.02	6.58%	$1,875.42	7.86%
1966-12-30	$412.16	−13.09%	$1,616.90	−2.79%	$1,928.31	−3.54%	$1,809.73	−3.50%
1967-12-29	$494.98	20.09%	$1,764.55	9.13%	$2,231.02	15.70%	$2,118.04	17.04%
1968-12-31	$532.89	7.66%	$1,840.20	4.29%	$2,326.67	4.29%	$2,244.97	5.99%

Date							
1969-12-31	$472.35	-11.36%	$1,780.55	-3.24%	$2,227.19	-4.28%	$2,138.55	-4.74%
1970-12-31	$472.04	-0.07%	$1,944.57	9.21%	$2,523.11	13.29%	$2,422.69	13.29%
1971-12-31	$523.09	10.82%	$2,104.17	8.21%	$2,804.97	11.17%	$2,569.19	6.05%
1972-12-29	$605.70	15.79%	$2,391.85	13.67%	$3,188.46	13.67%	$2,747.02	6.92%
1973-12-31	$500.52	-17.37%	$2,142.24	-10.44%	$2,885.99	-9.49%	$2,512.29	-8.55%
1974-12-31	$351.77	-29.72%	$2,142.24	0.00%	$2,885.99	0.00%	$2,512.29	0.00%
1975-12-31	$462.75	31.55%	$2,367.26	10.50%	$3,368.38	16.72%	$2,794.27	11.22%
1976-12-31	$551.36	19.15%	$2,713.31	14.62%	$3,860.78	14.62%	$3,220.36	15.25%
1977-12-30	$487.95	-11.50%	$2,599.94	-4.18%	$3,666.92	-5.02%	$3,019.69	-6.23%
1978-12-29	$493.13	1.06%	$2,494.21	-4.07%	$3,658.63	-0.23%	$3,183.15	5.41%
1979-12-31	$553.83	12.31%	$2,418.99	-3.02%	$3,659.00	0.01%	$3,336.29	4.81%
1980-12-31	$696.57	25.77%	$2,998.09	23.94%	$4,490.52	22.73%	$4,151.57	24.44%
1981-12-31	$628.79	-9.73%	$2,815.44	-6.09%	$4,196.43	-6.55%	$3,555.49	-14.36%
1982-12-31	$721.61	14.76%	$3,354.77	19.16%	$5,137.00	22.41%	$4,300.33	20.95%
1983-12-30	$846.23	17.27%	$3,940.61	17.46%	$6,034.08	17.46%	$4,869.61	13.24%
1984-12-31	$858.09	1.40%	$3,881.79	-1.49%	$6,272.36	3.95%	$5,061.91	3.95%
1985-12-31	$1,084.05	26.33%	$4,781.38	23.17%	$7,725.95	23.17%	$6,348.90	25.43%
1986-12-31	$1,242.54	14.62%	$5,175.52	8.24%	$8,494.45	9.95%	$6,948.51	9.44%
1987-12-31	$1,267.73	2.03%	$5,801.65	12.10%	$9,743.89	14.71%	$8,605.78	23.85%
1988-12-30	$1,424.94	12.40%	$6,327.75	9.07%	$9,770.16	0.27%	$8,052.22	-6.43%
1989-12-29	$1,813.25	27.25%	$8,052.09	27.25%	$12,432.57	27.25%	$10,246.49	27.25%
1990-12-31	$1,694.31	-6.56%	$7,177.33	-10.86%	$11,410.27	-8.22%	$9,811.79	-4.24%
1991-12-31	$2,140.03	26.31%	$8,320.14	15.92%	$14,222.82	24.65%	$12,032.63	22.63%
1992-12-31	$2,235.57	4.46%	$8,486.57	2.00%	$14,597.13	2.63%	$11,961.40	-0.59%
1993-12-31	$2,393.29	7.06%	$9,085.31	7.06%	$15,626.98	7.06%	$12,470.94	4.26%
1994-12-30	$2,356.45	-1.54%	$8,087.58	-10.98%	$14,533.37	-7.00%	$12,005.32	-3.73%

(continues)

TABLE 6.3 *(Continued)*

	SP 500		SP MA Test #1[a]		SP MA Test #2[b]		SP MA Test #3[c]	
1995-12-29	$3,160.25	34.11%	$10,846.30	34.11%	$19,490.80	34.11%	$16,050.09	33.69%
1996-12-31	$3,800.63	20.26%	$13,044.15	20.26%	$23,440.36	20.26%	$18,446.75	14.93%
1997-12-31	$4,979.14	31.01%	$17,088.89	31.01%	$30,708.79	31.01%	$22,470.73	21.81%
1998-12-31	$6,307.01	26.67%	$18,860.56	10.37%	$33,892.50	10.37%	$26,187.90	16.54%
1999-12-31	$7,538.52	19.53%	$21,587.95	14.46%	$38,793.59	14.46%	$28,777.76	9.89%
2000-12-29	$6,774.18	-10.14%	$18,782.81	-12.99%	$34,374.57	-11.39%	$22,687.15	-21.16%
2001-12-31	$5,890.64	-13.04%	$18,782.81	0.00%	$33,000.36	-4.00%	$21,780.17	-4.00%
2002-12-31	$4,514.23	-23.37%	$17,622.24	-6.18%	$29,276.01	-11.29%	$20,289.87	-6.84%
2003-12-31	$5,705.10	26.38%	$21,621.00	22.69%	$34,055.52	16.33%	$23,602.33	16.33%
2004-12-31	$6,218.19	8.99%	$23,004.94	6.40%	$35,350.70	3.80%	$24,571.10	4.10%
2005-12-30	$6,404.79	3.00%	$23,486.82	2.09%	$36,091.19	2.09%	$23,933.01	-2.60%
2006-12-31	$7,277.12	13.62%	$24,849.06	5.80%	$38,476.82	6.61%	$25,680.12	7.30%

Sources: CRB 1928–1980; Bloomberg 1980–2006.
[a]Test #1 = Positioned long when the price is above the MA and the MA is sloping up; positioned flat when price is below the MA and the MA is sloping down.
[b]Test #2 = Positioned long when price is above the MA; positioned flat when price is below MA and the MA is sloping down.
[c]Test #3 = Positioned long when price is above the MA; positioned flat when price is below the MA. Dividends not reinvested (price return only).

TABLE 6.4 S&P 200-Day Moving Average Study from October 10, 1928, to December 31, 2006

	SP 500		SP MA Test #1[a]		SP MA Test #2[b]		SP MA Test #3[c]	
Compound	5.46%		6.67%		7.14%		7.02%	
Average	7.35%		7.58%		8.20%		7.94%	
Annualized STD	19.25%		13.26%		13.54%		11.83%	
Max Drawdown	−86.03%		−56.50%		−62.11%		−50.94%	
	$100.00		$100.00		$100.00		$100.00	
1928-12-31	$110.81	10.81%	$110.81	10.81%	$110.81	10.81%	$110.81	10.81%
1929-12-31	$98.21	−11.36%	$111.45	0.58%	$111.45	0.58%	$121.79	9.92%
1930-12-31	$70.24	−28.48%	$111.45	0.00%	$106.42	−4.51%	$116.30	−4.51%
1931-12-31	$37.18	−47.07%	$111.45	0.00%	$106.42	0.00%	$116.30	0.00%
1932-12-30	$31.68	−14.78%	$87.98	−21.05%	$75.11	−29.42%	$82.08	−29.42%
1933-12-29	$45.65	44.08%	$107.65	22.35%	$93.75	24.82%	$90.68	10.48%
1934-12-31	$43.36	−5.02%	$112.94	4.91%	$96.65	3.09%	$90.09	−0.65%
1935-12-31	$61.49	41.82%	$155.56	37.74%	$139.00	43.81%	$129.56	43.81%
1936-12-31	$78.66	27.92%	$199.00	27.92%	$177.81	27.92%	$165.73	27.92%
1937-12-31	$48.31	−38.59%	$176.01	−11.55%	$157.27	−11.55%	$160.36	−3.24%
1938-12-30	$60.16	24.55%	$185.32	5.29%	$185.33	17.85%	$188.99	17.85%
1939-12-29	$57.05	−5.18%	$143.72	−22.45%	$142.27	−23.24%	$159.60	−15.55%
1940-12-31	$48.44	−15.09%	$139.34	−3.05%	$127.24	−10.56%	$140.42	−12.02%
1941-12-31	$39.79	−17.86%	$139.34	0.00%	$119.90	−5.77%	$132.32	−5.77%
1942-12-31	$44.73	12.43%	$155.58	11.66%	$133.09	10.99%	$146.87	10.99%
1943-12-31	$53.43	19.45%	$185.83	19.45%	$158.97	19.45%	$174.23	18.63%
1944-12-29	$60.81	13.80%	$202.93	9.20%	$176.81	11.22%	$189.72	8.89%
1945-12-31	$79.49	30.72%	$265.28	30.72%	$231.13	30.72%	$248.00	30.72%

(continues)

TABLE 6.4 (Continued)

	SP 500		SP MA Test #1[a]		SP MA Test #2[b]		SP MA Test #3[c]	
1946-12-31	$70.05	-11.87%	$255.65	-3.63%	$222.75	-3.63%	$245.13	-1.16%
1947-12-31	$70.05	0.00%	$252.95	-1.06%	$221.54	-0.54%	$237.76	-3.01%
1948-12-31	$69.60	-0.65%	$249.13	-1.51%	$218.19	-1.51%	$227.92	-4.14%
1949-12-30	$76.88	10.46%	$276.46	10.97%	$244.06	11.85%	$254.10	11.49%
1950-12-29	$93.54	21.68%	$336.40	21.68%	$296.97	21.68%	$295.82	16.42%
1951-12-31	$108.65	16.15%	$390.73	16.15%	$344.94	16.15%	$343.60	16.15%
1952-12-31	$121.66	11.97%	$424.65	8.68%	$374.88	8.68%	$373.66	8.75%
1953-12-31	$113.60	-6.62%	$393.48	-7.34%	$344.81	-8.02%	$353.04	-5.52%
1954-12-31	$164.74	45.02%	$556.73	41.49%	$500.05	45.02%	$511.99	45.02%
1955-12-30	$208.24	26.40%	$703.72	26.40%	$632.08	26.40%	$647.18	26.40%
1956-12-31	$213.69	2.62%	$701.10	-0.37%	$629.72	-0.37%	$642.01	-0.80%
1957-12-31	$183.10	-14.31%	$668.78	-4.61%	$625.75	-0.63%	$637.96	-0.63%
1958-12-31	$252.79	38.06%	$829.92	24.10%	$808.89	29.27%	$824.68	29.27%
1959-12-31	$274.22	8.48%	$900.27	8.48%	$877.46	8.48%	$857.53	3.98%
1960-12-30	$266.07	-2.97%	$828.77	-7.94%	$828.64	-5.56%	$835.06	-2.62%
1961-12-29	$327.61	23.13%	$1,020.45	23.13%	$1,020.29	23.13%	$1,028.20	23.13%
1962-12-31	$288.92	-11.81%	$916.48	-10.19%	$939.56	-7.91%	$1,000.39	-2.70%
1963-12-31	$343.50	18.89%	$1,039.37	13.41%	$1,117.05	18.89%	$1,143.85	14.34%
1964-12-31	$388.05	12.97%	$1,174.17	12.97%	$1,261.93	12.97%	$1,292.21	12.97%
1965-12-31	$423.21	9.06%	$1,209.71	3.03%	$1,300.13	3.03%	$1,387.45	7.37%
1966-12-30	$367.81	-13.09%	$1,095.04	-9.48%	$1,176.89	-9.48%	$1,336.87	-3.65%
1967-12-29	$441.71	20.09%	$1,207.99	10.31%	$1,360.19	15.57%	$1,507.55	12.77%
1968-12-31	$475.55	7.66%	$1,273.23	5.40%	$1,433.64	5.40%	$1,591.60	5.58%
1969-12-31	$421.52	-11.36%	$1,192.07	-6.37%	$1,342.26	-6.37%	$1,541.19	-3.17%

1970-12-31	$421.24	-0.07%	$1,257.69	5.50%	$1,491.04	11.08%	$1,712.02	11.08%
1971-12-31	$466.80	10.82%	$1,296.73	3.10%	$1,537.33	3.10%	$1,756.49	2.60%
1972-12-29	$540.52	15.79%	$1,501.51	15.79%	$1,780.11	15.79%	$1,994.54	13.55%
1973-12-31	$446.66	-17.37%	$1,330.69	-11.38%	$1,529.01	-14.11%	$1,785.54	-10.48%
1974-12-31	$313.92	-29.72%	$1,330.69	0.00%	$1,529.01	0.00%	$1,785.54	0.00%
1975-12-31	$412.96	31.55%	$1,390.68	4.51%	$1,767.05	15.57%	$1,936.44	8.45%
1976-12-31	$492.03	19.15%	$1,604.15	15.35%	$2,038.30	15.35%	$2,170.27	12.08%
1977-12-30	$435.44	-11.50%	$1,522.85	-5.07%	$1,917.12	-5.95%	$2,040.84	-5.96%
1978-12-29	$440.06	1.06%	$1,473.18	-3.26%	$1,941.88	1.29%	$2,031.49	-0.46%
1979-12-31	$494.23	12.31%	$1,465.18	-0.54%	$1,972.39	1.57%	$2,091.50	2.95%
1980-12-31	$621.61	25.77%	$1,706.98	16.50%	$2,297.90	16.50%	$2,562.58	22.52%
1981-12-31	$561.12	-9.73%	$1,550.66	-9.16%	$2,087.47	-9.16%	$2,344.49	-8.51%
1982-12-31	$643.95	14.76%	$1,777.67	14.64%	$2,528.48	21.13%	$2,839.81	21.13%
1983-12-30	$755.17	17.27%	$2,084.70	17.27%	$2,965.18	17.27%	$3,301.36	16.25%
1984-12-31	$765.75	1.40%	$2,020.10	-3.10%	$2,927.63	-1.27%	$3,321.55	0.61%
1985-12-31	$967.40	26.33%	$2,552.06	26.33%	$3,698.57	26.33%	$3,997.92	20.36%
1986-12-31	$1,108.83	14.62%	$2,925.18	14.62%	$4,239.32	14.62%	$4,424.33	10.67%
1987-12-31	$1,131.32	2.03%	$2,715.85	-7.16%	$3,935.95	-7.16%	$5,445.78	23.09%
1988-12-30	$1,271.61	12.40%	$2,763.01	1.74%	$3,997.49	1.56%	$5,249.41	-3.61%
1989-12-29	$1,618.13	27.25%	$3,515.94	27.25%	$5,086.82	27.25%	$6,679.90	27.25%
1990-12-31	$1,511.99	-6.56%	$3,201.71	-8.94%	$4,632.20	-8.94%	$6,121.38	-8.36%
1991-12-31	$1,909.75	26.31%	$3,882.78	21.27%	$5,771.08	24.59%	$7,526.23	22.95%
1992-12-31	$1,995.01	4.46%	$3,905.77	0.59%	$5,849.74	1.36%	$7,606.19	1.06%
1993-12-31	$2,135.76	7.06%	$4,181.33	7.06%	$6,262.44	7.06%	$8,142.81	7.06%
1994-12-30	$2,102.88	-1.54%	$3,785.85	-9.46%	$5,681.11	-9.28%	$7,636.11	-6.22%
1995-12-29	$2,820.19	34.11%	$5,050.83	33.41%	$7,618.97	34.11%	$10,240.83	34.11%

(continues)

TABLE 6.4 *(Continued)*

	SP 500		SP MA Test #1[a]		SP MA Test #2[b]		SP MA Test #3[c]	
1996-12-31	$3,391.67	20.26%	$6,074.31	20.26%	$9,162.84	20.26%	$11,976.77	16.95%
1997-12-31	$4,443.36	31.01%	$7,957.84	31.01%	$12,004.08	31.01%	$15,690.55	31.01%
1998-12-31	$5,628.34	26.67%	$10,080.08	26.67%	$15,205.40	26.67%	$18,407.71	17.32%
1999-12-31	$6,727.33	19.53%	$12,048.33	19.53%	$18,174.42	19.53%	$20,354.42	10.58%
2000-12-29	$6,045.24	−10.14%	$11,077.84	−8.05%	$16,710.47	−8.05%	$16,683.56	−18.03%
2001-12-31	$5,256.77	−13.04%	$11,077.84	0.00%	$16,710.47	0.00%	$16,683.56	0.00%
2002-12-31	$4,028.48	−23.37%	$11,077.84	0.00%	$15,885.95	−4.93%	$15,917.49	−4.59%
2003-12-31	$5,091.21	26.38%	$13,442.84	21.35%	$18,956.52	19.33%	$18,994.15	19.33%
2004-12-31	$5,549.08	8.99%	$14,337.97	6.66%	$20,255.44	6.85%	$19,591.48	3.14%
2005-12-30	$5,715.61	3.00%	$14,329.43	−0.06%	$20,243.37	−0.06%	$18,989.17	−3.07%
2006-12-31	$6,494.08	13.62%	$15,849.78	10.61%	$22,391.19	10.61%	$20,432.35	7.60%

Sources: CRB 1928–1980; Bloomberg 1980–2006.
Dividends not reinvested (price return only).
[a]Test #1 = Positioned long when the price is above the MA and the MA is sloping up; positioned flat when price is below the MA and the MA is sloping down.
[b]Test #2 = Positioned long when price is above the MA; positioned flat when price is below MA and the MA is sloping down.
[c]Test # 3 = Positioned long when price is above the MA; positioned flat when price is below the MA.

TABLE 6.5 S&P 250-Day Moving Average Study from October 10, 1928, to December 31, 2006

	SP 500		SP MA Test #1[a]		SP MA Test #2[b]		SP MA Test #3[c]	
Compound	5.31%		6.03%		6.14%		6.83%	
Average	7.18%		7.01%		7.26%		7.81%	
Annualized STD	19.22%		12.95%		13.36%		11.92%	
Max Drawdown	−86.03%		−43.42%		−60.94%		−51.91%	
	$100.00		$100.00		$100.00		$100.00	
1929-12-31	$86.46	−13.54%	$82.35	−17.65%	$82.35	−17.65%	$103.79	3.79%
1930-12-31	$61.83	−28.48%	$81.13	−1.48%	$81.13	−1.48%	$99.89	−3.76%
1931-12-31	$32.73	−47.07%	$81.13	0.00%	$81.13	0.00%	$99.89	0.00%
1932-12-30	$27.89	−14.78%	$81.13	0.00%	$56.28	−30.62%	$69.30	−30.62%
1933-12-29	$40.19	44.08%	$122.55	51.06%	$73.47	30.54%	$90.46	30.54%
1934-12-31	$38.17	−5.02%	$118.13	−3.61%	$70.82	−3.61%	$93.00	2.81%
1935-12-31	$54.13	41.82%	$161.88	37.04%	$101.39	43.18%	$133.16	43.18%
1936-12-31	$69.25	27.92%	$207.08	27.92%	$129.70	27.92%	$170.34	27.92%
1937-12-31	$42.52	−38.59%	$188.16	−9.14%	$117.85	−9.14%	$153.58	−9.84%
1938-12-30	$52.96	24.55%	$192.25	2.18%	$118.99	0.96%	$155.05	0.96%
1939-12-29	$50.22	−5.18%	$157.42	−18.12%	$93.63	−21.31%	$121.68	−21.52%
1940-12-31	$42.64	−15.09%	$129.88	−17.50%	$74.89	−20.02%	$112.12	−7.86%
1941-12-31	$35.03	−17.86%	$126.61	−2.52%	$72.00	−3.85%	$107.81	−3.85%
1942-12-31	$39.38	12.43%	$129.12	1.98%	$81.05	12.56%	$121.34	12.56%
1943-12-31	$47.04	19.45%	$154.23	19.45%	$96.81	19.45%	$139.24	14.75%
1944-12-29	$53.53	13.80%	$175.51	13.80%	$110.16	13.80%	$154.59	11.02%
1945-12-31	$69.97	30.72%	$229.43	30.72%	$144.01	30.72%	$202.08	30.72%
1946-12-31	$61.67	−11.87%	$198.37	−13.54%	$124.52	−13.54%	$204.41	1.15%

(continues)

TABLE 6.5 (Continued)

	SP 500		SP MA Test #1[a]		SP MA Test #2[b]		SP MA Test #3[c]	
1947-12-31	$61.67	0.00%	$189.54	-4.45%	$115.03	-7.61%	$194.52	-4.84%
1948-12-31	$61.27	-0.65%	$184.36	-2.73%	$110.03	-4.35%	$187.64	-3.53%
1949-12-30	$67.67	10.46%	$188.80	2.41%	$116.39	5.79%	$206.35	9.97%
1950-12-29	$82.35	21.68%	$229.73	21.68%	$141.63	21.68%	$242.87	17.70%
1951-12-31	$95.65	16.15%	$266.84	16.15%	$164.50	16.15%	$282.10	16.15%
1952-12-31	$107.09	11.97%	$298.78	11.97%	$184.19	11.97%	$308.33	9.29%
1953-12-31	$100.00	-6.62%	$270.89	-9.33%	$163.80	-11.07%	$280.11	-9.15%
1954-12-31	$145.02	45.02%	$373.57	37.91%	$237.55	45.02%	$406.23	45.02%
1955-12-30	$183.31	26.40%	$472.21	26.40%	$300.27	26.40%	$513.49	26.40%
1956-12-31	$188.11	2.62%	$479.70	1.59%	$305.03	1.59%	$487.61	-5.04%
1957-12-31	$161.18	-14.31%	$447.38	-6.74%	$287.49	-5.75%	$475.83	-2.42%
1958-12-31	$222.53	38.06%	$520.11	16.26%	$359.61	25.09%	$595.21	25.09%
1959-12-31	$241.39	8.48%	$564.20	8.48%	$390.10	8.48%	$613.86	3.13%
1960-12-30	$234.22	-2.97%	$512.71	-9.12%	$359.39	-7.87%	$592.31	-3.51%
1961-12-29	$288.39	23.13%	$623.78	21.66%	$442.51	23.13%	$729.30	23.13%
1962-12-31	$254.33	-11.81%	$575.31	-7.77%	$407.46	-7.92%	$680.20	-6.73%
1963-12-31	$302.38	18.89%	$630.53	9.60%	$484.43	18.89%	$808.69	18.89%
1964-12-31	$341.60	12.97%	$712.31	12.97%	$547.26	12.97%	$913.58	12.97%
1965-12-31	$372.55	9.06%	$739.60	3.83%	$568.23	3.83%	$966.45	5.79%
1966-12-30	$323.78	-13.09%	$715.28	-3.29%	$549.55	-3.29%	$917.88	-5.02%
1967-12-29	$388.83	20.09%	$781.55	9.26%	$621.95	13.17%	$1,038.81	13.17%
1968-12-31	$418.62	7.66%	$791.46	1.27%	$629.83	1.27%	$1,103.67	6.24%
1969-12-31	$371.06	-11.36%	$748.78	-5.39%	$595.87	-5.39%	$1,050.86	-4.79%
1970-12-31	$370.82	-0.07%	$766.10	2.31%	$637.86	7.05%	$1,124.90	7.05%

Date							
1971-12-31	$410.92	10.82%	$848.96	10.82%	$706.85	10.82%	$1,206.30	7.24%
1972-12-29	$475.82	15.79%	$983.03	15.79%	$818.47	15.79%	$1,396.80	15.79%
1973-12-31	$393.19	-17.37%	$825.21	-16.05%	$692.54	-15.39%	$1,226.69	-12.18%
1974-12-31	$276.34	-29.72%	$825.21	0.00%	$692.54	0.00%	$1,226.69	0.00%
1975-12-31	$363.52	31.55%	$821.38	-0.46%	$762.96	10.17%	$1,351.43	10.17%
1976-12-31	$433.13	19.15%	$978.66	19.15%	$909.05	19.15%	$1,594.04	17.95%
1977-12-30	$383.31	-11.50%	$917.46	-6.25%	$850.53	-6.44%	$1,515.11	-4.95%
1978-12-29	$387.38	1.06%	$832.83	-9.22%	$798.84	-6.08%	$1,442.67	-4.78%
1979-12-31	$435.07	12.31%	$907.94	9.02%	$870.89	9.02%	$1,454.63	0.83%
1980-12-31	$547.20	25.77%	$1,103.65	21.56%	$1,058.61	21.56%	$1,782.70	22.55%
1981-12-31	$493.95	-9.73%	$998.22	-9.55%	$957.48	-9.55%	$1,667.80	-6.45%
1982-12-31	$566.87	14.76%	$1,167.18	16.93%	$1,137.66	18.82%	$1,981.67	18.82%
1983-12-30	$664.77	17.27%	$1,368.77	17.27%	$1,334.15	17.27%	$2,323.92	17.27%
1984-12-31	$674.08	1.40%	$1,325.45	-3.17%	$1,291.92	-3.17%	$2,335.57	0.50%
1985-12-31	$851.59	26.33%	$1,674.48	26.33%	$1,632.13	26.33%	$2,950.61	26.33%
1986-12-31	$976.10	14.62%	$1,919.30	14.62%	$1,870.75	14.62%	$3,381.99	14.62%
1987-12-31	$995.89	2.03%	$1,781.95	-7.16%	$1,736.88	-7.16%	$3,948.01	16.74%
1988-12-30	$1,119.38	12.40%	$1,798.14	0.91%	$1,750.18	0.77%	$3,978.24	0.77%
1989-12-29	$1,424.42	27.25%	$2,288.14	27.25%	$2,227.11	27.25%	$5,062.34	27.25%
1990-12-31	$1,330.99	-6.56%	$2,232.84	-2.42%	$2,173.29	-2.42%	$4,790.70	-5.37%
1991-12-31	$1,681.13	26.31%	$2,781.82	24.59%	$2,707.63	24.59%	$5,968.56	24.59%
1992-12-31	$1,756.18	4.46%	$2,906.01	4.46%	$2,828.50	4.46%	$6,125.29	2.63%
1993-12-31	$1,880.08	7.06%	$3,111.03	7.06%	$3,028.06	7.06%	$6,557.44	7.06%
1994-12-30	$1,851.14	-1.54%	$2,675.98	-13.98%	$2,674.11	-11.69%	$6,038.68	-7.91%
1995-12-29	$2,482.58	34.11%	$3,486.15	30.28%	$3,575.06	33.69%	$8,073.20	33.69%

(continues)

TABLE 6.5 *(Continued)*

	SP 500		SP MA Test #1[a]		SP MA Test #2[b]		SP MA Test #3[c]	
1996-12-31	$2,985.64	20.26%	$4,192.57	20.26%	$4,299.50	20.26%	$9,709.12	20.26%
1997-12-31	$3,911.44	31.01%	$5,492.61	31.01%	$5,632.70	31.01%	$12,719.72	31.01%
1998-12-31	$4,954.56	26.67%	$6,372.58	16.02%	$6,535.12	16.02%	$14,687.93	15.47%
1999-12-31	$5,921.99	19.53%	$7,616.89	19.53%	$7,811.17	19.53%	$16,789.95	14.31%
2000-12-29	$5,321.54	−10.14%	$7,081.52	−7.03%	$7,262.14	−7.03%	$13,940.68	−16.97%
2001-12-31	$4,627.47	−13.04%	$7,081.52	0.00%	$7,262.14	0.00%	$13,940.68	0.00%
2002-12-31	$3,546.22	−23.37%	$7,081.52	0.00%	$7,088.77	−2.39%	$13,587.35	−2.53%
2003-12-31	$4,481.73	26.38%	$7,795.43	10.08%	$8,426.41	18.87%	$16,151.24	18.87%
2004-12-31	$4,884.79	8.99%	$8,496.51	8.99%	$9,184.23	8.99%	$16,892.91	4.59%
2005-12-30	$5,031.38	3.00%	$8,582.11	1.01%	$9,276.77	1.01%	$16,141.69	−4.45%
2006-12-31	$5,716.65	13.62%	$9,750.99	13.62	$10,540.27	13.62%	$17,562.16	8.80%

Sources: CRB 1928–1980; Bloomberg 1980–2006.
Dividends not reinvested (price return only).
[a]Test #1 = Positioned long when the price is above the MA and the MA is sloping up; positioned flat when price is below the MA and the MA is sloping down.
[b]Test #2 = Positioned long when price is above the MA; positioned flat when price is below MA and the MA is sloping down.
[c]Test # 3 = Positioned long when price is above the MA; positioned flat when price is below the MA.

TABLE 6.6 Summary of Table 6.3 through 6.5

A	B	C
Test—150 Days	Test—200 Days	Test—250 Days
#1 + 29.82%	#4 + 22.16%	#7 + 13.56%
#2 + 40.54%	#5 + 30.77%	#8 + 15.63%
#3 + 30.54%	#6 + 28.51%	#9 + 28.63%
+ **33.63% Ave**	+ **27.15% Ave**	+ **19.27% Ave**

Table 6.6 summarizes the results, illustrating the dramatic increase in returns.

- Average increased return was 26.68 percent for all nine samples
- Average standard deviation (STD) for the tests:
  - A STD 11.93 percent
  - B STD 12.87 percent
  - C STD 12.74 percent
- Average standard deviation (STD) for the S&P 500 index was 19.24 percent

This shows an average increased return of 26.68 percent, with an average standard deviation of only 12.51 percent for all nine tests, while the S&P 500 had a 19.24 percent standard deviation; that means the S&P 500 had 53.8 percent more risk. This translates to 3.16 times higher (risk-adjusted) return and "proves" over 78 years that trends exist, and random walk is not a valid theory.

SUMMARY

Although the random walk theory is considered a sound basis for investment strategies in some circles, I believe that if you study the material I have provided you with in this chapter, you will agree that trend following is a legitimate challenge to the random walk theory. It remains simply that—a theory, unproven and, in my mind, indefensible. More than 70 years of data show that trends do exist, and that while past prices may not be able to accurately predict the future perfectly, they certainly can provide a useful guide to help you know what to expect.

Remember, one of the main points that defenders of the random walk theory point to is that money managers often do not outperform their benchmarks. What they choose to forget is that whether individual money managers outperform benchmarks or not has as much to do with the fees they charge as any other reason.

Statistical analysis of the markets shows that trend following works over the long term. Like any other strategy, it produces better results during certain periods and market conditions, but properly used it is invaluable as a method of market analysis.

At best, the random walk theory is simply an argument in favor of indexing. At worst, it is wholly invalid. Just because a theory is well-known does not make it true, and it is important to resist the typical societal inclination to adopt something as unassailable truth simply because it is repeated again and again.

CHAPTER 7

The Rationale and Value of a Long/Short Futures Strategy

O ver the years I have followed and explored countless trading strate-gies. Some I developed myself, or in cooperation with people I worked with. Other times I purchased trading systems from outside vendors. It has always been my opinion that, in general, finding a trad-ing strategy that meets your style of trading, your objectives, and your risk tolerance is the equivalent of financial alchemy, since it allows you to eliminate the emotional aspect of trading commodities. If you maintain the discipline to follow the trading strategy (assuming you've chosen one that produces robust returns without large drawdowns), with the proper capitalization you should be profitable over the long term.

When choosing a trading strategy, it is important to understand the rationale behind it so that you have a thorough knowledge of whether it works, why it works, and why it works better than other strategies. As a hypothetical example, let us suppose I sold you a trading system that pur-ports to win 100 percent of its trades over the last 20 years. That alone should do nothing to convince you to follow the strategy. After all, per-haps it is as simple as saying, "If the New York Jets win a game by at least 9 points, the next trading day you buy the S&P 500 futures at the opening and hold them until you have a 7-point profit, at which point you sell them."

I am not going to go back and research this example, since, as I said, it is only hypothetical. But the point is as silly as that sounds, it *works*—or at least it has worked over the last 20 years up to today. Of course, it all depends on your definition of *works*. The fact remains that as I am writ-ing this, the S&P 500 has recently made new highs. Therefore, *any* trading strategy that tells you to go long the S&P 500, and then hold the position for an infinite period until the desired profit has been reached, has been successful. Naturally, you would need unlimited capital resources, as you might have suffered through years of losses in any given position before you were able to sell for the seven-point profit you were waiting for. But in the end, at least up to today, you've been profitable in every trade. However, the S&P drawdown lasted 83 months—almost seven years!

Forgetting the multitude of reasons such a trading strategy is illogical and undesirable, I think the point has been made that you need to understand the rationale behind any trading strategy so you can determine properly whether you truly believe in the strategy or not. For if you don't believe in it, no matter how you try to be open-minded and let the strategy work for you, in the end you will have occasion *not* to follow the system, to override it or even go directly against it. Emotional discipline rears its ugly head, and more often than not you will—in typical human nature—choose exactly the wrong time to deviate from the strategy. So first you need to understand the rationale, then decide if you believe in the evidence placed in front of you to the point that you can follow the strategies guidelines without interference.

One very important aspect of any strategy is whether it is a long-only strategy (like my fictitious New York Jets example) or whether it allows you to go both long and short in order to capitalize on price movements in both directions. Fundamentally, a long/short strategy is optimum in commodity trading, since it allows you to profit in the markets whether we are in an inflationary environment or not.

Although long/short (L/S) indicators and long-only commodity indexes may be considered the same asset class, because their structures are different their performance results diverge during differing market environments, especially when commodity prices decline. For example, long-only commodity indexes are generally heavily weighted to energy, and as such can generally only move up in value if oil prices increase. The S&P Goldman Sachs Commodity Index (GSCI) is one such example, currently weighted an estimated 75 percent to energy.

Fundamentally, it does not matter if an L/S indicator has financial components like bonds (used to provide liquidity and noncorrelation) because as commodities rise in general (i.e., due to inflation), financials will fall in general, as these movements are representative of the same economic condition—rising inflation. Thus, if a L/S indicator is long wheat, and short U.S. Treasury bonds, in an inflationary environment it accomplishes the same thing as a long-only commodity index. Examine Table 7.1, which compares annual directional price movement between different indicator classes.

To prove that an L/S strategy of commodities and (nonequity) financials could be more efficient and provides a smoother return compared to a long-only commodity index in inflationary environments (as well as

TABLE 7.1 Yearly Directional Correlations[a,b]

Yearly	Direction	Opposite	Same +	Same − = Years
1926 to 2006	S&P 500 vs. Bonds	42.0% (34)	51.9% (42)	6.2% (5) = 81
1970 to 2006	S&P 500 vs. Bonds	35.1% (13)	59.5% (22)	5.4% (2) = 37
1970 to 2006	S&P GSCI vs. Bonds	55.1% (20)	43.2% (16)	2.7% (1) = 37
1970 to 2006	LSM/DTI vs. Bonds	27.0% (10)	70.3% (26)	2.7% (1) = 37

Sources: S&P GSCI: The S&P Goldman Sachs Commodity Index, started 1970.
[a]LSM from 1970–1984 and S&P DTI from 1985–2006.
[b]Bonds: Long-term government bonds.

in other market environments, such as when financials rise), we measure the yearly percentage change directional movements of the strategy versus long-term government bonds—which in this instance are representing financials—and the comparison of various indexes and strategies. We measure these comparisons because stocks and bonds can be and are generally used for diversification. In other words, they can serve as noncorrelated asset classes within a portfolio, while long-only commodities indexes can be used as a negatively correlated asset class within a portfolio.

In the diversified world of modern portfolio theory, we can see a general noncorrelated directional pattern between the S&P 500 and bonds as they moved in opposite directions to each other 42.5 percent of the time on an annual basis from 1926 to 2006. Furthermore, they moved up together 51.2 percent and moved down together 6.3 percent of the time on an annual basis over 81 calendar years.

Comparing bonds to the LSM/S&P Diversified Trends Indicator (DTI), we see they moved opposite to each other 27.8 percent of the time, but moved up together 69.4 percent of the time and down together only 2.8 percent of the time. So as bonds move up, the noncorrelated LSM/S&P DTI (which is capable of being long financials and short commodities at the same time via its rules-based algorithm) is able to profit as well—as indicated by its correlation with bonds when bonds appreciate in the above simulation. Moreover, bonds and the LSM/S&P DTI moved down together only 2.8 percent of the calendar years on an annual basis, which is less than that for the S&P 500 versus bonds (5.6 percent). This provides negative correlation as commodities are long and financials are short.

Lastly, when the S&P GSCI is compared to bonds on an annual basis from 1970 to 2006 (the period Goldman Sachs began its simulations), they moved opposite to each other 52.8 percent of the time and up together 44.4 percent of the time, not much different than stocks, while moving down together 2.8 percent of the time, or the same as the LSM/S&P DTI—which is key to the conclusion of this analysis. After all, who does not want the potential to win more (LSM/S&P DTI +69.4 percent versus

+52.8 percent GSCI) when adding negatively correlated assets to a bond portfolio, especially when your loss frequency remains at 2.8 percent of the time, when bonds and commodities decline together?

This example helps illustrate that an L/S strategy like the S&P DTI is a commodities proxy that in the long run accomplishes the same goal as a long-only commodity index—it acts as a hedge against inflation. Yet by being more diversified, and functioning in an L/S capacity, not only can it provide a more effective hedge against inflation that is not centered in the energy sector, but it also provides the ability to take long financial and short commodity positions when bonds rise, which commodities long-only indexes cannot. Thereby an L/S strategy has the potential of creating a more efficient and smoother return.

The end result is that the S&P DTI, being a long/short commodities and financials futures strategy, is potentially more efficient (even with financials in it) than a long-only commodities index when used with a non- or negatively correlated investment asset, because the long/short concept is capable of adjusting to market conditions and is capable of profiting when bonds or commodities (or both) decline. Moreover, the S&P DTI, although an anomaly as an asset class to many investors, can certainly be a strategy used within the commodity asset class category.

In addition, while the idea of going long and short individual components may seem unusual, this construction also accurately adds another dimension of measure to an L/S strategy. A long/short construction measures what long-only indexes measure over long-term periods. However, what an L/S indicator can do, that a long-only indexes cannot, is measure the volatility of the markets it represents—and in this case, the S&P DTI has also historically been correlated to the CPI.

Stated differently, *long-only commodity indexes only measure commodity prices, but an L/S commodity indicator such as the S&P DTI not only measures commodity prices, but can also indirectly indicate something more: how volatile the period is and the rate of inflation (measured by the increase or decrease in the S&P DTI).* Therefore, small increases in volatility and the inflation rate should create small increases in the S&P DTI, and large increases in volatility and the CPI should create large increases in the S&P DTI, even though there does not have to be a true correlation between the S&P DTI and the CPI.

THE RELATIONSHIP BETWEEN THE S&P DTI AND INFLATION

All indicators or indexes with a significant commodities component will generally appreciate during inflationary environments, because tangible

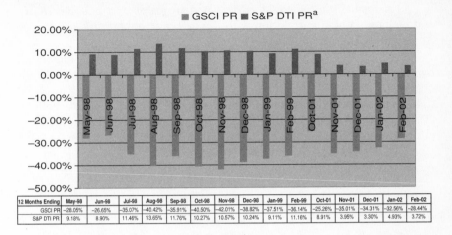

12 Months Ending	May-98	Jun-98	Jul-98	Aug-98	Sep-98	Oct-98	Nov-98	Dec-98	Jan-99	Feb-99	Oct-01	Nov-01	Dec-01	Jan-02	Feb-02
GSCI PR	-28.05%	-26.65%	-35.07%	-40.42%	-35.91%	-40.50%	-42.01%	-38.82%	-37.51%	-36.14%	-25.26%	-35.01%	-34.31%	-32.56%	-28.44%
S&P DTI PR	9.18%	8.90%	11.46%	13.65%	11.76%	10.27%	10.57%	10.24%	9.11%	11.16%	8.91%	3.95%	3.30%	4.93%	3.72%

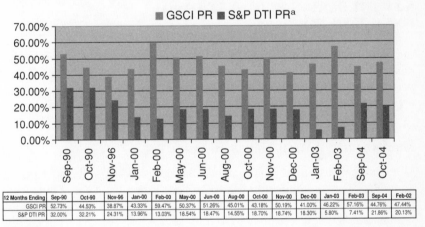

12 Months Ending	Sep-90	Oct-90	Nov-96	Jan-00	Feb-00	May-00	Jun-00	Aug-00	Oct-00	Nov-00	Dec-00	Jan-03	Feb-03	Sep-04	Feb-02
GSCI PR	52.73%	44.53%	38.87%	43.33%	59.47%	50.37%	51.26%	45.01%	43.18%	50.19%	41.00%	46.22%	57.16%	44.76%	47.44%
S&P DTI PR	32.00%	32.21%	24.31%	13.96%	13.03%	18.54%	18.47%	14.55%	18.70%	18.74%	18.30%	5.80%	7.41%	21.86%	20.13%

FIGURE 7.1 Simulated statistical information (gross performance—no fees included).
[a]PR means Price Return that does not include the return earned on the underlying portfolio (i.e. U.S. Treasury bills), which are used as collateral to acquire the S&P DTI or S&P GSCI futures exposure.

assets retain their value in such times. This is typical in long-only commodity indexes, such as the S&P GSCI and the Dow Jones AIG Commodity Index (DJAIG), as well as L/S concepts, such as the S&P DTI. The difference, however, occurs during deflation and or disinflationary environments. During these environments—when commodities often decline in price—the S&P GSCI and the DJAIG will decline and obviously underperform the CPI, because by their very nature they are always long commodities. The S&P DTI, by contrast, does not have this structural handicap because it is able to short its components in downtrends.

As a result, the S&P DTI is designed to produce a positive return and maintain a high correlation with the CPI over long-term periods. See Appendixes D and E.

The S&P DTI's structural advantage is most dramatically illustrated by examining its performance when commodities decline. As a proxy for declining commodity prices, the S&P GSCI performance results are used to measure declining 12-month rolling periods. Figure 7.1 shows the S&P DTI's performance during the GSCI's 15 best and worst 12-month rolling periods from 1985 to 2005. Also, from 1970 to 2005, in a total of 421 12-month rolling periods, the GSCI declined 164 times (a 61.1 percent win ratio); the S&P DTI appreciated during 154 of such 164 declines, or 94 percent of the time.

S&P DTI DURING DISINFLATIONARY ENVIRONMENTS

Indicators and asset classes perform differently during different economic periods. Even stable investments such as Treasury bills result in variable performance, depending on the interest rate environment and the general economic climate. The S&P DTI is no exception to this rule.

The Essence of What Makes an Index

There are two essential requirements that officially classify a structure as an index: (1) its composition has to be based on a fixed set of rules, and (2) its past and future performance has to be congruent with the economic fundamentals that it was created to represent.

Like an index, the S&P DTI has a fixed rules-based structure. The reason this requirement is important is that it allows investors to benchmark an index's performance during certain market environments, thus providing a reasonable expectation of similar future performance in similar conditions. (It is important to understand that the S&P DTI's performance is not the result of curve-fitted or optimized rules, and simulations have proven that its performance would not change drastically if the rules by which it operated were altered.)

More importantly, the S&P DTI's history is congruent with how it should perform in the future. Just as the S&P 500's return could be predicted if the economic fundamentals were known in advance, the S&P DTI's performance could generally be predicted. During inflationary or depressionary environments, the S&P DTI will generally outperform its median return; during disinflationary environments, the S&P DTI will generally produce a small or modest return; and during many (choppy) transitional periods, the S&P DTI may decline. However, there is no necessary correlation between such environments and the S&P DTI.

Long/Short Indicators and Long-Only Indexes: The Same Asset Class

Regardless of their construction, all equity indexes represent the same asset class. Yet, hundreds of different equity indexes exist, because it is possible to create different perspectives for the same asset class. By the same token, the S&P DTI and S&P GSCI merely represent different perspectives as to the commodity asset class. To prove this relationship, we recreated the S&P DTI history from 1985 to 2006 using the same components as the S&P DTI to create a "long-only" strategy (S&P DTI long only). The results showed similar performance; every year the S&P DTI long-only strategy declined, the S&P GSCI also declined. However, the S&P DTI long-only strategy, lost four times for an average loss of 8.51, while the S&P GSCI lost seven years during that period for an average annual loss of –20.11 percent. This difference in loss extent was due primarily to the S&P DTI long-only strategy's weighting to financials, which declined at a lower rate than commodities or rose when commodities declined (the normal case).

The S&P DTI: A Volatility Indicator

Because L/S concepts such as the S&P DTI can take either long or short positions, their return is more dependent on the extended volatility of the futures markets they represent, rather than on the specific direction. Stated differently, L/S indicators are designed to indirectly measure volatility. Volatility-based investments present investors with a significant advantage, since they are designed to allow investors to receive the same asset class exposure as their long-only index counterparts, with a much smoother return over cyclical periods.

To illustrate the relationship between volatility and L/S indicators, Table 7.2 shows the correlation between the return of several indexes/ indicators and their respective volatility, which was extracted from Table 7.2.

Notice the dramatic difference in correlations. In the S&P DTI, increased volatility almost always correspondingly produces increased positive returns, with a correlation of 83 percent! This is an entirely different relationship than that which exists in long-only indexes. However, the S&P GSCI at 34 percent and the SPCI at 37 percent do have a somewhat positive correlation. This is likely a result of the fundamental nature of

TABLE 7.2	Hypothetical Statistical Information Price Returns (PR) and Standard Deviations (STD)

	Correlation of STDs		
	Return	**Long-Only**	**S&P GSCI**	**SPCI**
Return	1.00	0.84	0.52	0.68
Long-only		1.00	0.65	0.82
S&P GSCI			1.00	0.78
SPCI				1.00

Correlation of each index's returns to its volatility			
Return	**Long-Only**	**S&P GSCI**	**SPCI**
0.84	0.51	0.31	0.36

The SPCI was discontinued recently by S&P, so these results are only through the end of 2005.

commodities, as they tend to move up quickly and down sharply. As you can see, stock indexes actually have negative correlations, because stock prices tend to move down far faster than they move up.

What is important to recognize is that the relationship between volatility and a L/S strategy is an inherent part of the S&P DTI's structure. The rules and components of L/S concepts such as the S&P DTI could be changed, without significantly changing the relationship of its return to volatility. This further suggests that going long and short captures a fundamental part of the futures markets core returns—that is, the risk transfer premiums.

CONCLUSION

The S&P DTI and long-only commodity indexes measure rising commodity prices in a similar fashion. What the S&P DTI can do through its long/short design that long-only indexes cannot, however, is measure the volatility of an aggregate of major commodity price movements. This, then, may indirectly act as a proxy for the rising and falling trends associated with inflation rates, which can be demonstrated mathematically and logically.

First we measure the volatility of the S&P DTI components using the DTI long-only strategy, then calculate the standard deviation (STD) of the aggregate of the components. The correlations of the S&P DTI to the DTI long-only returns from 1970 to 2005 are found to be a very high 0.70, while the correlation of the S&P DTI to the DTI long-only STD during this time period is an even higher 0.84 (see Table 7.2). Therefore, one can deduce the S&P DTI and the DTI long-only are highly correlated, deriving their returns from the same asset class fundamentals.

Subsequently, after comparing the DTI long-only to traditional long-only commodity indexes, such as the S&P GSCI and SPCI, it is evident that the DTI long-only returns from 1970 to 2005 are highly correlated to the S&P GSCI and the SPCI returns (0.73 and 0.77, respectively), while the DTI long-only STD is even more correlated to the S&P GSCI and SPCI's STD—0.66 and 0.84, respectively. The S&P GSCI and SPCI are logically correlated to each other in returns and STD, both by 0.79 (see Table 7.2). Therefore, the DTI long-only—and, by deduction, the S&P DTI—measure the same asset class fundamentals as do traditional long-only commodity indexes.

Ultimately, after comparing the annual returns of the S&P GSCI and the SPCI to their own annual STDs from 1970 to 2005, we noticed that they had little correlation, compared to the S&P DTI (0.34 and 0.37 versus 0.83—see Table 7.3). This very large number alludes to the very high correlation between high volatility and high returns, of which the S&P DTI is capable. In other words, the S&P DTI measures or reflects volatility in the commodity markets as a whole.

To logically conclude, if the S&P DTI and the DTI long-only are directly correlated, and the DTI long-only and S&P GSCI/SPCI are correlated, its plausible to assume that the S&P DTI and the S&P GSCI/SPCI are also correlated. As such, the S&P DTI is designed to measure the same things as the S&P GSCI/SPCI, but far more efficiently and profitably, since it is designed to obtain (or receive) a much smoother return.

Given that the S&P DTI clearly has measured volatility by the higher or lower returns it produces, it also may act as a proxy to inflation's rate of change. So if you think the CPI is going to rise, you buy the S&P DTI, and if you think the CPI is going to slow its appreciation, you sell your S&P DTI holdings (but you do *not*, then go short the S&P DTI). It seems

TABLE 7.3 Correlation Between Return and Standard Deviation (STD) of Each Investment from 1970 to 2005 Hypothetical Statistical Information—(Gross Returns—No Fees Included)

S&P DTI	S&P GSCI	SPCI	DTI LO
83%	34%	37%	51%
DJ Transport	DJ Utilities	Value Line	S&P 500
−16%	−16%	−30%	−28%

obvious that the S&P DTI is a far more efficient and profitable commodity investment as a long/short strategy than several other long-only commodity indexes, since futures need no real cash to own them. Collateral like stocks and bonds can be used as a deposit to own the futures contracts. This is especially true when seeking alpha or an equal, overlay-alternative asset exposure as it earns returns when commodities decline—but not as much as when they appreciate. The only disadvantage is not having a long exposure at all times—thus, its *asset class* classification is unclear to many. In other words, if the S&P DTI is flat the energy sector and crude oil suddenly spikes up, long-only indexes will be long and gain the return immediately, while the long/short strategy will not. However, if that spike quickly reverses itself, the S&P DTI will also avoid the losses that accompany the fall in prices that follows.

S&P DTI as an Asset Class

Outline

- The S&P GSCI is an index of commodity prices, and by nature long-only. A long/short indicator is clearly very similar in its asset class exposures. Therefore, the differences lie in how the S&P DTI represents the commodity and financial asset classes.
- Volatility in the commodities markets can be measured based on the performance of the S&P DTI given its long/short nature. The S&P GSCI and SPCI can only measure commodity prices—not the extent of up- and downtrends or volatility—since volatility that is negative causes losses when traded long-only.
- An index of volatility would be valuable, but it must be "investable" to be useful. It should have a capacity for billions of dollars, with the reasonable expectation of increased returns during times of volatility; the S&P DTI meets such criteria.
- The S&P DTI Snapshot: designed based on an asset class very similar to the S&P GSCI. However, unlike the S&P GSCI, it is capable of measuring volatility or the extent of trends.

Does It Work?   Although equity index returns are usually negatively correlated to volatility (since declines typically occur much faster than gains in equities), the S&P DTI and LSM returns are highly correlated, with a +0.83 correlation to its own volatility from 1970 to 2005. See Table 7.3.

Why So Highly Correlated?   Market volatility is generally associated with positive returns of the S&P DTI. In addition, significant negative results for the S&P DTI are rare because as an indicator, it tends to be forward looking, and futures usually anticipate short-term movements. This

TABLE 7.4 April 2006 S&P DTI Positions

Commodities				Financials			
Long	**Weight**	**Short**	**Weight**	**Long**	**Weight**	**Short**	**Weight**
Sugar	1.00%	Cotton	1.00%	Euro	13.00%	T-Notes	7.50%
Cocoa	1.00%	Coffee	1.50%	Yen	12.00%	Bonds	7.50%
Energy	18.75%	Grains	11.50%	Swiss	2.00%		
Copper	5.00%	Livestock	5.00%	Aussie	2.00%		
Gold/Silver	5.25%			Pound	5.00%		
				Canadian $	1.00%		
	31.00%		19.00%		35.00%		15.00%

perhaps is the reason that the S&P DTI reflects trends profitably. Also, its long and short positions act like a hedge fund. For example, in April 2006, the S&P DTI had the positions shown in Table 7.4.

Why the S&P DTI Must Include Financial Assets

For an index to be useful as a financial vehicle it must be investable. Financials, such as U.S. Treasury bonds or U.S. Treasury notes, as well as foreign currencies, play an integral part in the S&P DTI strategy. Not only do they add significantly to the indicator's liquidity, they allow the S&P DTI the ability to measure inflationary and deflationary trends. The S&P DTI can execute $20 billion in value—and with a small adjustment, $50 billion—because it uses financials in addition to commodities.

To repeat, fundamentally it does not matter if a long/short indicator has financials to provide liquidity, because in general as commodities rise (i.e. due to inflation), financials will fall in price, as these movements are representative of the same fundamental economic condition: rising inflation. With that in mind, you can see that being long wheat would accomplish the same thing in an inflationary environment as being short U.S. Treasury bonds.

Most importantly, when disinflation or deflation occurs—and the CPI increases incrementally—the S&P DTI accurately reflects this condition, because financials do not double or triple in value the way commodities are capable of doing. The percentage rate or increase for financials is, for all practical purposes, limited. Also, the rate of decline for commodities is limited when measured in percentage terms (i.e., a rise of 100 percent and a subsequent decline of 50 percent are the same in nominal terms, but half in percentage measures).

Combining commodity and financial exposures allows the indicator to resemble the rate of increase in the CPI, which virtually always increases (but at much lower rates in periods of disinflation). The S&P DTI will also increase, but at much lower rates. This is because of the lower percentage declines for commodities, and the advances in financials, which are highly correlated to the CPI. Even if commodity prices were secular, which of course they are not, a long-only commodity index would never be able to measure up to this phenomenon.

For practical reasons, the S&P DTI's 50 percent commodity/50 percent financial mix is noncorrelated within itself, further adding to the stability of the indicator as an investment, without causing performance to deviate.

Finally, investing in indexes has grown in recent history mainly because indexes (after fees) outperform 85 percent of money managers. It is the efficiency of an indicator that does this as well. An index does not predict anything. Rather it merely reflects fundamental trends in the economy, up or down, by discounting or anticipating short-term future events. This is similar to stock indexes or the Index of Leading Economic Indicators.

Hypothetical Statistical Information (Gross Returns—Fees Included)

Table 7.5 gives a simple overview to how various asset classes—stocks, bonds, and the S&P DTI—correlate to inflation. In this case, inflation is represented by the Consumer Price Index (CPI).

TABLE 7.5 The S&P DTI/LSM Has a High Correlation to the CPI [1961–2006, 1961–1984 (LSM), 1985–2006 (S&P DTI)][a]

	S&P 500 vs. CPI	LT Bonds[b] vs. CPI	LSM S&P DTI TR[c] vs. CPI	LSM/S&P DTI TR[c] vs.CPI w/ T-Bills
1 month	−15.48%	−11.74%	12.91%	17.45%
1 year	−18.76%	−28.86%	51.36%	49.52%
3 year	−19.67%	−32.93%	60.21%	52.73%
5 year	−19.6%	−29.47%	65.89%	52.86%
10 year	−33.17%	−37.89%	88.86%	70.54%

[a]The LSM uses the same algorithm as the S&P DTI—a 1.6 weighted 7-month moving average that rebalances monthly. However, the LSM has equal weightings for all of its futures contracts that are also not formed into sectors. The S&P DTI's futures contracts are weighted and are formed into sectors.
[b]"LT Bonds" means U.S. Government bonds.
[c]"TR" means Total Return, which includes the return earned on the underlying portfolio (i.e., U.S. Treasury bills), which is used as collateral to acquire the S&P DTI futures exposure.

TABLE 7.6 Gross Hypothetical Returns (Rolling Calendar Years)[a]

Rolling Calendar Years

10 Years	LSM PR	LSM TR	CPI	Ratio	S&P 500	LT Gov't Bonds	T-Bills
61–70	11.82%	16.53%	2.92%	4.05:1	8.18%	1.30%	4.26%
62–71	11.19%	16.14%	3.19%	3.51:1	7.06%	2.47%	4.49%
63–72	11.93%	17.03%	3.42%	3.49:1	9.93%	2.35%	4.60%
64–73	18.59%	24.41%	4.12%	4.51:1	6.00%	2.11%	4.98%
65–74	20.78%	27.22%	5.20%	4.00:1	1.24%	2.20%	5.43%
66–75	19.70%	26.31%	5.71%	3.45:1	3.27%	3.03%	5.62%
67–76	21.14%	27.86%	5.86%	3.61:1	6.63%	4.26%	5.65%
68–77	23.43%	30.38%	6.24%	3.75:1	3.59%	5.20%	5.74%
69–78	21.69%	28.79%	6.67%	3.25:1	3.16%	5.10%	5.94%
70–79	22.53%	30.13%	7.37%	3.06:1	5.86%	5.52%	6.31%
71–80	22.14%	30.29%	8.05%	2.75:1	8.44%	3.90%	6.77%
72–81	24.84%	34.39%	8.62%	2.88:1	6.47%	2.81%	7.78%
73–82	24.33%	34.67%	8.67%	2.81:1	6.68%	5.76%	8.46%
74–83	17.51%	27.54%	8.16%	2.15:1	10.61%	5.95%	8.65%
75–84	14.67%	24.69%	7.34%	2.00:1	14.76%	7.03%	8.83%
76–85	14.04%	24.22%	7.01%	2.00:1	14.33%	8.99%	9.03%
77–86	11.94%	22.07%	6.63%	1.80:1	13.82%	9.70%	9.14%
78–87	10.49%	20.60%	6.39%	1.64:1	15.26%	9.47%	9.17%
79–88	10.90%	21.04%	5.93%	1.84:1	16.33%	10.62%	9.09%
80–89	9.61%	19.50%	5.09%	1.88:1	17.55%	12.62%	8.89%
81–90	10.41%	20.03%	4.49%	2.32:1	13.93%	13.75%	8.55%
82–91	8.15%	16.68%	3.91%	2.08:1	17.59%	15.56%	7.65%
83–92	7.05%	14.77%	3.81%	1.85:1	16.19%	12.58%	6.95%
84–93	6.58%	13.67%	3.71%	1.77:1	14.94%	14.41%	6.35%

White Paper Pro Forma

10 Years	S&P DTI PR	S&P DTI TR	CPI	PR: CPI Ratio	S&P 500	LT Gov't Bonds	T-Bills
Dec–94	5.85%	12.32%	3.58%	1.63:1	14.40%	11.86%	5.76%
Dec–95	5.68%	11.97%	3.46%	1.65:1	14.84%	11.92%	5.55%
Dec–96	6.74%	12.99%	3.68%	1.83:1	15.28%	9.39%	5.46%
Dec–97	6.04%	12.20%	3.41%	1.78:1	18.05%	11.32%	5.44%
Dec–98	6.72%	12.69%	3.12%	2.15:1	19.19%	11.66%	5.29%
Dec–99	6.51%	12.05%	2.93%	2.22:1	18.20%	8.79%	4.92%
Dec–00	6.11%	11.42%	2.66%	2.27:1	17.46%	10.26%	4.74%
Dec–01	5.60%	10.66%	2.51%	2.20:1	12.93%	8.73%	4.56%
Dec–02	5.37%	10.20%	2.46%	2.13:1	9.33%	9.67%	4.37%
Dec–03	5.51%	10.12%	2.37%	2.28:1	11.06%	8.01%	4.18%
Dec–04	6.35%	10.66%	2.43%	2.61:1	12.07%	9.78%	3.90%
Dec–05	6.00%	9.97%	2.53%	2.37:1	9.08%	7.60%	3.64%
Dec–06	4.62%	8.43%	2.44%	1.89:1	8.42%	7.83%	3.60%

Source: All data compiled by Enhanced Alpha Management, LP.
[a]Each row represents a rolling 10-year period.

Gross Hypothetical Returns

Table 7.6 shows the gross hypothetical returns for a number of common as-set classes, as well as the LSM/S&P DTI. The returns are depicted in rolling ten-year periods, beginning with 1961 to 1970 and ending with 1997 to 2006.

Tables C.1 and C.2 in Appendix C offer detailed comparisons on an annual basis between commodity indexes and stock indexes. This should help illustrate the correlations we've discussed in this chapter.

CHAPTER 8

Why the S&P DTI Is an Indicator

The Standard & Poor's Diversified Trends Indicator (S&P DTI) is an investable index-like trading strategy, designed to reflect and capture the profit potential of price trends in the commodities and financials markets. Using an algorithm that is completely rules-based, the S&P DTI combines a diversified composite of 24 global commodity and financial futures that are grouped into 14 sectors and are highly liquid. Depending on recent price movements, each sector is represented by either a long or short position, except for energy, which is always either long or flat—the S&P DTI does not go short energies because of the risk of an unexpected market crisis.

With the ability to either go long or short, the S&P DTI was designed to capture the economic benefit derived from both rising and declining trends within a cross-section of the futures markets. It accomplishes this by reflecting price trends and, coincidentally, under most conditions, by receiving the risk transfer premium that hedgers pay to speculators for their capital.

The S&P DTI depicts the *diversified trends* of many different global markets that—as a whole—act as an *indicator*, by forecasting the trends within a cross-section of the global markets. A perfect example of another indicator is the Index of Leading Economic Indicators (LEI), which by Conference Board definition "is intended to predict future economic activity." One of the 11 components in the LEI is the S&P 500 Index.

The S&P DTI is an indicator that measures trends (not prices) in various global commodity and financial markets. These markets include U.S. bonds, U.S. Treasury notes, and many major global currencies, but does not include equities. Thereby, the S&P DTI reflects *the extent of trends* in its profit and loss outcome. Moreover, the value of the S&P DTI may be used to forecast the current trends in aggregate of such global commodity and financial markets. When the S&P DTI increases its value as a unit, continuing trends are demonstrated. Furthermore, when the level of profits is high, it depicts longer and larger trends, and when the level of profits is low, it depicts shorter and smaller trends. The changes in the level of profits reflect changes in the trends, and thereby the economic fundamentals creating those movements.

In addition, as the S&P DTI is completely rules-based, it has a predictive value similar to the predictive value of the LEI. Keep in mind that the LEI uses the S&P 500 Index as a discounting tool for future economic activity in order to predict economic growth. It is a known fact that markets discount the future, just not 100 percent of the time. As Charles Dow said, "If coming events cast their shadows, those shadows fall on the New York Stock Exchange."

PREDICTIVE VALUE OF THE S&P 500

To prove the predictive value of the S&P DTI, Enhanced Alpha Management, LP (EAM) measured the *net exposure* of the up (long) and down (short) price trends in the sectors. Surprisingly, it found that the more net long or net short the exposure, the higher the average profits of the S&P DTI. For example, when measured monthly, the highest category of average profits equaled +177 bps, and occurred when the net longs had the highest net long exposures of 71 to100 percent (maximum was 91 percent) of the S&P DTI's positions. The highest net short exposure of 50 to 100 percent (maximum was 75 percent) of the S&P DTI's positions produced a relatively high +58 bps per month. See Tables 8.1, 8.2, and 8.3.

Table 8.1 shows the monthly positions of the S&P DTI sectors or groups from 1995 to December 2006. The net exposures are longs minus shorts. Thereby, the net short position in August 2005 was −11% (the short being displayed as a negative). The sectors and groups are broken out as 50 percent financials, made up of 35 percent currencies and 15 percent U.S. government bonds/notes and 50 percent in various commodities. There are 144 monthly positions over the time period listed.

Table 8.2 distributes the 144 months of the study in high-low order of net exposure.

TABLE 8.1 S&P DTI Exposure[a]

	Overall View	
End Month	**Returns[b]**	**Net Exposure**
1995-01-31	−0.49%	−19%
1995-02-28	0.53%	18%
1995-03-31	2.42%	82%
1995-04-30	1.10%	79%
1995-05-31	−0.01%	74%
1995-06-30	−0.29%	69%
1995-07-31	−0.85%	61%
1995-08-31	0.40%	46%
1995-09-30	1.42%	0%
1995-10-31	0.60%	32%
1995-11-30	−0.21%	39%
1995-12-31	3.29%	7%
1996-01-31	0.34%	3%
1996-02-29	−0.31%	8%
1996-03-31	2.66%	0%
1996-04-30	2.86%	4%
1996-05-31	0.07%	−19%
1996-06-30	2.65%	−14%
1996-07-31	−1.25%	−30%
1996-08-31	0.21%	−11%
1996-09-30	0.94%	24%
1996-10-31	2.55%	−7%
1996-11-30	2.87%	7%
1996-12-31	1.13%	9%
1997-01-31	0.58%	7%
1997-02-28	−2.14%	−38%
1997-03-31	1.61%	−28%
1997-04-30	1.85%	−34%
1997-05-31	−1.90%	−36%
1997-06-30	0.51%	23%
1997-07-31	−0.49%	−2%
1997-08-31	0.39%	−21%
1997-09-30	1.44%	−26%
1997-10-31	0.20%	10%
1997-11-30	−0.96%	33%
1997-12-31	0.60%	−11%
1998-01-31	0.05%	−32%
1998-02-28	0.63%	−46%
1998-03-31	1.42%	−32%
1998-04-30	−0.04%	−70%

(continues)

TABLE 8.1   *(Continued)*

	Overall View	
End Month	**Returns[b]**	**Net Exposure**
1998-05-31	−0.22%	−16%
1998-06-30	0.27%	−24%
1998-07-31	1.88%	−48%
1998-08-31	2.39%	−14%
1998-09-30	−0.17%	−14%
1998-10-31	−1.03%	44%
1998-11-30	−0.66%	49%
1998-12-31	0.39%	−13%
1999-01-31	−0.91%	−11%
1999-02-28	2.58%	−63%
1999-03-31	−1.10%	−67%
1999-04-30	0.72%	−31%
1999-05-31	−1.31%	−24%
1999-06-30	1.96%	−54%
1999-07-31	0.75%	−45%
1999-08-31	1.54%	18%
1999-09-30	0.72%	−27%
1999-10-31	−2.76%	67%
1999-11-30	2.52%	9%
1999-12-31	1.34%	−3%
2000-01-31	1.37%	11%
2000-02-29	1.62%	13%
2000-03-31	−1.51%	−34%
2000-04-30	1.39%	3%
2000-05-31	2.98%	3%
2000-06-30	1.84%	−57%
2000-07-31	−1.97%	58%
2000-08-31	0.66%	−43%
2000-09-30	0.05%	−17%
2000-10-31	1.16%	−11%
2000-11-30	2.50%	−29%
2000-12-31	0.92%	5%
2001-01-31	−2.12%	49%
2001-02-28	1.17%	16%
2001-03-31	2.04%	6%
2001-04-30	−0.25%	−21%
2001-05-31	0.69%	−51%
2001-06-30	−1.15%	−51%
2001-07-31	−0.95%	−46%
2001-08-31	−0.02%	29%
2001-09-30	0.84%	64%
2001-10-31	0.52%	31%

TABLE 8.1 *(Continued)*

	Overall View	
End Month	**Returns[b]**	**Net Exposure**
2001-11-30	−1.85%	−11%
2001-12-31	0.62%	−75%
2002-01-31	−0.16%	−53%
2002-02-28	0.26%	−23%
2002-03-31	−1.73%	−18%
2002-04-30	0.20%	36%
2002-05-31	−0.37%	60%
2002-06-30	3.28%	87%
2002-07-31	−0.30%	85%
2002-08-31	2.57%	71%
2002-09-30	1.42%	65%
2002-10-31	−1.55%	58%
2002-11-30	0.49%	55%
2002-12-31	−2.50%	3%
2003-01-31	2.44%	62%
2003-02-28	1.83%	77%
2003-03-31	−2.35%	42%
2003-04-30	−0.58%	−14%
2003-05-31	1.99%	43%
2003-06-30	−1.56%	91%
2003-07-31	−2.41%	53%
2003-08-31	−1.38%	2%
2003-09-30	−2.18%	19%
2003-10-31	3.21%	91%
2003-11-30	0.79%	54%
2003-12-31	3.86%	91%
2004-01-31	1.63%	88%
2004-02-29	3.57%	84%
2004-03-31	1.39%	74%
2004-04-30	−2.20%	66%
2004-05-31	0.36%	−28%
2004-06-30	−0.17%	3%
2004-07-31	3.75%	−15%
2004-08-31	−2.41%	4%
2004-09-30	5.53%	26%
2004-10-31	1.63%	49%
2004-11-30	0.27%	51%
2004-12-31	−1.15%	60%
2005-01-31	0.67%	54%
2005-02-28	−2.52%	17%
2005-03-31	2.09%	57%

(continues)

TABLE 8.1   *(Continued)*

	Overall View	
End Month	**Returns[b]**	**Net Exposure**
2005–04–30	−3.50%	−13%
2005–05–31	1.14%	30%
2005–06–30	2.47%	−22%
2005–07–31	0.76%	17%
2005–08–31	1.88%	−11%
2005–09–30	2.16%	−9%
2005–10–31	−1.87%	−22%
2005–11–30	2.38%	−58%
2005–12–31	−0.91%	−58%
2006–01–31	0.01%	14%
2006–02–28	−1.81%	36%
2006–03–31	2.37%	−12%
2006–04–30	2.99%	2%
2006–05–31	0.15%	32%
2006–06–30	−2.40%	51%
2006–07–31	1.72%	2%
2006–08–31	−0.02%	42%
2006–09–30	−1.81%	35%
2006–10–31	0.08%	8%
2006–11–30	0.70%	−2%
2006–12–31	−0.43%	36%

Financials		**Commodities**	
Gross	**Net**	**Gross**	**Net**
61.5%	−38.2%	38.5%	19.4%
61.5%	24.6%	38.5%	−6.5%
61.5%	56.6%	38.5%	25.5%
50.0%	44.0%	50.0%	35.0%
50.0%	46.0%	50.0%	28.0%
50.0%	46.0%	50.0%	22.5%
61.5%	44.3%	38.5%	16.9%
61.5%	32.0%	38.5%	14.5%
61.5%	−17.2%	38.5%	16.9%
61.5%	0.0%	38.5%	32.3%
61.5%	29.5%	38.5%	9.5%
50.0%	−18.0%	50.0%	24.5%
50.0%	−20.0%	50.0%	22.5%
50.0%	−20.0%	50.0%	28.0%
50.0%	−36.0%	50.0%	36.0%

TABLE 8.1 *(Continued)*

Financials		Commodities	
Gross	**Net**	**Gross**	**Net**
50.0%	−44.0%	50.0%	48.0%
50.0%	−44.0%	50.0%	25.5%
50.0%	−36.0%	50.0%	22.5%
50.0%	−34.0%	50.0%	4.5%
50.0%	−10.0%	50.0%	−0.5%
50.0%	−4.0%	50.0%	27.5%
50.0%	−4.0%	50.0%	−2.5%
50.0%	−4.0%	50.0%	10.5%
50.0%	−4.0%	50.0%	12.5%
50.0%	−6.0%	50.0%	12.5%
50.0%	−48.0%	50.0%	10.5%
61.5%	−61.5%	38.5%	33.5%
61.5%	−56.6%	38.5%	23.1%
61.5%	−56.6%	38.5%	20.6%
50.0%	18.0%	50.0%	4.5%
61.5%	17.2%	38.5%	−18.8%
50.0%	−20.0%	50.0%	−0.5%
50.0%	−20.0%	50.0%	−5.5%
50.0%	10.0%	50.0%	0.0%
50.0%	20.0%	50.0%	12.5%
61.5%	−7.4%	38.5%	−4.0%
61.5%	−12.3%	38.5%	−19.4%
61.5%	−24.6%	38.5%	−21.8%
61.5%	−9.8%	38.5%	−21.8%
61.5%	−46.8%	38.5%	−23.1%
61.5%	−17.2%	38.5%	1.5%
61.5%	12.3%	38.5%	−36.0%
61.5%	−12.3%	38.5%	−36.0%
61.5%	12.3%	38.5%	−26.2%
61.5%	24.6%	38.5%	−38.5%
50.0%	46.0%	50.0%	−2.0%
61.5%	59.1%	38.5%	−10.2%
61.5%	−8.6%	38.5%	−4.0%
61.5%	23.4%	38.5%	−34.8%
61.5%	−24.6%	38.5%	−38.5%
61.5%	−54.2%	38.5%	−13.2%
50.0%	−44.0%	50.0%	13.5%
50.0%	−44.0%	50.0%	20.0%
50.0%	−44.0%	50.0%	−9.5%
50.0%	−44.0%	50.0%	−0.5%
50.0%	18.0%	50.0%	−0.5%

(continues)

TABLE 8.1 (Continued)

Financials		Commodities	
Gross	Net	Gross	Net
50.0%	−26.0%	50.0%	−0.5%
50.0%	20.0%	50.0%	47.0%
50.0%	−14.0%	50.0%	23.0%
50.0%	−24.0%	50.0%	21.0%
50.0%	−10.0%	50.0%	21.0%
50.0%	−23.0%	50.0%	35.5%
50.0%	−33.0%	50.0%	−0.5%
50.0%	−20.0%	50.0%	22.5%
50.0%	−20.0%	50.0%	22.5%
50.0%	−50.0%	50.0%	−6.5%
50.0%	38.0%	50.0%	20.0%
61.5%	−22.2%	38.5%	−21.2%
50.0%	−18.0%	50.0%	1.5%
50.0%	−20.0%	50.0%	9.5%
50.0%	−20.0%	50.0%	−8.5%
50.0%	−20.0%	50.0%	24.5%
50.0%	26.0%	50.0%	22.5%
50.0%	16.0%	50.0%	−0.5%
50.0%	6.0%	50.0%	−0.5%
50.0%	−20.0%	50.0%	−0.5%
50.0%	−50.0%	50.0%	−0.5%
50.0%	−50.0%	50.0%	−0.5%
61.5%	−22.2%	38.5%	−23.7%
61.5%	27.1%	38.5%	2.2%
61.5%	59.1%	38.5%	5.2%
61.5%	54.2%	38.5%	−23.1%
61.5%	24.6%	38.5%	−36.0%
61.5%	−56.6%	38.5%	−18.8%
61.5%	−44.3%	38.5%	−8.3%
61.5%	−24.6%	38.5%	1.5%
61.5%	−19.7%	38.5%	1.5%
50.0%	−4.0%	50.0%	40.0%
50.0%	50.0%	50.0%	10.0%
50.0%	50.0%	50.0%	37.0%
50.0%	50.0%	50.0%	35.0%
50.0%	44.0%	50.0%	26.5%
50.0%	48.0%	50.0%	16.5%
50.0%	20.0%	50.0%	38.0%
61.5%	32.0%	38.5%	23.1%
61.5%	−19.7%	38.5%	23.1%
50.0%	48.0%	50.0%	14.0%

TABLE 8.1 *(Continued)*

Financials		Commodities	
Gross	Net	Gross	Net
50.0%	50.0%	50.0%	27.0%
50.0%	40.0%	50.0%	1.5%
61.5%	19.7%	38.5%	−33.5%
61.5%	32.0%	38.5%	10.8%
50.0%	50.0%	50.0%	41.0%
50.0%	22.0%	50.0%	30.5%
50.0%	−18.0%	50.0%	20.0%
50.0%	−24.0%	50.0%	43.0%
61.5%	61.5%	38.5%	29.8%
61.5%	24.6%	38.5%	29.8%
50.0%	50.0%	50.0%	41.0%
50.0%	50.0%	50.0%	38.0%
50.0%	48.0%	50.0%	36.0%
50.0%	24.0%	50.0%	50.0%
50.0%	20.0%	50.0%	46.0%
50.0%	−50.0%	50.0%	22.5%
50.0%	−10.0%	50.0%	12.5%
50.0%	−14.0%	50.0%	−0.5%
50.0%	−8.0%	50.0%	11.5%
50.0%	6.0%	50.0%	20.0%
50.0%	26.0%	50.0%	23.0%
50.0%	50.0%	50.0%	1.0%
50.0%	35.0%	50.0%	25.0%
61.5%	61.5%	38.5%	−7.7%
61.5%	22.2%	38.5%	−5.2%
50.0%	9.0%	50.0%	48.0%
50.0%	−48.0%	50.0%	35.5%
50.0%	−6.0%	50.0%	35.5%
61.5%	−24.6%	38.5%	2.2%
50.0%	−18.0%	50.0%	35.0%
50.0%	−33.0%	50.0%	22.5%
50.0%	−18.0%	50.0%	9.5%
50.0%	−44.0%	50.0%	22.0%
61.5%	−59.1%	38.5%	1.5%
61.5%	−59.1%	38.5%	1.5%
61.5%	−22.2%	38.5%	36.0%
50.0%	−4.0%	50.0%	40.0%
61.5%	−29.5%	38.5%	17.5%
50.0%	−10.0%	50.0%	12.0%
50.0%	20.0%	50.0%	12.0%

(continues)

TABLE 8.1   *(Continued)*

Financials		Commodities	
Gross	Net	Gross	Net
50.0%	20.0%	50.0%	31.0%
50.0%	−8.0%	50.0%	9.5%
50.0%	24.0%	50.0%	18.0%
61.5%	32.0%	38.5%	2.8%
61.5%	−9.8%	38.5%	18.2%
61.5%	−7.4%	38.5%	5.8%
61.5%	29.5%	38.5%	6.5%

Financials Subsets			
Currencies		Bond-Notes	
Gross	Net	Gross	Net
43.1%	−38.2%	18.5%	0.0%
43.1%	6.2%	18.5%	18.5%
43.1%	38.2%	18.5%	18.5%
35.0%	29.0%	15.0%	15.0%
35.0%	31.0%	15.0%	15.0%
35.0%	31.0%	15.0%	15.0%
43.1%	25.8%	18.5%	18.5%
43.1%	13.5%	18.5%	18.5%
43.1%	−35.7%	18.5%	18.5%
43.1%	−18.5%	18.5%	18.5%
43.1%	11.1%	18.5%	18.5%
35.0%	−33.0%	15.0%	15.0%
35.0%	−35.0%	15.0%	15.0%
35.0%	−35.0%	15.0%	15.0%
35.0%	−21.0%	15.0%	−15.0%
35.0%	−29.0%	15.0%	−15.0%
35.0%	−29.0%	15.0%	−15.0%
35.0%	−21.0%	15.0%	−15.0%
35.0%	−19.0%	15.0%	−15.0%
35.0%	5.0%	15.0%	−15.0%
35.0%	11.0%	15.0%	−15.0%
35.0%	−19.0%	15.0%	15.0%
35.0%	−19.0%	15.0%	15.0%
35.0%	−19.0%	15.0%	15.0%
35.0%	−21.0%	15.0%	15.0%
35.0%	−33.0%	15.0%	−15.0%
43.1%	−43.1%	18.5%	−18.5%
43.1%	−38.2%	18.5%	−18.5%

TABLE 8.1 *(Continued)*

| | | **Financials Subsets** | |
| **Currencies** | | **Bond-Notes** | |
Gross	**Net**	**Gross**	**Net**
43.1%	−38.2%	18.5%	−18.5%
35.0%	3.0%	15.0%	15.0%
43.1%	−1.2%	18.5%	18.5%
35.0%	−35.0%	15.0%	15.0%
35.0%	−35.0%	15.0%	15.0%
35.0%	−5.0%	15.0%	15.0%
35.0%	5.0%	15.0%	15.0%
43.1%	−25.8%	18.5%	18.5%
43.1%	−30.8%	18.5%	18.5%
43.1%	−43.1%	18.5%	18.5%
43.1%	−28.3%	18.5%	18.5%
43.1%	−28.3%	18.5%	−18.5%
43.1%	1.2%	18.5%	−18.5%
43.1%	−6.2%	18.5%	18.5%
43.1%	−30.8%	18.5%	18.5%
43.1%	−6.2%	18.5%	18.5%
43.1%	6.2%	18.5%	18.5%
35.0%	31.0%	15.0%	15.0%
43.1%	40.6%	18.5%	18.5%
43.1%	−8.6%	18.5%	0.0%
43.1%	23.4%	18.5%	0.0%
43.1%	−6.2%	18.5%	−18.5%
43.1%	−35.7%	18.5%	−18.5%
35.0%	−29.0%	15.0%	−15.0%
35.0%	−29.0%	15.0%	−15.0%
35.0%	−29.0%	15.0%	−15.0%
35.0%	−29.0%	15.0%	−15.0%
35.0%	33.0%	15.0%	−15.0%
35.0%	−11.0%	15.0%	−15.0%
35.0%	35.0%	15.0%	−15.0%
35.0%	1.0%	15.0%	−15.0%
35.0%	−9.0%	15.0%	−15.0%
35.0%	5.0%	15.0%	−15.0%
35.0%	−23.0%	15.0%	0.0%
35.0%	−33.0%	15.0%	0.0%
35.0%	−35.0%	15.0%	15.0%
35.0%	−35.0%	15.0%	15.0%
35.0%	−35.0%	15.0%	−15.0%
35.0%	23.0%	15.0%	15.0%

(continues)

TABLE 8.1 *(Continued)*

Financials Subsets			
Currencies		Bond-Notes	
Gross	Net	Gross	Net
43.1%	−40.6%	18.5%	18.5%
35.0%	−33.0%	15.0%	15.0%
35.0%	−35.0%	15.0%	15.0%
35.0%	−35.0%	15.0%	15.0%
35.0%	−35.0%	15.0%	15.0%
35.0%	11.0%	15.0%	15.0%
35.0%	1.0%	15.0%	15.0%
35.0%	−9.0%	15.0%	15.0%
35.0%	−35.0%	15.0%	15.0%
35.0%	−35.0%	15.0%	−15.0%
35.0%	−35.0%	15.0%	−15.0%
43.1%	−40.6%	18.5%	18.5%
43.1%	8.6%	18.5%	18.5%
43.1%	40.6%	18.5%	18.5%
43.1%	35.7%	18.5%	18.5%
43.1%	6.2%	18.5%	18.5%
43.1%	−38.2%	18.5%	−18.5%
43.1%	−25.8%	18.5%	−18.5%
43.1%	−43.1%	18.5%	18.5%
43.1%	−38.2%	18.5%	18.5%
35.0%	11.0%	15.0%	−15.0%
35.0%	35.0%	15.0%	15.0%
35.0%	35.0%	15.0%	15.0%
35.0%	35.0%	15.0%	15.0%
35.0%	29.0%	15.0%	15.0%
35.0%	33.0%	15.0%	15.0%
35.0%	5.0%	15.0%	15.0%
43.1%	13.5%	18.5%	18.5%
43.1%	−1.2%	18.5%	−18.5%
35.0%	33.0%	15.0%	15.0%
35.0%	35.0%	15.0%	15.0%
35.0%	25.0%	15.0%	15.0%
43.1%	1.2%	18.5%	18.5%
43.1%	13.5%	18.5%	18.5%
35.0%	35.0%	15.0%	15.0%
35.0%	7.0%	15.0%	15.0%
35.0%	−3.0%	15.0%	−15.0%
35.0%	−9.0%	15.0%	−15.0%
43.1%	43.1%	18.5%	18.5%

TABLE 8.1 *(Continued)*

	Financials Subsets		
Currencies		**Bond-Notes**	
Gross	**Net**	**Gross**	**Net**
43.1%	43.1%	18.5%	−18.5%
35.0%	35.0%	15.0%	15.0%
35.0%	35.0%	15.0%	15.0%
35.0%	33.0%	15.0%	15.0%
35.0%	9.0%	15.0%	15.0%
35.0%	5.0%	15.0%	15.0%
35.0%	−35.0%	15.0%	−15.0%
35.0%	5.0%	15.0%	−15.0%
35.0%	1.0%	15.0%	−15.0%
35.0%	−23.0%	15.0%	15.0%
35.0%	−9.0%	15.0%	15.0%
35.0%	11.0%	15.0%	15.0%
35.0%	35.0%	15.0%	15.0%
35.0%	35.0%	15.0%	0.0%
43.1%	43.1%	18.5%	18.5%
43.1%	3.7%	18.5%	18.5%
35.0%	9.0%	15.0%	0.0%
35.0%	−33.0%	15.0%	−15.0%
35.0%	−21.0%	15.0%	15.0%
43.1%	−43.1%	18.5%	18.5%
35.0%	−33.0%	15.0%	15.0%
35.0%	−33.0%	15.0%	0.0%
35.0%	−33.0%	15.0%	15.0%
35.0%	−29.0%	15.0%	−15.0%
43.1%	−40.6%	18.5%	−18.5%
43.1%	−40.6%	18.5%	−18.5%
43.1%	−40.6%	18.5%	18.5%
35.0%	11.0%	15.0%	−15.0%
43.1%	−11.1%	18.5%	−18.5%
35.0%	5.0%	15.0%	−15.0%
35.0%	35.0%	15.0%	−15.0%
35.0%	35.0%	15.0%	−15.0%
35.0%	7.0%	15.0%	−15.0%
35.0%	9.0%	15.0%	15.0%
43.1%	13.5%	18.5%	18.5%
43.1%	−28.3%	18.5%	18.5%
43.1%	−25.8%	18.5%	18.5%
43.1%	11.1%	18.5%	18.5%

(continues)

TABLE 8.1 *(Continued)*

Commodities Subsets				
Agriculture		Metals-Materials		Energy
Gross	Net	Gross	Net	Gross & Net (same)
Grains, Livestock, Edible Softs		All Metals plus Cotton		
24.6%	18.5%	13.8%	0.9%	0.0%
24.6%	−7.4%	13.8%	0.9%	0.0%
24.6%	24.6%	13.8%	0.9%	0.0%
20.0%	5.0%	11.3%	11.3%	18.8%
20.0%	8.0%	11.3%	1.3%	18.8%
20.0%	3.0%	11.3%	0.8%	18.8%
24.6%	16.0%	13.8%	0.9%	0.0%
24.6%	16.0%	13.8%	−1.5%	0.0%
24.6%	16.0%	13.8%	0.9%	0.0%
24.6%	18.5%	13.8%	13.8%	0.0%
24.6%	20.9%	13.8%	−11.4%	0.0%
20.0%	15.0%	11.3%	−9.3%	18.8%
20.0%	15.0%	11.3%	−11.3%	18.8%
20.0%	8.0%	11.3%	1.3%	18.8%
20.0%	18.0%	11.3%	−0.8%	18.8%
20.0%	18.0%	11.3%	11.3%	18.8%
20.0%	8.0%	11.3%	−1.3%	18.8%
20.0%	15.0%	11.3%	−11.3%	18.8%
20.0%	−3.0%	11.3%	−11.3%	18.8%
20.0%	−8.0%	11.3%	−11.3%	18.8%
20.0%	18.0%	11.3%	−9.3%	18.8%
20.0%	−10.0%	11.3%	−11.3%	18.8%
20.0%	−7.0%	11.3%	−1.3%	18.8%
20.0%	−5.0%	11.3%	−1.3%	18.8%
20.0%	−5.0%	11.3%	−1.3%	18.8%
20.0%	−7.0%	11.3%	−1.3%	18.8%
24.6%	22.2%	13.8%	11.4%	0.0%
24.6%	24.6%	13.8%	−1.5%	0.0%
24.6%	22.2%	13.8%	−1.5%	0.0%
20.0%	−13.0%	11.3%	−1.3%	18.8%
24.6%	−19.7%	13.8%	0.9%	0.0%
20.0%	−8.0%	11.3%	−11.3%	18.8%
20.0%	−13.0%	11.3%	−11.3%	18.8%
20.0%	−18.0%	11.3%	−0.8%	18.8%
20.0%	5.0%	11.3%	−11.3%	18.8%
24.6%	9.8%	13.8%	−13.8%	0.0%
24.6%	−18.5%	13.8%	−0.9%	0.0%

TABLE 8.1 *(Continued)*

Agriculture		Metals-Materials		Energy
				Commodities Subsets
Gross	Net	Gross	Net	Gross & Net (same)
Grains, Livestock, Edible Softs		All Metals plus Cotton		
24.6%	−20.9%	13.8%	−0.9%	0.0%
24.6%	−20.9%	13.8%	−0.9%	0.0%
24.6%	−24.6%	13.8%	1.5%	0.0%
24.6%	−9.8%	13.8%	11.4%	0.0%
24.6%	−24.6%	13.8%	−11.4%	0.0%
24.6%	−24.6%	13.8%	−11.4%	0.0%
24.6%	−24.6%	13.8%	−1.5%	0.0%
24.6%	−24.6%	13.8%	−13.8%	0.0%
20.0%	−20.0%	11.3%	−0.8%	18.8%
24.6%	3.7%	13.8%	−13.8%	0.0%
24.6%	9.8%	13.8%	−13.8%	0.0%
24.6%	−20.9%	13.8%	−13.8%	0.0%
24.6%	−24.6%	13.8%	−13.8%	0.0%
24.6%	−12.3%	13.8%	−0.9%	0.0%
20.0%	6.0%	11.3%	−11.3%	18.8%
20.0%	−10.0%	11.3%	11.3%	18.8%
20.0%	−17.0%	11.3%	−11.3%	18.8%
20.0%	−18.0%	11.3%	−1.3%	18.8%
20.0%	−18.0%	11.3%	−1.3%	18.8%
20.0%	−18.0%	11.3%	−1.3%	18.8%
20.0%	17.0%	11.3%	11.3%	18.8%
20.0%	−5.0%	11.3%	9.3%	18.8%
20.0%	−7.0%	11.3%	9.3%	18.8%
20.0%	−7.0%	11.3%	9.3%	18.8%
20.0%	16.0%	11.3%	0.8%	18.8%
20.0%	−10.0%	11.3%	−9.3%	18.8%
20.0%	13.0%	11.3%	−9.3%	18.8%
20.0%	15.0%	11.3%	−11.3%	18.8%
20.0%	−16.0%	11.3%	−9.3%	18.8%
20.0%	−8.0%	11.3%	9.3%	18.8%
24.6%	−19.7%	13.8%	−1.5%	0.0%
20.0%	−18.0%	11.3%	0.8%	18.8%
20.0%	−8.0%	11.3%	−1.3%	18.8%
20.0%	−18.0%	11.3%	−9.3%	18.8%
20.0%	15.0%	11.3%	−9.3%	18.8%
20.0%	15.0%	11.3%	−11.3%	18.8%
20.0%	−8.0%	11.3%	−11.3%	18.8%
20.0%	−8.0%	11.3%	−11.3%	18.8%

(continues)

TABLE 8.1 *(Continued)*

Agriculture		Metals-Materials		Energy
Gross	Net	Gross	Net	Gross & Net (same)
Grains, Livestock, Edible Softs		All Metals plus Cotton		
20.0%	−8.0%	11.3%	−11.3%	18.8%
20.0%	−8.0%	11.3%	−11.3%	18.8%
20.0%	−8.0%	11.3%	−11.3%	18.8%
24.6%	−9.8%	13.8%	−13.8%	0.0%
24.6%	16.0%	13.8%	−13.8%	0.0%
24.6%	6.2%	13.8%	−0.9%	0.0%
24.6%	−22.2%	13.8%	−0.9%	0.0%
24.6%	−22.2%	13.8%	−13.8%	0.0%
24.6%	−19.7%	13.8%	0.9%	0.0%
24.6%	−7.4%	13.8%	−0.9%	0.0%
24.6%	−9.8%	13.8%	11.4%	0.0%
24.6%	−9.8%	13.8%	11.4%	0.0%
20.0%	10.0%	11.3%	11.3%	18.8%
20.0%	−18.0%	11.3%	9.3%	18.8%
20.0%	7.0%	11.3%	11.3%	18.8%
20.0%	5.0%	11.3%	11.3%	18.8%
20.0%	17.0%	11.3%	−9.3%	18.8%
20.0%	7.0%	11.3%	−9.3%	18.8%
20.0%	20.0%	11.3%	−0.8%	18.8%
24.6%	22.2%	13.8%	0.9%	0.0%
24.6%	22.2%	13.8%	0.9%	0.0%
20.0%	−6.0%	11.3%	1.3%	18.8%
20.0%	−3.0%	11.3%	11.3%	18.8%
20.0%	−18.0%	11.3%	0.8%	18.8%
24.6%	−22.2%	13.8%	−11.4%	0.0%
24.6%	24.6%	13.8%	−13.8%	0.0%
20.0%	13.0%	11.3%	9.3%	18.8%
20.0%	13.0%	11.3%	−1.3%	18.8%
20.0%	−8.0%	11.3%	9.3%	18.8%
20.0%	15.0%	11.3%	9.3%	18.8%
24.6%	16.0%	13.8%	13.8%	0.0%
24.6%	16.0%	13.8%	13.8%	0.0%
20.0%	13.0%	11.3%	9.3%	18.8%
20.0%	8.0%	11.3%	11.3%	18.8%
20.0%	8.0%	11.3%	9.3%	18.8%
20.0%	20.0%	11.3%	11.3%	18.8%
20.0%	18.0%	11.3%	9.3%	18.8%
20.0%	15.0%	11.3%	−11.3%	18.8%

TABLE 8.1 *(Continued)*

Agriculture		Metals-Materials		Energy
Gross	Net	Gross	Net	Gross & Net (same)
Grains, Livestock, Edible Softs		All Metals plus Cotton		
20.0%	−5.0%	11.3%	−1.3%	18.8%
20.0%	−8.0%	11.3%	−11.3%	18.8%
20.0%	−6.0%	11.3%	−1.3%	18.8%
20.0%	−8.0%	11.3%	9.3%	18.8%
20.0%	−5.0%	11.3%	9.3%	18.8%
20.0%	−17.0%	11.3%	−0.8%	18.8%
20.0%	−3.0%	11.3%	9.3%	18.8%
24.6%	−6.2%	13.8%	−1.5%	0.0%
24.6%	−3.7%	13.8%	−1.5%	0.0%
20.0%	18.0%	11.3%	11.3%	18.8%
20.0%	16.0%	11.3%	0.8%	18.8%
20.0%	16.0%	11.3%	0.8%	18.8%
24.6%	3.7%	13.8%	−1.5%	0.0%
20.0%	5.0%	11.3%	11.3%	18.8%
20.0%	5.0%	11.3%	−1.3%	18.8%
20.0%	−8.0%	11.3%	−1.3%	18.8%
20.0%	−8.0%	11.3%	11.3%	18.8%
24.6%	−9.8%	13.8%	11.4%	0.0%
24.6%	−9.8%	13.8%	11.4%	0.0%
24.6%	24.6%	13.8%	11.4%	0.0%
20.0%	10.0%	11.3%	11.3%	18.8%
24.6%	6.2%	13.8%	11.4%	0.0%
20.0%	−16.0%	11.3%	9.3%	18.8%
20.0%	−16.0%	11.3%	9.3%	18.8%
20.0%	3.0%	11.3%	9.3%	18.8%
20.0%	−8.0%	11.3%	−1.3%	18.8%
20.0%	−10.0%	11.3%	9.3%	18.8%
24.6%	−8.6%	13.8%	11.4%	0.0%
24.6%	19.7%	13.8%	−1.5%	0.0%
24.6%	19.7%	13.8%	−13.8%	0.0%
24.6%	7.4%	13.8%	−0.9%	0.0%

[a]Past performance is no guarantee of future results.
[b]The S&P DTI returns on this report are those of the "DTI-O" prior to 2004. The DTI-O is the original S&P DTI calculation method, with position adjustments occurring on the last trading day of each month. The S&P DTI as published by S&P (and used since 1-1-2004 in this table) has variable adjustment dates.
[c]"Gross Exposure" is always a positive number and is equal to the sum of the absolute values of each sector position.

TABLE 8.2 S&P DTI Exposure—Sorted[a,b]

Summary Table of Net Exposure Ranges and Average Return

Lower limit	>0.80	>0.60	>0.40	>0.20	>0.00	>−0.20	>−0.40	>−0.60	>−0.80
Higher limit		<0.80	<0.60	<0.40	<0.20	<0.00	<−0.20	<−0.40	<−0.60
Avg. return	2.01%	0.46%	−0.40%	0.31%	0.74%	0.63%	0.19%	0.63%	0.52%

	Overall View	
End Month	**Returns**	**Net Exposure**
2003–10–31	3.21%	91%
2003–12–31	3.86%	91%
2003–06–30	−1.56%	91%
2004–01–31	1.63%	88%
2002–06–30	3.28%	87%
2002–07–31	−0.30%	85%
2004–02–29	3.57%	84%
1995–03–31	2.42%	82%
1995–04–30	1.10%	79%
2003–02–28	1.83%	77%
2004–03–31	1.39%	74%
1995–05–31	−0.01%	74%
2002–08–31	2.57%	71%
1995–06–30	−0.29%	69%
1999–10–31	−2.76%	67%
2004–04–30	−2.20%	66%
2002–09–30	1.42%	65%
2001–09–30	0.84%	64%
2003–01–31	2.44%	62%
1995–07–31	−0.85%	61%
2004–12–31	−1.15%	60%
2002–05–31	−0.37%	60%
2002–10–31	−1.55%	58%
2000–07–31	−1.97%	58%
2005–03–31	2.09%	57%
2002–11–30	0.49%	55%
2003–11–30	0.79%	54%
2005–01–31	0.67%	54%
2003–07–31	−2.41%	53%
2004–11–30	0.27%	51%
2006–06–30	−2.40%	51%
2004–10–31	1.63%	49%
1998–11–30	−0.66%	49%
2001–01–31	−2.12%	49%
1995–08–31	0.40%	46%

TABLE 8.2 *(Continued)*

End Month	Overall View	
	Returns	**Net Exposure**
1998-10-31	−1.03%	44%
2003-05-31	1.99%	43%
2006-08-31	−0.02%	42%
2003-03-31	−2.35%	42%
1995-11-30	−0.21%	39%
2006-02-28	−1.81%	36%
2002-04-30	0.20%	36%
2006-12-31	−0.43%	36%
2006-09-30	−1.81%	35%
1997-11-30	−0.96%	33%
1995-10-31	0.60%	32%
2006-05-31	0.15%	32%
2001-10-31	0.52%	31%
2005-05-31	1.14%	30%
2001-08-31	−0.02%	29%
2004-09-30	5.53%	26%
1996-09-30	0.94%	24%
1997-06-30	0.51%	23%
2003-09-30	−2.18%	19%
1995-02-28	0.53%	18%
1999-08-31	1.54%	18%
2005-07-31	0.76%	17%
2005-02-28	−2.52%	17%
2001-02-28	1.17%	16%
2006-01-31	0.01%	14%
2000-02-29	1.62%	13%
2000-01-31	1.37%	11%
1997-10-31	0.20%	10%
1999-11-30	2.52%	9%
1996-12-31	1.13%	9%
2006-10-31	0.08%	8%
1996-02-29	−0.31%	8%
1997-01-31	0.58%	7%
1996-11-30	2.87%	7%
1995-12-31	3.29%	7%
2001-03-31	2.04%	6%
2000-12-31	0.92%	5%
1996-04-30	2.86%	4%
2004-08-31	−2.41%	4%
2002-12-31	−2.50%	3%

(continues)

TABLE 8.2 *(Continued)*

	Overall View	
End Month	Returns	Net Exposure
2004–06–30	−0.17%	3%
2000–04–30	1.39%	3%
1996–01–31	0.34%	3%
2000–05–31	2.98%	3%
2003–08–31	−1.38%	2%
2006–04–30	2.99%	2%
2006–07–31	1.72%	2%
1996–03–31	2.66%	0%
1995–09–30	1.42%	0%
1997–07–31	−0.49%	−2%
2006–11–30	0.70%	−2%
1999–12–31	1.34%	−3%
1996–10–31	2.55%	−7%
2005–09–30	2.16%	−9%
2005–08–31	1.88%	−11%
1996–08–31	0.21%	−11%
2000–10–31	1.16%	−11%
1997–12–31	0.60%	−11%
1999–01–31	−0.91%	−11%
2001–11–30	−1.85%	−11%
2006–03–31	2.37%	−12%
2005–04–30	−3.50%	−13%
1998–12–31	0.39%	−13%
1996–06–30	2.65%	−14%
1998–08–31	2.39%	−14%
1998–09–30	−0.17%	−14%
2003–04–30	−0.58%	−14%
2004–07–31	3.75%	−15%
1998–05–31	−0.22%	−16%
2000–09–30	0.05%	−17%
2002–03–31	−1.73%	−18%
1996–05–31	0.07%	−19%
1995–01–31	−0.49%	−19%
2001–04–30	−0.25%	−21%
1997–08–31	0.39%	−21%
2005–10–31	−1.87%	−22%
2005–06–30	2.47%	−22%
2002–02–28	0.26%	−23%
1998–06–30	0.27%	−24%
1999–05–31	−1.31%	−24%

TABLE 8.2 *(Continued)*

	Overall View	
End Month	**Returns**	**Net Exposure**
1997-09-30	1.44%	-26%
1999-09-30	0.72%	-27%
2004-05-31	0.36%	-28%
1997-03-31	1.61%	-28%
2000-11-30	2.50%	-29%
1996-07-31	-1.25%	-30%
1999-04-30	0.72%	-31%
1998-01-31	0.05%	-32%
1998-03-31	1.42%	-32%
2000-03-31	-1.51%	-34%
1997-04-30	1.85%	-34%
1997-05-31	-1.90%	-36%
1997-02-28	-2.14%	-38%
2000-08-31	0.66%	-43%
1999-07-31	0.75%	-45%
2001-07-31	-0.95%	-46%
1998-02-28	0.63%	-46%
1998-07-31	1.88%	-48%
2001-05-31	0.69%	-51%
2001-06-30	-1.15%	-51%
2002-01-31	-0.16%	-53%
1999-06-30	1.96%	-54%
2000-06-30	1.84%	-57%
2005-12-31	-0.91%	-58%
2005-11-30	2.38%	-58%
1999-02-28	2.58%	-63%
1999-03-31	-1.10%	-67%
1998-04-30	-0.04%	-70%
2001-12-31	0.62%	-75%

[a]Past performance is no guarantee of future results.
[b]The S&P DTI returns on this report are those of the "DTI-O" prior to 2004. The DTI-O is the original S&P DTI calculation method, with position adjustments occurring on the last trading day of each month. The S&P DTI as published by S&P (and used since 1-1-2004 in this table) has variable adjustment dates.

TABLE 8.3 Exposure Averages

Seven Categories		Four Categories		
Net Exposures (range)	Average Profit per month	# of Months[a]		Ave. Profit
71–100%	1.77%	13		
51–70%	−0.39%	18	31	0.52%
26–50%	0.04%	20		
1–25%	0.74%	31	51	0.46%
<0%> – <25%>	0.50%	33		
<26%> – <49%>	0.38%	18	51	0.46%
<50%> – <100%>	0.61%	11	11	0.61%
	Total	**144**	**144**	

[a]Monthly distributions of "net exposures" of the S&P DTI long and short sectors.

DISTRIBUTION CLASSES

Table 8.3 places the results into distribution classes such as 71 to 100 percent (maximum was 91 percent) net longs, and 50 to 100 percent (maximum was 75 percent) net shorts, and then averages the monthly occasions in each class, to see which areas are the most profitable. Normally, the highest exposures *on average* earn and lose the most. However, in the S&P DTI's case, when the net longs and shorts have the highest net exposure, it earns the highest average returns, which is very unusual because human intervention is not implemented in the S&P DTI. Therefore, the S&P DTI as an indicator provides strong evidence that the markets themselves are predictive by their nature and discount what is known in advance of the actual occurrence.

In theory, the longs make more than the shorts. This is because the short positions can only drop 100 percent. The price for a bushel of corn could theoretically drop from $2.00 to $0.00 (not that it ever would), but it cannot drop below $0. Meanwhile, long positions can appreciate to an infinite amount. For example, the same bushel of corn could increase in price from $2.00 to $5.00 (an increase of 150 percent) or $8.00 or, in theory, to $100.00 if circumstances and markets so dictated. So, there is a price appreciation bias that makes more on the upside than on the downside.

In reality, since commodities can't go bankrupt or decline by 100 percent, they all have a below-production cost price that acts as a floor. In addition, there are government price supports in several commodities markets. If corn drops from $3 to $2 a bushel, where it likely runs into potential price supports, the maximum decline is 33 percent. However, if a drought occurs, it can go from $3 a bushel to $6 a bushel, thereby yielding 100 percent appreciation. Clearly, the bias is all on the upside. The short exposure of net 50 to 100 percent (maximum was 75 percent) of the S&P DTI's positions had a lower, but relatively high, average of +61 bps per monthly occasion profit, since $3 can only drop to $2 in this example.

CONCLUSION

The value of the S&P DTI as an indicator is proven in that the highest returns, long or short, occur when the greatest number of trends have the highest exposure as a consensus. This implies a highly predictable tool for forecasting trends in the global markets, in that the positions are not based on human intervention.

In conclusion, the LEI as a leading indicator uses the stock market to predict upcoming economic activity; the S&P DTI uses a global basket, encompassing 16 commodities markets and 8 financial markets. The S&P DTI also acts as a forecaster of future trends, by the strength and consensus of its current trends, as shown in its profitability.

CHAPTER 9

The Fundamental Reason the S&P DTI Generates Core Returns

T he idea that an investment has fundamental source returns should give an investor confidence that its future performance will not be dependent on management skill nor past performance. Commodities derive their source returns differently than financial assets. Understanding this difference is the key to understanding why the Standard & Poor's Diversified Trends Indicator (S&P DTI) total return is so consistently profitable over 12-month periods, with a win ratio of over 97 percent.

CORE RETURNS IN DIFFERENT ASSET CLASSES

Charles Dow and William Peter Hamilton said that the stock market was a barometer of things to come, not a thermometer of current events. Stated differently, stocks derive their source (core) returns from the discounted present value of a future flow of income. And generally—aside from sudden, unforeseeable political events—markets discount the visibility of the next quarter's earnings quite accurately. As Gordon A. Holmes proved in his book *Capital Appreciation in the Stock Market*, it is statistically significant (a high probability) that the slope of a stock's trend line (log) is virtually the same as the rate of growth or slope of a company's earnings percentage increases or decreases.

In equities, earnings eventually become dividends. The percentage of dividends distributed from earnings varies directly with the maturity and size of the company. GE, for example, pays more than 50 percent of its earnings in dividends. Google and eBay pay no dividends at all. In the last 81 years the S&P 500 returned 10.42 percent compounded, and dividends accounted for 42.5 percent of the return (or a net 4.43 percent), while the capital appreciation accounted for 57.5 percent (the other 5.99 percent) of the return. Dividends reflect past earnings, and price appreciation reflects the future of dividend payouts.

For bonds, virtually all core returns come from interest payments. The total returns from long-term government bonds are 5.42 percent compounded, while corporate bonds yielded 5.89 percent compounded over the last 81 years. This is virtually identical to the 5.99 percent compounded capital appreciation return from equities.

Commodities, however, are different. Futures contract prices often sell above or below the actual spot price. Most people mistakenly see this *premium* or *discount* as the market's view of discounting where the spot price will be in the future. In most cases, this is not true. The spot price itself (or the front month), not the future contract price, reflects the market's discounting of the future.

A future contract's price is a function of interest rates and other carrying costs (i.e., storage, insurance, transportation and the convenience yield), plus a risk transfer premium. This means that the futures contract prices for commodities and financials are distinctly different from stock prices in that, unlike stocks, the prices do not represent future streams of anything, including the supply/demand equilibrium. In fact, they only represent current spot prices, plus all the other factors mentioned. Futures do often move faster than spot prices because of leverage and short covering, but it is the spot price that controls the futures price, which is a fundamental phenomenon.

For example, on November 24, 1999, the December 2000 S&P 500 Index futures closed at 1,494.70, while the spot (cash) price closed at 1,417.08. This 13-month future contract was 5.48 percent above the market. This premium reflected the interest carrying costs of 6.10 percent, less dividends, plus execution fees and slippage to swap cash for the futures. It was priced at virtual parity to the spot S&P 500 Index and did not at all reflect where the S&P 500 would be in December 2000!

To Recap

For equities, investors are offered future dividends as a core return, which allows businesses to obtain capital to grow; for debt, investors are offered interest as a core return on loans; and for commodities, investors are paid a *risk transfer premium* for their capital to hedge and ensure an edge to obtaining their profits.

In the S&P DTI, this amounts to a simulated and real compounded price return of 5.81 percent between 1985 and 2006, and a total return of 11.04 percent. During the same time period, compounded returns for the S&P 500 were 12.95 percent, and 9.98 percent for corporate bonds.

THE SOURCE RETURNS OF COMMODITIES

Most commodity futures contract prices are similar to the process of a discount wholesaler, such as Sam's or Costco, when it buys merchandise from a producer and in turn, hopes (and expect) to resell it at a profit to a future consumer. In this process, *generally*, the futures contract price is in *backwardation* (discounted) after cost adjustments with commodities in uptrends, and in *contango* (premium) with commodities in downtrends.

The reasons are the same as the producer-wholesaler-retailer conse-quence of common business practices. When Sam's or Costco buys mer-chandise (in bulk), it buys it at a lower price than they believe it is worth to a consumer in order to have a better than even chance of selling it (retail) at a profit, after overhead costs. To illustrate, if Sam's believes a consumer would pay $300 for a television set, then it would only pay $150 to a pro-ducer (SONY) to better ensure it can make a profit after interest, storage, and insurance costs.

This same principle applies to the futures markets.

Backwardation or Discount Markets

In early 1999, oil hit a low price of less than $10 a barrel because of a world-wide glut. In March 1999, OPEC cut supplies sharply. In response, spot oil shot to $16 a barrel in one month. The spot price discounted the adjust-ment of lower future supply and a higher price resulted. Bear in mind that current supplies were, in fact, still plentiful. If future contract prices were the source of the discounting, then spot prices should have remained the same and only the futures should have risen. But, holders of oil withheld supplies knowing the market of oil would rise, and the futures contract prices merely adjusted to the spot for the same reason.

Oil rose to $28 a barrel in December 1999. However, while it was rising, the futures contracts traded at *backwardation*—a discount to spot prices. On November 26, 1999, spot (West Texas crude) was $27.28 a barrel while the January 2000 futures were at $26.87 and March 2000 futures were at $24.87. This was the case since the mid-teens for crude (see Table 9.1). The reason is, again, fundamental to futures markets and related to normal business practices.

TABLE 9.1 Backwardation and Contango in Crude Oil

	Futures Prices[b]		Trend
West Texas Crude Spot[a]	**Spot Month**		**Backwardation/Contango**
Spot on 2/12 $11.89	March 1999	$11.88	Downtrend
	April 1999	$11.96	Contango
	May 1999	$12.09	Contango
Spot on 3/12 $14.49	April 1999	$14.49	Uptrend
	May 1999	$14.49	Backwardation
	June 1999	$14.40	Backwardation
Spot on 4/14 $16.47	May 1999	$16.47	Uptrend
	June 1999	$16.55	Contango
	July 1999	$16.54	Contango
Spot on 5/14 $18.04	June 1999	$18.04	Uptrend
	July 1999	$17.98	Backwardation
	August 1999	$17.87	Backwardation
Spot on 6/14 $18.34	July 1999	$18.33	Uptrend
	August 1999	$18.44	Contango
	September 1999	$18.43	Contango
Spot on 7/15 $20.63	August 1999	$20.16	Uptrend
	September 1999	$20.40	Contango
	October 1999	$20.44	Contango
Spot on 8/13 $21.68	September 1999	$21.67	Uptrend
	October 1999	$21.77	Contango
	November 1999	$21.62	Backwardation
Spot on 9/15 $24.13	October 1999	$24.13	Uptrend
	November 1999	$23.88	Backwardation
	December 1999	$23.40	Backwardation
Spot on 10/15 $22.83	November 1999	$22.82	Uptrend
	December 1999	$22.82	Backwardation
	January 2000	$22.60	Backwardation
Spot on 11/15 $25.13	December 1999	$25.13	Uptrend
	January 2000	$25.05	Backwardation
	February 2000	$24.64	Backwardation

Source: Compiled by Enhanced Alpha Management, LP.
Backwardation is based on spot to future and prior future month's price.
[a]Bloomberg WTI Cushing Spot Index.
[b]Interactive Data Corp (IDC).

For example, Exxon, the producer, wants to hedge its future production price. As a result, it is willing to pay the equivalent of *business insurance* fees by selling oil at a discount to a speculator. Exxon can sell its current production at spot prices, but if it wants to hedge its future production and sell at a price it thinks is high, it can only sell it to a speculator who thinks (hopes) he can sell it for more over time. Just like Sam's, the speculator has to buy his product (oil) at a discount to the market to potentially make a profit. The speculator needs this business (and statistical) edge to make a consistent return over time. This business/statistical edge is no different than the one casino owners use. Although they don't win every bet, over the long run they always win because the odds are in their favor.

As the spot price goes higher, producers have a greater desire to lock in these high prices for their future production, while speculators demand a higher compensation for their risk exposure of being long at higher prices. Consequently, this normal backwardation process must occur in order for the spot price to continue to rise. Volatility also moves the discount or premium higher or lower based on normal risk assessment measures. Of course there are always exceptions. For example, in March 2005, a major brokerage firm put out a very convincing bullish report on the energy sector, predicting that oil was going to go up in price from $40 a barrel to over $100. From that time until April 2007, oil has traded contango but recently reverted to backwardation.

Therefore, this transfer of risk from a producer (acting as a hedger) to a speculator (who acts as a wholesaler demanding a business edge) is why backwardation is not a prediction of future price declines. Instead, in most cases, a discount actually means the opposite, as it usually accompanies rising prices. The exception is for *cash and carry* commodities such as gold, which should trade at a premium, or T-bonds futures, which should trade at a discount due to arbitrage of the interest rate carry.

Contango or Premium Markets

Contango or premium futures markets are a characteristic of downtrend markets. In this case, the producers are unwilling to lock in their future production at prices they believe are too low while consumer-producers (like Kellogg, Armour, etc.) still need cost certainty for their own production. Additionally, these consumer-producers have a desire to lock in low prices, so they are willing to pay a premium to speculators willing to sell future production.

In the paper "Stocks of Staple Commodities" (1923), John Maynard Keynes posited that the natural course of commodities was toward backwardation. He called it *normal backwardation*. In general, the long-run average future price for a commodity is below the spot price. This is the reflection of producers paying an insurance premium to protect against the risk of adverse price declines. It suggests that the nature of commodity producers is to transfer risk to protect themselves, and thereby, sell future production at a discount under certain conditions.

An example of a contango market was corn in late 1999 and 2000. With corn in a major downtrend and near a contract low of 193 (November 26, 1999) and approaching government price supports, corn producers refused to sell future production at *current prices* because they were very low. Therefore, March 2000 corn was 205, May 2000 was 212, July 2000 was 219, and so on. During such time, if Kellogg's wanted to purchase corn for corn-flakes because it needed product for its consumers, but farmers would not sell because they would be paid the same price from the government anyway, Kellogg's would have had to buy from speculators, who would have demanded a risk premium to be short. Thus, downtrending commodities take on a premium at some point, but this premium does not necessarily predict an uptrend. Cyclically as production is cut, prices, of course, will rise. However, there is no guarantee when production will be cut and at what price.

The cocoa market in late 1999 and 2000 provides an additional example (Table 9.2). An article in *Barron's* on November 8, 1999, by Cheryl S. Einhorn provides the following background:

> *"Cocoa prices have fallen to a seven-year low amid anorexic demand ... " Walter Spilka, a commodities analyst at Salomon Smith Barney, says prices could melt another 8.5 percent, to $800 in coming weeks ... The Ivory Coast, which is the world's largest cocoa producer turning out over 40 percent of the global production, is harvesting a record crop now. But with the relentless global price slump this year, they haven't had any opportunities to sell, so commercial selling has been all but absent from the market in past*

TABLE 9.2 Cocoa Prices 1999 to 2001

Futures Dates	Cocoa Prices
December 1999	833
March 2000	854
May 2000	878
July 2000	900
September 2000	928
December 2000	963
March 2001	1,000
May 2001	1,026
July 2001	1,052
September 2001	1,078

Compiled by Enhanced Alpha Management, LP.

> *months ... "It has become a spot market," says a cocoa dealer, explaining that shippers are selling the cocoa only after it is in their possession, and that is "making prices volatile on the downside." "There is no sign that we've come to the bottom," says Ganes. "So prices aren't going to recover any time soon. They are only beginning to approximate the fundamentals now."*

But with all this negative sentiment, bearish future fundamentals, oversupply, and withholding of demand, the cocoa futures complex prices, as shown in *The Wall Street Journal* on November 24, 1999, depicted a rising contango (premium) market. This demonstrates solid evidence of the reasons speculators must be paid an edge to sell future production short.

Currently an exception to a general rule has occurred. Goldman Sachs, one of the most respected firms in the world, put out a report in March 2005 making the case for crude oil to increase in price to $105 a barrel. It was a great analysis, by the way. This sort of opinion became more widespread, and thereby oil started to trade in contango. In effect, oil has now become an asset class investment. This contango situation will continue until supply eventually overtakes demand, as opinions change.

WHY THE S&P DTI GENERATES CORE RETURNS

Because the Standard & Poor's Diversified Trends Indicator goes long and short according to its long-term trend, the *bulk* of the S&P DTI's returns come simply from buying uptrend commodities at backwardation and selling downtrend commodities at contango, not from price changes in and of themselves. This means that most of the S&P DTI's performance comes from the source returns available to commodity investors. Table 9.3 breaks down the amount of S&P DTI/LSM return that came from backwardation and contango during two periods: inflationary (1/31/61 to 1/30/81) and noninflationary (2/27/81 to 7/31/99).

Notice that the inflationary period made an average +0.44 percent (0.98 percent – 0.54 percent) of its monthly return from price changes whereas the noninflationary period made only 0.06 percent (0.48 percent – 0.42 percent) of its monthly return from price changes. See the charts that are included.

Most important to this analysis and its conclusions is that the S&P DTI's returns are not stochastic, but deterministic. In other words, they

TABLE 9.3   Portion of S&P DTI/LSM Return from Backwardation/Contango[a]

	1/31/61 to 1/30/81	2/27/81 to 7/31/99
	Inflationary	Noninflationary
Average monthly return	0.98%	0.48%
Average monthly backwardation/contango return	0.54%	0.42%

Source: Compiled by Enhanced Alpha Management, LP. All results simulated. Gross results were performed by an independent CFA, who is believed to be reliable, but the accuracy was not verified by EAM.
[a]"Amount of LSM/S&P DTI monthly return resulting from backwardation or contango. LSM, or long/short methodology," is a proxy for the S&P DTI before 1985. LSM is a basket of similar, but different commodities and financials (after 1975) that equally weights each component, while the S&P DTI weights each component differently. Also, the LSM does not create sectors from the components, but the S&P DTI does.

do not come only from prices, which can never be as consistent and as smooth as the S&P DTI returns demonstrate. Instead, they come from the nature of the construction of the S&P DTI, which is fundamentally driven, providing the investor a business-based return similar to traditional assets.

TABLE 9.4   Historical Convenience Yields (1970 to 1992)[a]

	Spot Price	Avg. Total Compounded Returns	Profit from Backwardation
Goldman Sachs Commodity Index	2.58%	13.81%	11.23%
Goldman Sachs Energy Index	−0.74%	14.93%	18.67%
Goldman Sachs Non-Energy Index	3.01%	12.72%	9.71%
Goldman Sachs Agricultural Index	2.85%	8.76%	5.91%
Goldman Sachs Livestock Index	2.96%	15.48%	12.52%
Goldman Sachs Precious Metals Index	6.18%	5.80%	−0.38%
Goldman Sachs Industrial Metals Index	2.68%	10.23%	7.55%

Source: Compiled by Enhanced Alpha Management, LP. All results simulated.
[a]Beginning in 2007, all of these Goldman Sachs indexes were purchased by Standard and Poors, and are now known as the S&P Goldman Sachs indexes, respectively.

As an aside, one additional idea readers might find useful is that of *convenience yield.* The concept of convenience yield is equivalent to a net earning or yield accruing to the owner of a physical commodity. The owner may forgo this yield and allow arbitrage profits to the market for the convenience of having ready the physical commodity. This allows the markets to profit from this choice. (Satyajit Das, "Swap & Derivative Financing," Probus Publishing, 1994). Table 9.4 demonstrates the historical convenience yields found in various Goldman Sachs commodity index sectors.

CHAPTER 10

The Nature of the S&P DTI Returns

A s I have stated in prior chapters, the Standard & Poor's Diversified Trends Indicator (S&P DTI) is an investable trading methodology that attempts to reflect, and thereby measure, the approximate extent of trends covering an aggregate composite of futures. Those futures are then formed into sectors on a variety of global currencies, financials, and commodities.

One might wonder whether it is intellectually appropriate to create an indicator. Consider the following quote by Khalid Ghayur CFA:

> *Indicators are indexes that do not possess the qualities of a good* performance benchmark *or a benchmark index. One of the most popular market indicators is* 'the Dow Jones Industrial Average' ... *[which] does not meet the criteria of a good performance benchmark. ... On a broader end of the indicator spectrum is the* Wilshire 5000, *which, while covering the entire U.S. equity market capitalization, includes many illiquid stocks and must be optimized to form the basis for a fund portfolio* (The Journal of Indexes, *2003. Roman added for emphasis.)*

Thereby, indicators can be custom designed to reflect different phenomena.

DESIGN OF THE S&P DTI MOVING AVERAGE ALGORITHM

The S&P DTI is an indicator that reflects the extent of trends, not prices. This is possible because the S&P DTI universal algorithm (a 1.6-weighted

115

exponential seven-month moving average) determines the direction of each of the S&P DTI sectors. Those determinations of direction specify whether the sector should be held long or short (or flat, in regards to the energy sector). Therefore, *the S&P DTI is capable of appreciating in value regardless of whether prices are moving up or down, but not if they are moving sideways.* The same moving average (MA) was arbitrarily selected to determine each sector's approximate trend, based on its percent change being above or below the MA within the S&P DTI. However, the particular MA used is not optimized, or curve-fitted, and not important to the results; switching to a different MA will change the specific profitability, but not the overall function as an indicator. Its influence is only to the degree of the returns, more or less, depending on the environment being analyzed.

WHY THE PARTICULAR MOVING AVERAGE USED IS NOT IMPORTANT TO THE RESULTS

To demonstrate why the particular MA used is not important, we count the S&P DTI's monthly losses (T-bill interest not included) of different long-term periods. If the numbers of losses are stable, it provides strong evidence that long-term (months to years) trends, not the economic environments, dominate the wide basket of objects within the S&P DTI, and are a part of the reason for the robust results. This can be seen from Table 10.1 comparing the S&P 500 to the long/short methodology (LSM) from 1961 to 1984 and the S&P DTI from 1985 to 2005.

The LSM is a proxy for the S&P DTI. From 1961 to 1984 we use a similar (but not the same) basket of futures in the LSM, as compared to that used in the S&P DTI. The only difference is that in the LSM the individual components are *equally weighted* and are *not* formed into sectors as in the S&P DTI. Also, there is a *different basket of components* to some degree in the LSM. This is because there were less liquid futures contracts trading during that period of time.

THE S&P DTI COMPARED TO LONG-ONLY INDEXES

A long-only index such as the S&P 500 generally experiences higher returns when the number of monthly losses is lower. By contrast, a long/short methodology using a futures portfolio, such as the LSM and the S&P DTI,

TABLE 10.1 S&P 500 versus LSM/S&P DTI

S&P 500 Index
All Economic Periods Simulated Gross Returns

Total Months	Decade/Period	# Monthly Losses	% Monthly Losses	Yearly Compounded Return
120	Jan/1961–Dec/1970	44	36.70%	8.98%
120	Jan/1971–Dec/1980	51	42.50%	8.44%
120	Jan/1981–Dec/1990	48	40.00%	13.93%
120	Jan/1991–Dec/2000	38	31.67%	17.50%

S&P 500

Bear Market (Ended July 1982) vs. Bull Market
Simulated Gross Returns

Total Months	Decade/Period	# Monthly Losses	% Monthly Losses	Yearly Compounded Return
115	Dec/1972–July/1982	56	48.70%	3.70%
217	Aug/1982–Aug 2000	61	28.10%	19.36%

Based on S&P 500 highs and lows using month-end closes.

LSM + S&P DTI (PR) By Decade
Hypothetical Gross Returns

Total Months	Decade/Period w/o T-bills	# Monthly Losses	% Monthly Losses	Yearly Compounded Return
120	Jan/1961–Dec/1970	36	30.00%	10.65%
120	Jan/1971–Dec/1980	40	33.30%	22.53%
120	Jan/1981–Dec/1990	44	36.70%	9.71%
120	Jan/1991–Dec/2000	40	33.30%	6.12%

has almost the same number of monthly losses in any given period. For example, in the LSM/S&P DTI the returns (without T-bills) broken out by decade from 1961 to 2000 have varied 268 percent, from a low of 6.12 percent to a high of 22.55 percent, yet the percentage of losses ranged only 10 percent from its mean! This proves that the extents of the trends are responsible for the degree of the yearly returns within the LSM/S&P DTI, not the number of monthly profits as in long-only indexes. It also is a measure of volatility, as the higher the standard deviation the greater the returns. This is the exact opposite of the result for equities in general.

THE MOVING AVERAGE RULE ALLOWS ONLY FOR THE APPROXIMATE MEASURE OF THE EXTENT OF THE RETURNS, BUT DOES NOT DETERMINE THEM

In other words, the MA does not predict anything, but only reflects the trends in force. An MA smoothes prices to better define the trend. Moreover, all MAs are strictly approximates of trends in any particular environment. Although the LSM and S&P DTI use a 1.6 weighting and a seven-month MA, in different periods alternative MAs would have resulted in superior returns.

Specifically, in 1973, the longer the MA and the lower the weighting, the higher the returns. However, in 1992, the shorter the MA and the higher the weighting, the higher the returns. As an example, the LSM PR simulation earned 87.4 percent in 1973 when utilizing a 1.6 weighting and a seven-month MA. However, if it had used a 12-month simple (unweighted) MA, the price return would have been 94.0 percent; with a two weighting and a seven-month MA the price return would have been 83.2 percent; and with a four-month MA and a 1.6 weighting the price return would have been 74.2 percent. The 12-month MA worked best during that period, because the markets were in strong longer-term uptrends.

Conversely, in 1992 (a low return year), the shorter the MA and the higher the weighting, the higher the returns, while the longer the MA and the lower the weighting, the smaller the returns. For example, the S&P DTI PR simulation earned 3.7 percent in 1992 utilizing a 1.6 weighting and a seven-month MA. However, if it had used a seven-month MA and a two weighting the price return would have been 5.9 percent; with a four-month MA and a 1.6 weighting the price return would have been 6.7 percent; with a 12-month simple (1 weighting) MA the price return would have been 1.0 percent; and with a 12-month MA and a 1.6 weighting the price return would have been 2.9 percent. The higher weighting and shorter MA worked best because choppy trends dominated.

The point to focus on in these examples of best case/poor case is that *they all profited, only to different degrees of measure, no matter what the MA design was.* For example, 1973 was a peak growth year with rising inflation and interest rates, while 1992 was a low interest rate, CPI, and growth period. Economic fundamentals, not the particular MA used, cause the market trends that create returns, and those same fundamentals determine whether the returns are large or small.

The only way to make a precise MA is to be able to adapt it before the economic period and know the type of environment, which is impossible unless someone was a soothsayer. Therefore, the MA selected will act better in some periods than in others in defining its results. The important thing to remember is that it doesn't matter what the short-term results are—the indicator works over time, whether to a greater or lesser extent.

WHIPSAWS AND SHORT-TERM TRENDS CANNOT DOMINATE THE S&P DTI'S MOVEMENTS FOR LONG

A percentage of whipsaws are embedded in all strategies that use trend-following MAs as a trading rule, or that utilize trend-direction-measuring methodology. The trade-off is, if MAs are structured to reflect longer steady up- or downtrends, then they will not be in sync with short choppy periods. *No MA can adapt by predicting the future*, so lower returns or losses will reflect the environment the MA is not structured to benefit from—in this case, short-term trends (i.e., days to weeks). However, all long-term MAs have the opportunity to reflect returns over longer periods, especially when used in a diversified and noncorrelated mix of components. The critical reason for this is that when fundamental economic events create long-term trends, they take a longer time to change. Long-term trends were defined by Charles Dow as lasting months to years (*months* in this case is at least three).

Macrofundamental events are created by government monetary, taxation, and political decisions throughout the world, the most powerful being the United States. In addition, microfundamental supply and demand forces for each component create specific long-term trends for each object separately. All markets adjust to these policies and individual forces (the most influential being U.S. Fed policy), and maintain a bullish or bearish bias until something affects the forces in place.

Whipsaws take place due to short-term, technical, unimportant, or unforeseen events that influence and cause a percentage of losses not structured to benefit the indicator's MA. Short-term trends are basically of minor consequence in the long-term process. If the percentages of losses are stable when compared to each other and to long-only indexes, this analysis supplies the reason to be optimistic that the results of the LSM or the

S&P DTI are due to long-term trends. Short-term trends cannot dominate the S&P DTI's movements for long, and they caused only a minor number of 12-month price return (not including T-bills) losses (32) in the 46-year history tested (1961 to 2006).

In the last 46 years there was only one totally unforeseen Fed policy change that caused a major loss and was a surprise to the LSM/S&P DTI markets. That was in 1978's last quarter, when a sudden decision by Paul Volker—which was influenced by Milton Friedman—called for a change in monetary policy, away from pegging interest rates to money supply and instead fixing money supply to a specific growth rate (e.g., 6 percent). All markets reversed, as they were all in sync with an inflationary policy, or pegging interest rates. This is a determinant of the *price of credit*, but not the *quantity of money*, which is the actual cause of inflation according to monetary theory. Moreover, on Wall Street, anything can happen. Therefore, this cannot be assumed to be the only instance where the markets will be shocked by the Fed, as undoubtedly there will be other events that cannot be predicted or discounted in advance.

BASIS OF RETURNS AT ANY PARTICULAR TIME PERIOD IS THE EXTENT OF THE LONG-TERM TRENDS

Finally, similar to the characteristics of a stock or bond index, it did not matter in 46 years if the S&P DTI was weighted, or the LSM was not, what they were composed of, what the weighting per sectors were, or if they had more commodities than financials, or vice versa. *The basis to the returns at any particular time period is the extent of the long trends*, not the number of months of profits, and not the occasional quantity of whipsaws from surprise events that will always occur at certain time periods.

THE NATURE OF LSM AND S&P DTI LOSSES

I believe I have established empirically that the extent and duration of long-term trends caused by fundamental developments determine the consistent profitability of the S&P DTI. The returns were reduced by monthly losses approximately 33 percent of the time, which were counter short-term trends (i.e., whipsaws). Overall, however, long-term trends dominated the returns and have outperformed the short-term offsets, which only lowered the median returns and caused small losses.

NONCORRELATION WITHIN ITS TWO MAJOR GROUPS

In addition to the fact that long-term trends provide the bulk of the returns, *the S&P DTI itself is noncorrelated within its two major groups—the financials and commodities.* This also provides real diversification of each sector, and therefore a more stable investment methodology. Although the universal moving average (MA) is identically used on all components and sectors, in 46 years the actions of the two groups and components have generally offset one another. Please see Table 10.2, which shows a very low correlation of LSM/S&P DTI financials to its commodities and the CPI from 1961 to 2006. Interestingly, the LSM/S&P DTI and financials have a higher correlation to the CPI as a whole rather than commodities alone.

A more visual and simple, common-sense method of correlation is set forth in Table 10.3, "Correlation of S&P DTI Price Return to Its Major Groups." This table shows the percentage returns of the weighted S&P DTI (from 1985) of the financials and commodities, and the directional percentage changes—up or down—indicating how each acted from the year before and compared to each other. After 1990, the rate of percentage change of the two groups moved up or down together from the year before only once. This demonstrates that when one group is returning less than the year before, the other group is earning more or losing less. This offset is a primary reason for the consistency of the S&P DTI returns. This aspect of the S&P DTI is far more significant than just diversification, as the S&P DTI is structured like a hedge fund, made up of noncorrelated longs and shorts in and of itself.

The importance of this noncorrelation can be viewed historically, by keeping in mind that the financials were not offered as futures contracts until September 1975. The S&P DTI proxy, the LSM, missed this noncorrelation feature within itself during the period of 1961 to 1975. This

TABLE 10.2 Correlation of Financials to Commodities and CPI (1961 to 2006, Based on Hypothetical Gross Returns)[a]

	FIN vs. CDYS	FIN vs. CPI	CDYS vs. CPI	LSM/S&P DTI vs. CPI
1 month	5.12%	2.48%	7.25%	12.91%
1 year	−20.58%	11.83%	30.41%	51.36%
3 years	−32.75%	28.89%	32.06%	60.21%
5 years	−13.79%	46.26%	32.47%	65.89%
10 years	−17.87%	87.37%	52.04%	88.86%

[a]These figures were calculated using Lotus 1-2-3 correlation function.

TABLE 10.3	Correlation of S&P DTI Price Return to Its Major Groups [50 percent Financials (FTI) and 50 percent Commodities (CTI)][a]

	S&P DTI %	Dir.[b]	LT Gov't Bonds	Dir.	Fin. %	Dir.	Com.%	Dir.	Fin/Com same % Direction[c]
1985	9.81%	−	30.97%	+	18.06%	+	1.18%	−	
1986	4.65%	−	24.55%	−	6.00%	−	0.54%	−	Same—both were lower
1987	8.51%	+	−2.71%	−	8.60%	+	7.90%	+	Same—rate of increase higher
1988	−1.51%	−	9.66%	+	−5.30%	−	2.07%	−	Same—both were lower
1989	8.15%	+	18.12%	+	0.25%	−	15.50%	+	
1990	15.68%	+	6.16%	−	8.60%	+	22.38%	+	Same—higher
1991	4.43%	−	19.32%	+	12.58%	+	−5.49%	−	
1992	3.67%	−	8.06%	−	1.23%	−	6.72%	+	
1993	2.09%	−	18.26%	+	1.90%	+	1.99%	−	
1994	3.97%	+	−7.80%	−	−2.28%	−	9.17%	+	
1995	8.09%	+	31.67%	+	8.30%	+	6.57%	−	
1996	15.62%	+	−0.92%	−	5.70%	−	26.16%	+	
1997	1.61%	−	15.85%	+	8.27%	+	−5.44%	−	
1998	4.95%	+	13.08%	−	7.27%	−	3.63%	+	
1999	6.05%	+	−8.99%	−	4.23%	−	7.10%	+	
2000	11.45%	+	21.48%	+	2.43%	−	19.96%	+	
2001	−0.55%	−	3.72%	−	2.01%	−	−4.35%	−	Same—both were lower
2002	1.46%	+	17.84%	+	6.30%	+	−4.64%	−	
2003	3.42%	+	1.44%	−	1.49%	−	4.54%	+	
2004	12.56%	+	9.34%	+	−2.30%	−	32.07%	+	
2005	4.61%	−	7.81%	−	1.61%	+	9.33%	−	
2006	1.42%	−	1.18%	−	−1.46%	−	5.23%	−	

[a]Simulated S&P DTI statistical information—gross returns (T–bill interest is not included). No fees included. All results use the end of the month trade date as in the historical simulations. The S&P DTI "Live" starting in 2004 uses a random 1- to 5-day trade date after the end of the month.
[b]"Dir." + and − symbols depict whether the return for the given year was higher or lower than the return for the prior year.
[c]Yearly increasing or decreasing % directional (dir) changes.

was because it had only commodities, and was heavily weighted to the grains from 1961 to 1971. This fact causes more 12-month losses than using the S&P DTI methodology, which includes 50 percent financials.

The importance of noncorrelation is demonstrated by viewing the 12-month rolling periods of price returns—without T-bills added—of the

TABLE 10.4 1961 to 1971 Composition

#	Sector	Percent
5	Grains	41.7%
4	Softs	33.3%
2	Livestock	16.7%
1	Prec. metals	8.3%
12		100.0%[a]

[a]The contracts were equally weighted at 8.33% each.

simulated 24-year history of the long/short methodology (LSM) and the 22-year history of the S&P DTI. There were only 32 losing fiscal periods (including one calendar year) out of 541 periods. However, 11 of the 32 12-month losses took place in the first 121 rolling 12-month periods. (All S&P DTI numbers used are end of the month simulations, not S&P DTI Live, which use random trade dates.)

Therefore, the first 22.4 percent of the history using this methodology had 34.4 percent of all the 12-month losses, or stated differently, the first 121 12-month rolling periods had 9.1 percent losses, and thereafter it dropped to only 5.0 percent losses. From December of 1971 to date, the win ratio increased from 90.9 percent to 95.0 percent, in large part due to the noncorrelation of the two different groups. The lower win ratio prior to 1971 was, in part, due to the limited and more correlated concentration of contracts in the LSM methodology. Table 10.4 shows the breakdown of the weights by adding the number of futures contracts together in the same group.

See Table 10.9 for a complete list of the components of the LSM and S&P DTI and the date each component was added to the methodology.

TRUE DIVERSIFICATION WITHIN ITS COMPONENTS

In addition to noncorrelation, the S&P DTI provides true diversification within its components. Stock indexes have stocks that diversify the index, but are very much correlated to one another at approximately 0.65. By comparison, the S&P DTI has commodities that have absolutely no relation to one another. The supply and demand of silver, cocoa, and soybeans move individually and independent of one another. Stocks generally move together when interest rates and GDP increase or decline. However, supply and demand for each component in the S&P DTI are the primary influence on price movements, and are based on fundamental events specific to the component. The MA used does have an influence on individual components, but not on the S&P DTI overall.

DIVERSIFICATION AND NONCORRELATION PROVIDES STABLE RETURNS

We can conclude that all long-term moving averages have similar characteristics: During choppy markets (low growth, CPI, and interest rates) they are likely to experience whipsaws, and during long-trending markets they are likely to capture part of the trend. The problem with MAs when used on individual components is that the whipsaws to one component can be devastating, creating sizable losses, but historically not when diversified and weighted into sectors, and when used as a basket.

The S&P DTI's MA displays the same characteristics of other moving averages. Its moving average has no special ability to avert whipsaws. In fact, in historical simulations, the highly volatile commodities such as sugar and silver have experienced 40 percent whipsaws. But, because the S&P DTI's individual positions are fundamentally diversified—except in extreme macroeconomic events—when one commodity is experiencing a whipsaw, the other commodities are just as likely *not* to be experiencing one. This is to say, the fundamental supply and demand factors that would cause a sugar whipsaw are likely to be completely unrelated to those factors affecting oil, gold, or T-notes. As such, within the S&P DTI structure, the inherent propensity of moving averages to have periodic whipsaws is offset by the inherent noncorrelation between the S&P DTI individual components. The result is extremely stable returns.

LSM AND S&P DTI LOSES BECAUSE OF SHORT-TERM TRENDS

Finally, to better understand why the LSM or S&P DTI has losses because of short-term countertrends, we have analyzed the history of the 12-month losses from 1961 to 2006. The basis to a loss is made up of each sector being in position of its long-term trend, established by fundamental events particular to each sector. Then a surprise news or macro-occurrence of importance causes profit taking by traders and a pause by large commercial hedgers to the components, or a reassessment of the markets due to the important event, such as the following:

- War or the threat of war
- U.S. president:
  - Assassinated: Kennedy
  - Scandals: Nixon and Clinton
  - Threat to interfere in the free-market process (i.e., socialistic proposals): Kennedy—steel prices; Nixon—wage and price controls; Clinton—nationalized health care
- Abrupt change of Fed policy: Under Volker, 1978
- Incorrect Fed policy: Under Greenspan, 2001 to 2002
- International crisis of important nations, such as China, Russia, the Middle East or former USSR

LARGEST DRAWDOWN ANALYSIS

The worst drawdown for the S&P DTI from 1985 to 2006 was −8.24 percent price return only (PR) and occurred between the end of February and September 30, 2003. Below is a time line of the market events that transpired over this time period to cause the drawdown.

- Jan/Feb 2003 +4.31 percent PR—Energy up due to threat of invasion of Iraq (war).
- March/April 2003 –2.92% percent PR—Energy declines discounting the victory for the U.S. versus Iraq.
- May 2003 rally bounce +1.99 percent PR.
- June to September 2003–5.85 percent PR. Change in Fed policy from decrease in Fed funds rate from 50 bps to 25 bps, which surprised the markets. All markets reversed and July was the largest monthly decline for U.S. government bonds in history –9.82 percent TR. U.S. government bonds declined 12.10 percent PR in June and July.

In 1963, a drawdown of 8.92 percent PR was actually the largest in 46 years of using a *long/short strategy*. However, as the LSM only had commodities in it and no financials, such drawdown is not as critical to analyze, as more importantly it was a very different long/short structure.

1. Please note the "official" LSM used was unweighted from 1961 to 1984 and the S&P DTI is weighted from 1985 to 2006.
2. The LSM does not officially use any weighting methodology from 1961 to 1984, because of the difficulty of assigning realistic weights to the simulations for legal purposes (i.e., a hypothetical weighting on top of a P&L simulation). Also, the lawyers for a public offering thought it

would be imprudent to show the public the "very high returns" of the 1970s. This is the reason an attestation (audit) by a big four accounting firm only goes back to 1985 for the S&P DTI, when the LSM could be realistically attested as well. For a detailed discussion of all thirty-two 12-month losses, and the reasons I observed as the cause, see Tables 10.5 through 10.9.

TABLE 10.5 LSM Returns during Inflationary Periods without T-bills[a]

12-month # Ending	12-month % Losses	# Contracts	LSM S&P DTI Key Monthly Loss	Probable Cause
1 Apr 1962	<0.14%>	9	<1.44%>	Due to Kennedy critique to steel prices
2 Jan 1964	<1.14%>	9	11/63: <4.44%>	Due to Kennedy assasination
3 Feb 1964	<1.59%>	9		" "
4 May 1964	<0.69%>	10		Carry forward Nov. 1963 loss caused 12-month loss
5 Jun 1967	<0.37%>	12	5/67: <3.81%>	Arab & Israeli war S&P <4.77%>
6 Aug 1967	<0.43%>	12		" "
7 Jun 1971	<2.23%>	12	2/71: <0.89%>	Discounted Nixon wage price controls 8/15/71
8 Aug 1971	<2.39%>	12	3/71: <2.35%>	" "
9 Sep 1971	<2.25%>	12	4/71: <0.18%>	" "
10 Oct 1971	<5.30%>	12	5/71: <1.04%>	" "
11 Nov 1971	<2.97%>	12	6/71: <0.25%>	" "
			7/71: <0.19%>	" "
12 Dec 1978	<5.10%>	20	11/78: <5.23%>	Paul Volker announced Fed switch from Fed funds to money supply as target
13 Jan 1979	<2.89%>	20	12/78: <2.84%>	
14 Mar 1979	<2.84%>	20		" "
15 May 1979	<0.44%>	20		" "

[a]% Win Ratio: 93.8%. # of Losses: 15 of 241. 12-Month Periods 1961–1981. Inflationary Period. Compounded Returns: +17.39%.

TABLE 10.6	LSM/S&P DTI Returns without T-bills during Disinflationary Periods[a, b, c]

12-month Ending	12-month % Losses	# Contracts	LSM S&P DTI Key Monthly Loss	Probable Cause
16 Jul 1988	<2.37%>	24	8/87: <2.22%>	Change of Fed policy
			9/87: <0.70%>	Interest rates increase
			10/87: <2.64%>	James Baker: threatens devaluation of the dollar
17 Dec 1988	<1.51%>	24	1/88: <2.41%>	1. Currencies −2.61% Central Bank intervention to protect the dollar. Interest rates decline.
			3/88: <2.27%>	2. Copper drops 24.8% due to fundamental factors. Interest rates rise.
			7/88: <2.31%>	3. Grains −2.48%, rained after expected drought.
	w/o T-bills			

12-month Ending	12-month % Losses	# Contracts	LSM S&P DTI Key Monthly Loss	Probable Cause
18 Sep 1991	<0.50%>	24	10,11,12/90: <2.08>	Profit Taking after +7.57% 9/90 Iraq War
19 Feb 1994	<1.49%>	24	1/94: <1.15%>	Clinton health care proposal
20 Mar 1994	<0.72%>	24	2/94: <1.80%>	Clinton health care proposal
21 Apr 1994	<2.19%>	24		Clinton health care proposal
22 May 1994	<1.08%>	24		Clinton health care proposal

Source: Compiled By Enhanced Alpha Management, LP. Source: LSM Futures Data Commodity Research Bureau. Past performance is not necessarily indicative of future results.
[a]% Win Ratio: 96.9%. # of Losses: 7 of 228. 12-Month Periods 1982–2000 / March. Disinflationary Period. Compounded Returns: +7.03%.
[b]1982–2000 March is based on using the month when most market indexes made highs.
[c]The S&P 500 made a high in August of 2000.

TABLE 10.7   LSM/S&P DTI Returns during Recession and Recovery Periods[a]

12-month Ending	w/o T-Bills 12-month % Losses	# Contracts	S&P DTI Key Monthly Loss	Probable Cause
23 Nov-01	−0.26	24	6/01: −1.15%	Greenspan change in Fed policy lowers Fed funds by 0.25%
24 Dec-01	−0.55	24	7/01: −0.95%	
25 Mar-02	−3.19	24	11/01: −1.85%	Change Fed Policy back to −0.50%
26 Apr-02	−2.76	24		" "
27 May-02	−3.77	24		" "
28 Jul-03	−0.43	24	3/03: −2.35%	Iraq War discounts victory, oil declines
29 Aug-03	−4.27	24	4/03: −0.58%	
30 Sep-03	−7.67	24	6/03: −1.56%	Unexpectedly Fed cuts
31 Oct-03	−3.20	24	7/03: −2.41%	rate, causes largest
32 Nov-03	−2.91	24	8/03: −1.38%	monthly decline for
			9/03: −2.18%	bonds in history, (−10.20% PR, −9.82% TR) in July. Also, major transition in currencies which turned into several whipsaws.

[a]% Win ratio: 76.2%. # of Losses: 5 of 21. 12-Month Periods March/ 2000–2002. Deflationary Period. Compounded Returns: +3.81%. % Win Ratio: 79.2% # of Losses 5 of 24. 12-Month Periods 2003–2004. Recovery Period 2003–2004. Compounded Returns +7.89%.

Several things should be noted when reading Table 10.8. Note that it examines the history of LSM/S&P DTI TR between 1961–1984; there was one 12-month rolling period loss. This was for the period ending 10/31/71 and was caused by the denial of Richard Nixon that he would institute "wage and price controls." This denial was disbelieved by the markets and caused a "slow erosion" until the event happened on August 15, 1971.

The history of S&P DTI TR between 1985 and 2006 showed seven losses that were caused primarily by the 55-year low in T-bill rates, which are 44% of the S&P DTI total return.

The T-bill compounded return was 4.74%, and when adjusted to the historical period from the periods of loss (i.e., 2002–2003), T-bill rates were lower by 75%. If T-bills were earning 4.74%, it would have caused only

TABLE 10.8 LSM/S&P DTI Returns during Recapitulation

Various WIN Ratios for Decades	Rolling 12 Months	# Contracts	T-Bills	CPI	PR # of Losses	TR # of Losses	PR [a] w/o T-Bills	TR [b] w/ T-Bills	PR WIN Ratio	TR WIN Ratio
9 years	97 12-month periods 1961–1969	12	4.02%	2.64%	6	0	11.90%	16.35%	93.81%	100.00%
10 years	120 12-month periods 1970–1979	20	6.31%	7.37%	9	1	22.53%	30.13%	92.50%	99.20%
10 years	120 12-month periods 1980–1989	24	8.89%	5.09%	2	0	11.22%	19.50%	98.33%	100.00%
10 years	120 12-month periods 1990–1999	24	4.92%	2.93%	5	0	6.51%	12.05%	95.83%	100.00%
7 years	84 12-month periods 2000–2006	24	3.04%	2.63%	10	7	4.80%	7.94%	86.30%	90.41%
					32	8				

Source: Compiled By Enhanced Alpha Management, LP. Past performance is not necessarily indicative of future results.
[a]Price Return used with other investments as an overlay.
w/o: without T-bill interest (Price Return)
[b]T-bills used as a collateral (margin) but without leverage to purchase the S&P DTI Futures as a stand alone investment.
w/T-bills: with T-bill interest (Total Return)
S&P DTI is weighted from 1985 to date, LSM was unweighted from 1961–1984.

TABLE 10.9 LSM/S&P DTI Component History

	Futures Market	Exchange	Symbol	Start Date	Contract #	
1	Wheat	CBOT	W	1-Jan-61	1	**LSM**
2	Cotton	NYCE	CT	1-Jan-61	2	
3	Corn	CBOT	C	1-Jan-61	3	
4	Copper	COMEX	HG	1-Jan-61	4	
5	Soybeans	CBOT	S	1-Jan-61	5	
6	Cocoa	CSCE	CC	1-Jan-61	6	
7	Soybean oil[a]	CBOT		1-Jan-61 Discontinued 1/1/91	7	
8	Soybean meal[a]	CBOT		1-Jan-61 Discontinued 1/1/91	8	
9	Sugar	CSCE	SB	1-Jan-62	9	
10	Silver	COMEX	SI	1-Jun-64	10	
11	Live cattle	CME	LC	1-Dec-65	11	
12	Lean hogs	CME	LH	1-May-67	**1960s = 12**	
13	Coffee	CSCE	KC	1-Sep-73	13	
14	British pound	CME	BP	1-Sep-75	14	
15	Swiss franc	CME	SF	1-Nov-75	15	
16	Deutsche mark[b]	CME	DM	1-Dec-75 Discontinued 1/1/00	16	
17	Gold	COMEX	GC	1-Jan-76	17	
18	Canadian dollar	CME	CD	1-Apr-76	18	
19	Japanese yen	CME	JY	1-Feb-77	19	
20	U.S. Treasury bond	CBOT	US	1-Aug-78	**1970s = 20**	
21	Heating oil	NYMEX	HO	1-Dec-80	21	
22	U.S. 10-year Treasury note	CBOT	TY	1-May-83	22	
23	Light crude oil	NYMEX	CL	1-Oct-84	23	**LSM**
24	Unleaded gasoline	NYMEX	HU	1-Mar-86 Discontinued 10/1/06	24	**S&P DTI**
25	Australian dollar	CME	AD	1-Jun-88	**1980s = 25**	
26	Natural gas	NYMEX	NG	2-Jan-91	**1990s = 24**	
27	Euro currency[b]	CME	EU	1-Jan-00	**2000s = 24**	
27	RBOB[c]	NYMEX	RB	1-Oct-06	**2000s = 24**	
				Total	**24**	

[a]Soybean oil and Soybean meal were removed from the S&P DTI simulation as of January 1, 1991.
[b]The Deutsche mark was replaced by the euro in January 2000.
[c]Unleaded gasoline was replaced by RBOB on October 1, 2006.
The Long/short methodology (LSM) is a proxy for the S&P DTI. From 1961 to 1984 we use a similar (but not the same) basket of futures in the LSM compared to that used in the S&P DTI. The only difference is in the LSM the individual components are equally weighted and are not formed into sectors as in the S&P DTI. Also, there is a different basket of components to some degree in the LSM as there were less futures contracts trading during that period.

one loss for the period ending 9/30/03, which would have been −2.91%, not −6.47%.

The point is, the increase in 12-month total return losses were caused by extremely low T-bills rates, not S&P DTI price return anomalies.

SUMMARY

The S&P DTI uses a universal algorithm: a 1.6-weighted exponential seven-month moving average. The position in each sector is then determined by examining whether the price of the sector is above or below that moving average. In analyzing the various sectors and their historical price movements, you can always find a different moving average that yields slightly better results, either by changing the weighting or by changing the period. Yet in constructing the DTI it was decided that it was best to use a universal algorithm in order to remove the appearance of data mining or curve-fitting from which so many trading systems or investment guidelines suffer from.

Remember, similar results in the S&P DTI are experienced regardless of the specific moving average selected. Most telling is the fact that in general, the frequency of winning months versus losing months remains static over any specific period of time.

Unlike a typical long-only index, the S&P DTI experiences its degree of yearly returns from the extent of the market trends, as opposed to the number of monthly profits. Also, the higher the volatility the greater the overall returns, which is the exact opposite of the result for equities.

The component groups within the S&P DTI are not correlated to each other, which provides additional diversification. The combination of diversification and noncorrelation helps provide stable returns to the indicator. This has the effect of producing smoother results, which should lessen the drawdowns overall.

CHAPTER 11

A Fundamental Hedge

The Standard & Poor's Diversified Trends Indicator (S&P DTI) (1985 to present) and the long/short methodology (LSM) (1961 to 1984) are a fundamental hedge to stocks. However, they are *not* structured to be a direct monthly hedge to falling equity or bond prices, so you should not expect them to display negative correlation to either market.

From 1961 to 2006 (552 months of observation), the LSM/S&P DTI on a monthly basis moved in the same direction as the S&P 500 index (S&P 500) 52.2 percent of the time, and in the opposite direction 47.8 percent of the time. A more important observation is that the LSM/S&P DTI and S&P 500 were both down only 12.1 percent of the time, but were both up 40.4 percent of the time. (See Table 11.3, later in this chapter.) However, even on a monthly basis, for marked-to-market reasons, there is a fundamental statistical bias to needing the LSM/S&P DTI as a hedge.

In the top and bottom 3.8 percent (20 occasions) of monthly changes, when the S&P 500 declined the largest percentage (Table 11.1), the LSM/S&P DTI was up for the month 75.0 percent of the time, and during the months when the S&P 500 gained the largest percentage (Table 11.2), the LSM/S&P DTI still rose 55 percent of the time.

What is more telling from a diversification standpoint is that when the S&P 500 had its greatest 20 monthly declines, the bond market also declined 70.0 percent of the time, or 14 of 20 occasions. Furthermore, when the S&P 500 had its greatest declines, the LSM/S&P DTI hedge ratio more than offset the total loss in 35 percent of the occasions, or in seven monthly periods. This is using a recommended three-times leverage structure that approximately equally weights the standard deviations of both asset classes. Tables 11.1 and 11.2 depict this study and its results.

TABLE 11.1 S&P 500 Index 20 Largest Monthly Declines

Number	S&P 500 Index Percent	Total Return Date	Largest Declines LT Gov't Bonds	Largest Declines LSM/S&P DTI	Offset Decline[a] 3X Leverage
1	−21.52	Oct 87	+	−2.64%	−7.92
2	−14.46	Aug 98	+	2.39	7.17
3	−11.7	Sep 74	+	6.77	Net +20.31
4	−10.87	Sep 2	−	0.48	1.44
5	−10.82	Nov 73	−	−0.47	−1.41
6	−9.87	Mar 80	−	−1.19	−3.57
7	−9.13	Feb 00	+	1.62	4.86
8	−9.03	Aug 90	−	4.58	Net 13.74
9	−8.91	Oct 78	−	4.55	Net +13.65
10	−8.89	Apr 70	−	2.79	8.37
11	−8.29	Aug 74	−	−3.75	−11.25
12	−8.22	Sep 86	−	−1.86	−5.58
13	−8.19	Nov 87	+	2.84	Net +8.52
14	−8.17	Sep 1	−	0.84	2.52
15	−8.11	May 62	+	3.91	Net +11.73
16	−8.03	Jun 62	−	0.35	1.05
17	−7.88	Nov 00	−	2.5	7.5
18	−7.59	Jul 74	−	4.58	Net +13.74
19	−7.43	Jan 70	−	0.7	2.1
20	−7.3	Jun 2	−	3.28	Net +9.84
			30%	75%	Net +35%

Source: Compiled by Enhanced Alpha Management, LP. All results simulated. Past performance is not necessarily indicative of future results.
[a]Net indicates a complete offset of the S&P 500 loss that occurred 35 percent of the time.

TABLE 11.2 S&P 500 Index 20 Largest Monthly Increases

	S&P 500 Index	Total Return	Largest Increases	
Number	%	Date	Bonds	LSM/S&P DTI
1	16.57	Oct 74	+	2.44
2	13.43	Jan 87	+	0.83
3	12.67	Aug 82	+	1.13
4	12.51	Jan 75	+	3.19
5	11.99	Jan 76	+	1.96
6	11.43	Dec 91	+	2.68
7	11.26	Oct 82	+	0.21
8	11.25	Aug 84	+	−2.55
9	10.95	Nov 80	+	0.54
10	10.86	Nov 62	+	1.06
11	9.78	Mar 00	−	−1.51
12	9.75	May 90	+	−1.53
13	8.98	Jul 89	+	−0.94
14	8.8	Oct 2	−	−1.48
15	8.77	Dec 71	+	6.45
16	8.7	Apr 78	−	−1.41
17	8.34	Apr 68	+	1.21
18	8.13	Oct 98	−	−1.03
19	7.98	Jan 67	+	−0.25
20	7.94	Jul 97	+	−0.49
			80%	55%

Source: Compiled by Enhanced Alpha Management, LP. All results simulated. Past performance is not necessarily indicative of future results.

TIME AS A FACTOR IN HEDGE RESULTS

The critical aspect of the relationship between the S&P 500 and the LSM/S&P DTI, and the fundamental nature of the hedge, is depicted by time in the *various results* table (Table 11.3). The saying that "a picture is worth a thousand words" certainly applies here. Observe that the occasions when the S&P 500 and the LSM/S&P DTI both declined diminished to 2.02 percent after nine months. Also, both the S&P 500 and the LSM/S&P DTI increased in profitability, the longer the time invested.

TABLE 11.3 Correlation between S&P DTI, Stocks, and Bonds, 1961 to 2006

	LSM/S&P DTI		Percent	
	S&P	**Bonds**	**S&P**	**Bonds**
Monthly (552 Months)				
Same direction	288	274	52.17%	49.64%
Opposite direction	264	278	47.83%	50.36%
Same direction profit	221	205	40.04%	37.14%
Same direction loss	67	69	12.14%	12.50%
Quarterly (550 Rolling 3-Month Periods)				
Same direction	316	311	57.45%	56.55%
Opposite direction	234	239	42.55%	43.45%
Same direction profit	278	268	50.55%	48.73%
Same direction loss	38	43	6.91%	7.82%
Semi-Annually (547 Rolling 6-Month Periods)				
Same direction	331	356	60.51%	65.08%
Opposite direction	216	191	39.49%	34.92%
Same direction profit	315	331	57.59%	60.51%
Same direction loss	16	25	2.93%	4.57%
Nine Months (544 Rolling 9-Month Periods)				
Same direction	378	377	69.49%	69.30%
Opposite direction	166	167	30.51%	30.70%
Same direction profit	367	367	67.46%	67.46%
Same direction loss	11	10	2.02%	1.84%
Annually (541 Rolling 12-Month Periods)				
Same direction	397	391	73.38%	72.27%
Opposite direction	144	150	26.62%	27.73%
Same direction profit	392	390	72.46%	72.09%
Same direction loss	5	1	0.92%	0.18%

Source: Compiled by Enhanced Alpha Management, LP. All results simulated. Past performance is not necessarily indicative of future results.

The source returns of both indexes are proven by this analysis. A price-driven (system trading) strategy could never achieve these robust and stable results. Furthermore, any index of commodities chosen would yield a positive return, more or less as shown, regardless of the specific markets included. However, only liquid commodities can be practically applied. For example, the S&P DTI does not use illiquid commodities such as orange juice, but it would be profitable if used.

Lastly, we define the trend based on a moving average, and use that moving average to determine whether to be long or short in our structure.

This is *primarily* to capture the risk transfer premium of futures (backwardation and contango), or discount and premium business returns. Thus, any long-term moving average that defines trend direction would achieve similar results.

The LSM was equally weighted from 1961 to 1984. The S&P DTI was weighted, and the similar components were formed into sectors from 1985 to date when this study was initiated.

A big-four accounting firm has attested to the S&P DTI from 1985 to May of 2001 for a major brokerage firm.

The long/short methodology (LSM) is a proxy for the S&P DTI. From 1961 to 1984 we use a similar (but not the same) basket of futures in the LSM compared to that used in the S&P DTI.

CHAPTER 12

S&P DTI Subindexes

The S&P Commodity Trends Indicator and the S&P Financial Trends Indicator

I If you break the S&P Diversified Trends Indicator (S&P DTI) in half, you're left with the commodity-based piece and the financial-based piece. This is more of an asset-class investment process in the eyes of the public. Of course, in essence, being short financials and long commodities is virtually the same position. This is because economic events that cause bonds to go down generally cause commodities to go up—although not necessarily to the same extent. But investors don't always see that clearly, and when you look at something from a trading standpoint (as I might), you get a very different view than the public (or those who might be selling a product to the public). In particular, institutions like to put things into some sort of logical box to benchmark investments. Something multifaceted can actually be a negative in their eyes, instead of a diversified positive, if it is hard to explain or isn't comparable to common alternatives or benchmarks.

Institutions, and institutional salesmen, also like to allocate investments directly to specific classes. Is the item in question stocks, bonds, cash, real estate, oil, or gold? If it can't be classified in simplistic terms, it can become very confusing for them, or difficult to apply to their models. If that happens, they usually take the easy way out and toss the investment presentation in the garbage. So for those who desire clear asset class exposure, the S&P DTI has been split into the S&P Commodity Trends Indicator (S&P CTI) and the S&P Financial Trends Indicator (S&P FTI). The administration and position determination for both are the same as the S&P DTI, but the asset percentages are doubled. See Tables 12.1 through 12.3 for the

TABLE 12.1 S&P CTI Component Breakdown—Long Energy

Market	Market Weight	Sector	Sector Weight	Component	Component Weight
Commodities	100.00%	Energy	37.50%	Heating oil	6.00%
				Light crude	17.00%
				Natural gas	8.50%
				RBOB gasoline	6.00%
		Industrial metals	10.00%	Copper	10.00%
		Precious metals	10.50%	Gold	7.00%
				Silver	3.50%
		Livestock	10.00%	Lean hogs	4.00%
				Live cattle	6.00%
		Grains	23.00%	Corn	8.00%
				Soybeans	10.00%
				Wheat	5.00%
		Softs	9.00%	Cocoa	2.00%
				Coffee	3.00%
				Cotton	2.00%
				Sugar	2.00%

TABLE 12.2 S&P CTI Component Breakdown—Flat Energy

Market	Market Weight	Sector	Sector Weight	Component	Component Weight
Commodities	100.00%	Energy	0.00%	Heating oil	0.00%
				Light crude	0.00%
				Natural gas	0.00%
				Unleaded gasoline	0.00%
		Industrial metals	16.00%	Copper	16.00%
		Precious metals	16.80%	Gold	11.20%
				Silver	5.60%
		Livestock	16.00%	Lean hogs	6.40%
				Live cattle	9.60%
		Grains	36.80%	Corn	12.80%
				Soybeans	16.00%
				Wheat	8.00%
		Softs	14.40%	Cocoa	3.20%
				Coffee	4.80%
				Cotton	3.20%
				Sugar	3.20%

TABLE 12.3 S&P FTI Component Breakdown

	Market Weight	Sector	Sector Weight	Component	Component Weight
Financials	100.00%	Financials	100.00%	Australian dollar	4.00%
				British pound	10.00%
				Canadian dollar	2.00%
				Euro	26.00%
				Japanese yen	24.00%
				Swiss franc	4.00%
				U.S. Treasury bonds	15.00%
				U.S. Treasury notes	15.00%

breakdown of percentages. The S&P CTI requires two tables, one for when it is long the energy group, and one for when it is flat.

A PURE COMMODITY PLAY

When it comes to commodities, the S&P CTI is what is in demand. In my opinion, it is a better mousetrap than any long-only commodity index. Theoretically it should be, as it gives you both sides of commodity movement. In actuality, it seems that in the long run those theories play out to be truthful, as the S&P CTI outperforms them—with less volatility, more return, and less drawdown risk. To me, that's like meeting a woman who is a Texas 10 but enjoys discussing derivatives. (If you happen to find one, let me know; I might be willing to offer a reward!)

In any respect, to be entirely fair, it can be argued that since you can go short within the S&P CTI, you don't have the same kind of constant exposure as a long-only index, and therefore they are different asset classes and should not be compared directly. In theory I agree, but in reality anything with commodity exposure winds up being compared, and it does outperform. I suppose it is a gray area of debates.

BUILDING S&P CTI-BASED PRODUCTS

Commodities are in vogue at the moment, and some professional firms believe this will be the case for many decades. A major bank has recently asked me to trade and execute the S&P CTI as it structures products based on the S&P CTI. HSBC is an extremely bright firm that deals in structured products. It is not often that I am impressed with the personnel involved in structured products. The reason is that they usually seem to be like traders in a Casablanca street market: They only care about "one trade," and not developing a long-term relationship with investors. HSBC is a welcome exception to that rule.

Generally, all structured note desks are filled with smart people. They have to be—after all, it is a complex business. But, like chess masters, they are not as likeable as Oprah Winfrey, Jay Leno, or David Letterman; they are numbers people, not people people! Fortunately, not everybody is that way. After all, we work for money (for ourselves, for our families, our significant others, and our parents—and sometimes for all four). The challenge is to be productive and successful while still having fun.

Sadly, most of the time relationships are difficult to build—almost like trying to stick to a diet. If you find smart, trustworthy people who are fun to deal with, this is a rare event indeed. I am glad to report that I have found the people at HSBC to be all that and more. Over the years, I have been fortunate enough to discover a very small number of individuals and firms who fit that description—HSBC is just the latest one to be added to the list. HSBC has taken on the role of S&P CTI specialists, and they are structuring many different products around it.

Other top-notch firms are also doing this. HSBC's leading role is probably because it has the think-outside-the-box mentality. Like the New York Mets slogan of yesteryear, "You Gotta Believe." I appreciate its interest and support, as I believe this is a winning investment.

Lastly, I can't resist paraphrasing the famous saying: With the Victor go the spoils!

And yes, the pun is intended!

Afterword

C ommodities and futures can appear very complicated, but I hope that through this book I was able to demystify some of the more confusing aspects of their operation and their successful utilization, either as trading vehicles or as part of a structured portfolio. Properly handled, commodity futures are simply another (albeit slightly more volatile) method of profiting from market movements. In many ways, they are one of the truest and purest forms of speculation, because they are closely tied to the real world. A biotech stock that has never shown a penny of profit may trade above $75 per share for many years, simply on speculation that some new drug or process it is developing will become the next big thing. But commodity futures have to take current cash prices and world supply and demand factors into account at all times, as almost all contracts can be used to receive or deliver the physical commodity after first notice day. Despite their name, commodity *futures* contracts often trade with more focus on the present or near term compared to other assets!

SUMMARIZING AND CLARIFYING

Before you prepare to close this book and jump into the markets head-first, let's take a moment and summarize some of the major points touched on in the preceding chapters.

- There are known knowns, unknown knowns, known unknowns, and (most importantly) unknown unknowns. All of these can be important factors in success with commodities.
- Commodity futures were created not to make you rich, nor for you to trade them, but to allow the producers of the commodity to hedge their risk. And they pay you to take that risk!
- The recent rise in commodity prices has been caused by a number of diverse factors, and has helped generate increasing interest in the commodities markets.

- *Trading* in commodities and *investing* in commodities as an asset class require different strategies, and have different pros and cons.
- The three most common reasons traders lose money are the effects of *leverage*, *gambling* for a home run, and not *cutting their losses*.
- Fold your bad hands. Cut your losses, and let your profits run.
- Losses are a part of the commodities game. But if you make the right bets, you can lose four out of five times and still come out ahead in the end.
- Pay attention to what the market is telling you.
- Never use oscillators to try and pick the bottom or the top. Use them as indicators to confirm a change in trend.
- When sentiment is nearly universal on one side or the other, that is the time to play the other side, and fade the consensus.
- Professionals and big speculators usually are on the right side more often than the general public.
- Long-only commodity indexes can usually be a good play for traders, and occasionally a good investment.
- Rebalancing is critical to the long-term success of a diversified commodities strategy.
- If you're going to read charts, it is important to learn how to draw a trendline properly.
- The 2B rule is a powerful tool that can anticipate changes in trend, and it allows you to enter trades with very limited risk (but attractive returns).
- Curve-fitted or data-mined trading systems cannot be successful over the long term.
- Long-only commodity indexes not only are unable to profit from downtrends, they actually have to stay invested through the entire move, and thereby sustain losses while also paying the contango premium.
- The S&P DTI, as a long/short indicator, can profit whether market trends are up or down, but not when sideways.
- The S&P DTI will not go short energy, due to the risk of ruin in the case of a catastrophic event. It will only go long or flat.
- The S&P DTI uses a seven-price exponential moving average that is 1.6 times weighted to determine positional direction. However, any moving average would be profitable. This is because if trends exist, the concept of trend following will earn a return in virtually any market and in any environment over longer term periods.
- The S&P DTI sectors are rebalanced monthly, but the individual components are rebalanced annually. This rebalancing helps to keep volatility low.
- Trend following is a legitimate challenge to the random walk theory, and is the basis of the S&P DTI.

- A long/short strategy like the S&P DTI accomplishes the same goal as a long-only commodity index—it acts as a hedge against inflation. Yet it has the potential of creating a more efficient and smoother return.
- The S&P DTI is an indicator that measures trends, not prices.
- Backwardation and contango in commodities markets are important sources of core returns in the S&P DTI.
- The S&P DTI enjoys noncorrelation between its two major groups, commodities and financials.
- The S&P DTI provides true diversification within its components.
- The S&P DTI acts as a fundamental hedge to stocks.
- The S&P CTI and S&P FTI provide more specific asset-class investments compared to the diversified S&P DTI.

S&P DTI Methodology and Implementation

The Standard & Poor's Diversified Trends Indicator (S&P DTI) is a diversified composite of global commodity and financial futures that are highly liquid. The components are formed into sectors that are long or short (except energy) the underlying futures using a rules-based methodology. The indicator measures the extent (and duration)—that is, the extended volatility—of the trends of these sectors in aggregate.

Futures derive their returns differently from other financial assets. Unlike declining equities, where usually only short-sellers benefit, declining futures prices have as much benefit as rising futures prices: Rising prices benefit producers; declining prices, consumers. As such, within the futures markets both buying and selling play an equally important economic role. Futures prices reflect not only current cash prices, but also expectations of future prices as well as general economic and fundamental factors. The S&P DTI methodology is investable, intending to reflect and capture the profit potential in price trends.

Speculators play an important role in the economics of futures markets. They provide liquidity and accept the risk of price fluctuations in return for a premium from hedgers who are unwilling to bear that risk.

This appendix discusses the economic function of the futures market and how it relates to the rationale behind the S&P DTI. We describe how the indicator is constructed and what the methodology is designed to achieve. Weighting decisions, method for determining direction of position, rebalancing, and execution are explained. We consider the indicator's internal diversification and how the long exposure tends to capture inflation over long periods. We describe how exposure to the indicator tends to mitigate and even profit from commodity and financial price cyclicality.

147

There is a discussion of long/short measures compared to long-only commodity indexes and why the indicator tends to be profitable in a variety of market conditions. Finally, there is a brief discussion of two variations on the S&P DTI based on its sector subcomponents: the S&P Commodity Trends Indicator (CTI), and the S&P Financial Trends Indicator (FTI).

INTRODUCTION

Through a licensing agreement with Alpha Financial Technologies, LLC (AFT), Standard & Poor's offers the S&P DTI. AFT's CEO, Victor Sperandeo, is recognized as offering futures market trading expertise as a commodity trading advisor and has for some time implemented a number of successful strategies that are designed to profit from futures price trends. The S&P DTI is an evolution of these strategies in that it constitutes the intellectual property of AFT, but is constructed, calculated, and maintained by Standard & Poor's with participation from AFT.

The indicator follows a quantitative methodology to track prices of a diversified portfolio of 24 commodity and financial futures contracts. The *contracts* (also called *components*) are grouped into sectors, and each sector is represented on either a long or short basis, depending on recent price trends of that sector. With the ability to go long or short sectors, the S&P DTI is designed to capture the economic benefit over long time periods derived from both rising and declining trends within a cross-section of futures markets.

The primary objective of the indicator is to measure in aggregate the component trends based on price movement and premium discount expansion and contraction of certain highly liquid futures. Limiting the volatility of the indicator was a guide in the determination of the methodology. The methodology is implemented in a rules-based, systematic manner. The indicator is not intended to be representative of a particular futures market or group of markets.

DESCRIPTION

The key characteristics of the S&P DTI include the following:

- 24 components (futures contracts), equally divided by weight, grouped into 14 sectors—8 financial and 6 commodity sectors
- Long or short positions are determined by comparing the current sector price to a moving exponential average (i.e., most recent price weighted most heavily, etc.)

- Sectors are rebalanced monthly; components are rebalanced annually
- Performance has a positive correlation to its own standard deviation (i.e., performance tends to increase/decrease with increased/decreased volatility)
- Exposure offers potential to mitigate the negative effect of commodity and financial price cyclicality

Table A.1 illustrates the sector weightings of the indicator, including a reference to the component weights. Note that in some cases there is only one component.

Figure A.1 offers an overview of the construction and maintenance process of the S&P DTI and serves as an introduction to the description following.

TABLE A.1   S&P DTI Weighting Scheme

Market	Market Weight	Sector	Sector Weight	Component	Component Weight
Commodities	50%	Energy	18.75%	Heating oil	3.00%
				Light crude	8.50%
				Natural gas	4.25%
				Unleaded gasoline	3.00%
		Industrial metals	5.00%	Copper	5.00%
		Precious metals	5.25%	Gold	3.50%
				Silver	1.75%
		Livestock	5.00%	Lean hogs	2.00%
				Live cattle	3.00%
		Grains	11.50	Corn	4.00%
				Soybeans	5.00%
				Wheat	2.50%
		Softs	4.50%	Cocoa	1.00%
				Coffee	1.50%
				Cotton	1.00%
				Sugar	1.00%
Financials	50%	Currencies	35.00%	Australian dollar	2.00%
				British pound	5.00%
				Canadian dollar	1.00%
				Euro	13.00%
				Japanese yen	12.00%
				Swiss franc	2.00%
		Treasuries	15.00%	U.S. Treasury bonds	7.50%
				U.S. Treasury notes	7.50%

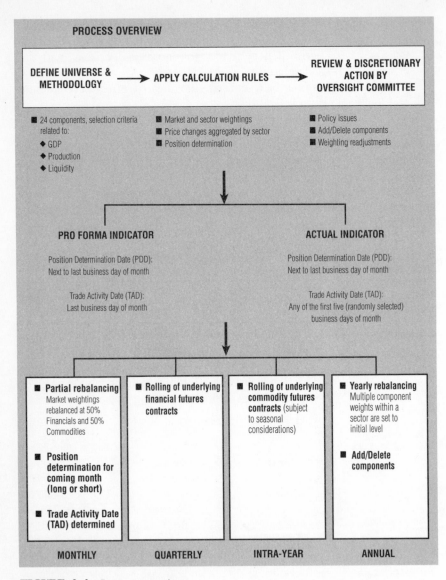

FIGURE A.1 Process overview.

METHODOLOGY AND MAINTENANCE

The methodology of the S&P DTI is designed with a focus on capturing both up and down price trends, yet moderating volatility. Components of the indicator are chosen based on fundamental characteristics and liquidity (necessary for an investable model), as opposed to a means for achieving performance per se.

Selection Criteria

Of the factors considered in determining the S&P DTI components and weights, *liquidity*—the volume and notional size of futures contracts traded—is one of the most important. Liquidity is an indication both of the significance of a particular market and the ability to trade with minimal market impact. All the components of the indicator are consistently in the lists of top contracts traded in the United States.

Investability is another important consideration. Other liquid contracts may exist, but exceptionally large contract values (i.e., $1,000,000 per contract for Eurodollar futures) would make the cost to replicate the indicator very inefficient. Contracts are limited to those traded on U.S. exchanges to minimize any impact from major differences in trading hours, avoid currency exchange calculations, and allow for similar closing times and holiday schedules. This may expand in the future.

Initial Weightings

For commodities, production is an indication of the significance of a given component to the world economy and of such component's significance within the futures markets themselves. (In the case of the natural gas component included in the energy sector, North American rather than world production has been used as the relevant factor due to constraints linked to transporting natural gas internationally.) Since there is often no single recognized source for a commodity's production figures, estimates are used in selecting and making allocations.

Gross domestic product (GDP), is an indication of economic significance and is used in selecting and making allocations to financials. The Swiss franc is an exception: This currency is allocated a weighting slightly disproportionate (1 percent) to the Swiss GDP due to the Swiss franc's liquidity and Switzerland's political significance. Table A.2 shows worldwide GDP by major industrial nation.

Markets are divided equally between tangible commodities and financials (excluding equities) in order to increase the internal noncorrelation among the components. This is not done to reflect their relative notional values outstanding, but rather, to produce a smoother, less-volatile return.

Weightings of the financial sectors are based on, but not directly proportional to, GDP. Instead, the financials of the countries with a GDP of

TABLE A.2 Gross Domestic Product, 2004

Related Sector Weight	Region	GDP (USD Trillion)
15%	United States	$11.67
13%	European Monetary Union	$9.37
12%	Japan	$4.62
5%	United Kingdom	$2.14
1%	Canada	$0.98
2%	Australia	$0.63
2%	Switzerland	$0.36

Source: World Bank, World Development Indicators Database, March 2006.

greater than $3 trillion are placed into tier 1 and countries with a GDP of less than $3 trillion are placed in tier 2. Tier 1 financials are meant to be close in weight, with slight relative tilts toward those from the larger economies. Thus, the U.S.-based financials have a higher importance than the euro currency. Tier 2 markets are weighted approximately proportionate to each other, but have some adjustments for liquidity, trading significance, and potential correlation to tier 1 markets. For example, the Canadian dollar component receives a 1 percent weighting due to Canada's historical economic connection with the United States. By not weighting the financials of the largest GDP countries so high, the tier weighting approach increases diversification.

Commodity weights are based on generally known world production levels. A reasonability test is to compare weights with established commodity-specific indexes, such as the Goldman Sachs Commodity Index (GSCI) and Dow Jones-AIG Commodity Index (DJAIG). As shown in Table A.3, when divided in half to match the fact that commodities are only half the weight of the S&P DTI, the production allocations compare fairly

TABLE A.3 Production Allocation

	S&P Goldman Sachs Commodity Index	Half Weight	Dow Jones–AIG Commodity Index	Half Weight	S&P DTI
Energy	74.56%	37.38%	33.00%	16.50%	18.75%
Industrial metals	8.49%	4.25%	18.09%	9.05%	5.00%
Precious metals	2.20%	1.10%	8.22%	4.11%	5.25%
Livestock	4.20%	2.10%	10.45%	5.23%	5.00%
Grains	6.67%	3.34%	21.18%	10.59%	11.50%
Softs	3.88%	1.94%	9.06%	4.53%	4.50%

closely. The exception to this is the significantly higher energy weighting in the GSCI due to strict adherence to production figures.

S&P GSCI weightings are as of April 2006, DJ AIG are as of January 2006, and the DTI are as of any given month end.

REBALANCING

The monthly and annual rebalancing of the S&P DTI is one of its most powerful and important aspects. This keeps volatility lower, and assures the indicator is properly diversified.

Monthly Rebalancing for Sector Weights

Sectors are rebalanced monthly to their fixed weights. The rebalance date is the second to the last business day of the month, with an effective date randomly selected from any of the first five business days of the next month.

Rebalancing monthly helps to keep volatility low, since otherwise an extended move in one group or sector would overweight the S&P DTI and potentially lead to significantly higher volatility of the indicator. Because the sectors are rebalanced, it follows that every month the aggregate markets are rebalanced to equal weighting (e.g., 50 percent commodities/50 percent financials). An exception to this (described more fully below) is when the energy sector has a neutral position.

Variability of Component Weights

Although sectors are always rebalanced monthly back to their fixed weights, the component weightings are allowed to vary. A hypothetical example is described below and shown in Table A.4.

In the livestock sector, for the two months ending February 2000, the cumulative year-to-date return is 5.26 percent for the lean hogs component and −0.68 percent for the live cattle component. To determine the weight of each component within the livestock sector for March 2000, we multiply one plus the component's year-to-date return by its initial weight and divide by one plus the sector's year-to-date return.

Thus, the weight for lean hogs in March is: $(1 + 5.26\%) \times 2.00\% / (1 + 1.70\%) = 2.07\%$.

For live cattle, the March weight is: $(1 - 0.68\%) \times 3.00\% / (1 + 1.70\%) = 2.93\%$.

TABLE A.4 Example of Multiple Component Weight Changes in a Sector

| | Lean Hogs | Lean Hogs Components | | Live Cattle | Live Cattle Components | | Livestock | Sector | |
	Monthly Return	YTD Return	Monthly Weight	Monthly Return	YTD Return	Monthly Weight	Monthly Return	YTD Return	Monthly Weight
Initial Weight			2.00%			3.00%			5.00%
Jan 00	6.04%	6.04%	2.00%	0.29%	0.29%	3.00%	2.59%	2.59%	5.00%
Feb 00	0.74%	5.26%	2.07%	−0.97%	−0.68%	2.93%	−0.87%	1.70%	5.00%
Mar 00	10.27%	16.07%	2.19%	0.07%	−0.61%	2.81%	4.29%	6.06%	5.00%

154

The two components weights sum to 5.00 percent, which is the target livestock sector weight.

Annual Rebalancing for Component Weights

At the end of each year, each of the 24 components is rebalanced. It is expected that the component weights will not vary significantly from those shown in Table A.2. Although production and GDP figures change over time, in a relative sense as it affects component weights, that change is small.

Rebalancing components only annually allows a degree of microeconomic influence among the correlated sector components so that market actions can determine which components are relatively more important.

Position Determination

The rule for the indicator regarding long or short positions can be summarized as follows:

- Long positions are tracked when a component's current price input is equal to or greater than an exponential average of the past seven price inputs.
- Short positions are tracked when a component's current price input is less than an exponential average of the past seven price inputs.
- Track a flat (zero weight) position for the energy sector when a short position is indicated; in this case, the 18.75 percent weight for energy is distributed proportionately to the other 13 sectors.

Position is determined on the second to the last business day of the month (defined as the position determination day or PDD) when the monthly percentage change of a sector's price is compared to past monthly price changes exponentially weighted to give greatest weight to the most recent return and least weight to the return seven months prior. The weighted sum of the percentage changes of all the sector prices equals the daily movement of the indicator.

After the market closes on the trade activity date (TAD), active S&P DTI contracts are replaced either because (1) a new long/short signal has been generated for a particular sector or component; or (2) to roll into a further dated contract as required by the roll schedule (see Table A.7), or both. Therefore, new contracts become active as of the day following the TAD. The TAD is randomly selected and is one of the first five business days of each month. S&P acknowledges that limit closes that occur on the

TAD in active S&P DTI contracts can restrict, and in some cases eliminate, the liquidity required for perfect replication of the S&P DTI.

Price Input

The price input for a particular contract is based on the cumulative percentage price change. For example, assume the March euro contract goes from 100 to 102 in January and from 102 to 104 in February. At the end of February/beginning of March, the S&P DTI represents a selling of the March euro contract and a buying of the June euro contract that is trading at 110 and that then experiences a decline to 106 by month end. The price input for this hypothetical euro contract would be as shown in Table A.5.

Sectors versus Components

For those sectors with only one component (industrial metals and the eight financial sectors), the price input calculations to determine position are at the component level. For the energy, precious metals, livestock, and grains sectors, the price inputs from the respective underlying components are aggregated to determine position for that sector as a whole. In this case, aggregating the components reduces minor and unnecessary minor fluctuations, or whipsaws. An exception exists in the calculation of the softs sector. Here, since there is no fundamental tie between each of its components (coffee, cocoa, cotton, and sugar), the position of each is determined separately. For example, coffee could be long while sugar is short.

Energy's Short Exemption—Risk of Ruin

Energy, due to the significant level of its continuous consumption, limited reserves, and oil cartel controls, is subject to rapid price increases in the event of perceived or actual shortages. Because no other sector is subject to the same continuous demand with supply and concentration risk, the energy sector is never positioned short in the S&P DTI methodology.

TABLE A.5 Example of Price Input Calculation

Month	Price Percentage Change	Calculation of Price Input	Price Input
January	$2.00\% = (102/100) - 1$		2.00%
February	$1.96\% = (104/102) - 1$	$((1 + 2.00\%) \times (1 + 1.96\%)) - 1$	4.00%
March	$-3.96\% = (106/110) - 1$	$((1 + 2.00\%) \times (1 + 1.96\%) \times$ $(1 - 3.64\%)) - 1$	0.21%

TABLE A.6 S&P DTI Weighting Scheme without Energy

Market	Market Weight	Sector	Sector Weight	Component	Component Weight
Commodities	38.50%	Energy	0.00%	Heating oil	0.00%
				Light crude	0.00%
				Natural gas	0.00%
				Unleaded gasoline	0.00%
		Industrial metals	6.15%	Copper	6.15%
		Precious metals	6.46%	Gold	4.31%
				Silver	2.15%
		Livestock	6.15%	Lean hogs	2.46%
				Live cattle	3.69%
		Grains	14.15%	Corn	4.92%
				Soybeans	6.15%
				Wheat	3.08%
		Softs	5.54%	Cocoa	1.23%
				Coffee	1.85%
				Cotton	1.23%
				Sugar	1.23%
Financials	61.50%	Currencies	43.07%	Australian dollar	2.46%
				British pound	6.15%
				Canadian dollar	1.23%
				Euro	16.00%
				Japanese yen	14.77%
				Swiss franc	2.46%
		Treasuries	18.46%	U.S. Treasury bonds	9.23%
				U.S. Treasury notes	9.23%

Table A.6 shows how the 18.75 percent weight of the energy sector would be allocated to the other sectors if it were not positioned long.

Mathematically, original weights are divided by one minus 18.75 percent. Weights in Table A.6 do not sum to one due to rounding.

Contract Maintenance

The S&P DTI is an indicator of futures contract price trends, and futures contracts have limited durations. Consequently, in order for the indicator to be calculated on an ongoing basis, it must change (or roll) from tracking contracts that are approaching expiration to tracking new contracts. Currently, each contract has three to four roll periods each year and its own roll pattern based on historical liquidity. The following rules are observed in rolling the indicator futures contracts from an expiring contract to the next contract:

- The noncurrency component contracts are rolled over from the current contract to the next contract beginning with the TAD for the month that is two months before the current contract matures.
- The currency contracts are rolled over from the current contract to the next maturing futures contract four times per year as of the TAD for the month prior to the contract's final maturity month.

See Table A.7 for a schedule of the active contracts used for price inputs of the indicator.

The risk of aberrational liquidity or pricing around the maturity date of a commodity futures contract is greater than in the case of other futures contracts because (among other factors) a number of market participants take delivery of the underlying commodities. Spot markets in commodities occasionally have delivery problems, related to, for example, weather conditions disrupting transportation of cattle to a delivery point. Such a delay could cause the spot market to skyrocket, while later-dated futures contracts are little changed. The indicator avoids delivery issues by owning contracts that are outside of nearby delivery.

S&P DTI Oversight Committee

In order to provide for the smooth functioning of the S&P DTI, the S&P DTI Oversight Committee will make any decisions that cannot be systematized or that occur on an ad hoc basis. The Oversight Committee will implement established methodology or determine new policy if market conditions warrant change. For example, an exchange might substantially change the contract terms or even discontinue trading a component contract. In such cases, the Oversight Committee would determine any component or weighting changes. The Oversight Committee does not, however, use discretion to affect performance. Always, the goal is to maintain liquidity and low volatility in the indicator.

S&P DTI Performance

There are two kinds of returns for a futures-based index or indicator. The first is a simple combination of the weighted price percentage changes on a daily basis: This will be referred to as the S&P DTI price return (PR). The second return stream represents a simple, but realistic, rate of return for an actual implementation of the indicator. Since futures contracts are bought on margin rather than with an actual cash investment, it is useful to have a return that uses a fully collateralized margin account consisting of 90-day U.S. Treasury bills. This collateralized return will be known as the S&P DTI total return (TR). Compounding of the interest on the U.S. Treasury bill is on a quarterly basis.

TABLE A.7 Schedule of Contracts

Contract Name	Jan	Feb	Mar	Apr	May	Jun	Jul	Aug	Sep	Oct	Nov	Dec
Heating oil	H	M	M	M	U	U	U	Z	Z	Z	H	H
Crude oil (light)	H	M	M	M	U	U	U	Z	Z	Z	H	H
Natural gas	H	M	M	M	U	U	U	Z	Z	Z	H	H
RBOB gas blend	H	M	M	M	U	U	U	Z	Z	Z	H	H
Copper	H	N	N	N	N	U	U	Z	Z	Z	H	H
Gold	M	M	M	M	V	V	V	V	Z	Z	G	G
Silver	H	N	N	N	N	U	U	Z	Z	Z	H	H
Lean hogs	M	M	M	M	Q	Q	Z	Z	Z	Z	G	G
Live cattle	M	M	M	M	Q	Q	Z	Z	Z	Z	G	G
Corn	H	N	N	N	N	U	U	Z	Z	Z	H	H
Soybeans	H	N	N	N	N	X	X	X	X	H	H	H
Wheat	H	N	N	N	N	U	U	Z	Z	Z	H	H
Cocoa	H	N	N	N	N	U	U	Z	Z	Z	H	H
Coffee	H	N	N	N	N	U	U	Z	Z	Z	H	H
Cotton	H	N	N	N	N	Z	Z	Z	Z	Z	H	H
Sugar	H	K	K	N	N	V	V	V	H	H	H	H
Australian dollar	H	H	M	M	M	U	U	U	Z	Z	Z	H
British pound	H	H	M	M	M	U	U	U	Z	Z	Z	H
Canadian dollar	H	H	M	M	M	U	U	U	Z	Z	Z	H
Euro	H	H	M	M	M	U	U	U	Z	Z	Z	H
Japanese yen	H	H	M	M	M	U	U	U	Z	Z	Z	H
Swiss franc	H	H	M	M	M	U	U	U	Z	Z	Z	H
U.S. Treasury bond	H	M	M	M	U	U	U	Z	Z	Z	H	H
U.S. Treasury note	H	M	M	M	U	U	U	Z	Z	Z	H	H

Key:

Contract Expiration	Letter
January	F
February	G
March	H
April	J
May	K
June	M
July	N
August	Q
September	U
October	V
November	X
December	Z

S&P Diversified Trends Pro Forma Indicator Performance Analysis

For purposes of analysis, I constructed a pro forma version of the S&P DTI from January 1985 through December 2003. This methodology differs only slightly from the current methodology of the S&P DTI:

S&P DTI	S&P DT Pro Forma Indicator
Includes November Soybean contract	Includes September Soybean contract
Includes December Cotton contract	Includes October Cotton contract
TAD any of first five business days	TAD always last business day
Quarterly compounding of T-bill	Monthly compounding of T-bill interest for total return interest for total return

Furthermore, minor changes were made to the component composition to accommodate market changes, specifically prior to January 2000 the Deutsche mark futures contract was used instead of the euro contract. Two contracts were not used until they demonstrated sufficient liquidity after their respective launch: Before May 1991, natural gas was not included as a component, and before February 1988, the Australian dollar was not included.

The S&P Diversified Trends Pro Forma Indicator price return stream is based on data that were (for the period January 1, 1985, through May 31, 2001) attested to by a big-four accounting firm that was engaged for a fee. Using the same methodology for the period June 1, 2001, through December 31, 2003, the pro forma performance history for the price return series has been calculated and replicated by S&P using historical price data from Bloomberg. Since January 1, 2004, S&P has calculated the value of the S&P DTI price return and total return series (the *live* series).

All references to the performance of the S&P DTI in this section refer to the combined pro forma and live series history of the S&P DTI PR and the S&P DTI TR.

A history of returns combining live results with a modified pro forma implementing the current (effective January 1, 2004) methodology of the S&P DTI is shown in Table A.8 and Table A.9. Because the difference between the two methodologies is minor, the returns are similar: The annualized S&P Diversified Trends Pro Forma Indicator price return for the 22-year period is 6.03 and 5.90 for the modified pro forma series. The correlation between the two series is 0.99.

Past performance during the pro forma period is based on back-tested results that do not represent the results of concurrent calculation but are achieved instead through retroactive application of a methodology that

TABLE A.8 Monthly and Annual Returns of the S&P DTI (without T-bills), Combined Pro Forma and Live Price Return Series, January 1985 to December 2006

Year	Jan	Feb	Mar	Apr	May	Jun	Jul	Aug	Sep	Oct	Nov	Dec	Annual/YTD
2006	0.01%	-1.81%	2.37%	2.99%	0.15%	-2.40%	1.72%	-0.02%	-1.81%	0.08%	0.70%	-0.42%	1.42%
2005	0.67%	-2.52%	2.09%	-3.50%	1.14%	2.47%	0.76%	1.88%	2.16%	-1.87%	2.38%	-0.91%	4.59%
2004	1.63%	3.57%	1.39%	-2.20%	0.36%	-0.17%	3.75%	-2.41%	5.53%	1.63%	0.27%	-1.15%	12.56%
2003	2.44%	1.83%	-2.35%	-0.58%	1.99%	-1.56%	-2.41%	-1.38%	-2.18%	3.21%	0.79%	3.86%	3.43%
2002	-0.16%	0.26%	-1.73%	0.20%	-0.37%	3.28%	-0.30%	2.57%	1.42%	-1.55%	0.49%	-2.50%	1.46%
2001	-2.12%	1.17%	2.04%	-0.25%	0.69%	-1.15%	-0.95%	-0.02%	0.84%	0.52%	-1.85%	0.62%	-0.55%
2000	1.37%	1.62%	-1.51%	1.39%	2.98%	1.84%	-1.97%	0.66%	0.05%	1.16%	2.50%	0.92%	11.45%
1999	-0.91%	2.58%	-1.10%	0.72%	-1.31%	1.96%	0.75%	1.54%	0.72%	-2.76%	2.52%	1.34%	6.05%
1998	0.05%	0.63%	1.42%	-0.04%	-0.22%	0.27%	1.88%	2.39%	-0.17%	-1.03%	-0.66%	0.39%	4.95%
1997	0.58%	-2.14%	1.61%	1.85%	-1.90%	0.51%	-0.49%	0.39%	1.44%	0.20%	-0.96%	0.60%	1.61%
1996	0.34%	-0.31%	2.66%	2.86%	0.07%	2.65%	-1.25%	0.21%	0.94%	2.55%	2.87%	1.13%	15.62%
1995	-0.49%	0.53%	2.42%	1.10%	-0.01%	-0.29%	-0.85%	0.40%	1.42%	0.60%	-0.21%	3.29%	8.09%
1994	-1.15%	-1.80%	1.09%	0.93%	1.37%	2.72%	1.14%	-1.56%	0.37%	1.33%	0.22%	-0.66%	3.97%
1993	0.23%	0.36%	0.30%	2.45%	0.23%	-1.83%	1.08%	-1.18%	1.53%	-1.31%	0.28%	-0.01%	2.09%
1992	-1.71%	-0.11%	0.43%	-0.12%	-0.26%	1.79%	3.34%	1.68%	0.48%	-2.16%	0.55%	-0.18%	3.67%
1991	1.05%	-1.09%	1.34%	-0.12%	0.25%	0.67%	-2.94%	0.88%	1.64%	0.85%	-0.76%	2.68%	4.43%
1990	0.84%	0.24%	1.34%	1.90%	-1.53%	1.87%	0.28%	4.58%	7.57%	-0.70%	-0.28%	-1.10%	15.68%
1989	0.45%	0.12%	4.30%	1.17%	2.57%	-0.11%	-0.94%	-2.81%	-0.01%	-0.92%	1.45%	2.80%	8.15%
1988	-2.41%	0.91%	-2.27%	1.43%	2.16%	-0.71%	-2.31%	0.48%	-0.60%	-0.95%	2.76%	0.15%	-1.51%
1987	0.83%	-0.98%	0.18%	3.53%	0.37%	1.03%	2.39%	-2.22%	-0.70%	-2.64%	2.84%	3.81%	8.51%
1986	0.00%	2.59%	1.68%	0.80%	-1.99%	-0.54%	1.96%	0.56%	-1.86%	-1.48%	0.41%	2.57%	4.65%
1985	0.33%	1.42%	-5.44%	-0.96%	2.45%	0.41%	3.32%	1.98%	2.35%	2.06%	2.54%	-0.75%	9.81%

TABLE A.9 Monthly and Annual Returns of the S&P DTI (Total Return with T-bills), Combined Pro Forma and Live Total Return Series, January 1985 to December 2006

Year	Jan	Feb	Mar	Apr	May	Jun	Jul	Aug	Sep	Oct	Nov	Dec	Annual/YTD
2006	0.35%	-1.46%	2.62%	3.21%	0.52%	-1.96%	2.03%	0.36%	-1.36%	0.46%	1.02%	-0.05%	5.74%
2005	0.86%	-2.34%	2.27%	-3.26%	1.39%	2.68%	1.00%	2.13%	2.37%	-1.55%	2.61%	-0.62%	7.55%
2004	1.71%	3.64%	1.47%	-2.12%	0.44%	-0.09%	3.85%	-2.29%	5.63%	1.77%	0.42%	-1.00%	13.92%
2003	2.54%	1.92%	-2.25%	-0.48%	2.08%	-1.46%	-2.33%	-1.30%	-2.01%	3.23%	0.87%	3.93%	4.53%
2002	-0.01%	0.40%	-1.59%	0.37%	-0.22%	3.40%	-0.15%	2.71%	1.56%	-1.41%	0.61%	-2.38%	3.17%
2001	-1.56%	1.57%	2.44%	0.13%	1.02%	-0.85%	-0.62%	0.28%	1.09%	0.74%	-1.67%	0.77%	3.30%
2000	1.85%	2.08%	-1.01%	1.86%	3.51%	2.28%	-1.46%	1.20%	0.58%	1.73%	3.02%	1.40%	18.30%
1999	-0.54%	2.93%	-0.66%	1.10%	-0.91%	2.34%	1.16%	1.96%	1.12%	-2.36%	2.99%	1.78%	11.29%
1998	0.49%	1.03%	1.88%	0.39%	0.18%	0.71%	2.32%	2.80%	0.22%	-0.67%	-0.28%	0.78%	10.24%
1997	1.04%	-1.73%	2.06%	2.31%	-1.45%	0.97%	-0.02%	0.83%	1.91%	0.67%	-0.55%	1.08%	7.24%
1996	0.82%	0.10%	3.04%	3.33%	0.51%	3.02%	-0.77%	0.67%	1.40%	3.00%	3.27%	1.56%	21.75%
1995	0.03%	1.00%	2.92%	1.57%	0.53%	0.19%	-0.36%	0.89%	1.85%	1.09%	0.26%	3.70%	14.47%
1994	-0.87%	-1.55%	1.39%	1.22%	1.73%	3.05%	1.49%	-1.15%	0.77%	1.75%	0.65%	-0.17%	8.51%
1993	0.49%	0.59%	0.58%	2.70%	0.46%	-1.54%	1.34%	-0.90%	1.78%	-1.06%	0.57%	0.27%	5.33%
1992	-1.37%	0.21%	0.80%	0.23%	0.05%	2.12%	3.66%	1.95%	0.74%	-1.93%	0.82%	0.11%	7.52%
1991	1.64%	-0.58%	1.82%	0.44%	0.75%	1.12%	-2.41%	1.38%	2.11%	1.32%	-0.35%	3.06%	10.65%
1990	1.58%	0.87%	2.00%	2.62%	-0.83%	2.50%	1.02%	5.23%	8.04%	-0.01%	0.35%	-0.45%	25.08%
1989	1.22%	0.81%	5.02%	1.91%	3.36%	0.62%	-0.20%	-2.07%	0.68%	-0.17%	2.13%	3.40%	17.83%
1988	-1.94%	1.43%	-1.73%	1.92%	2.70%	-0.16%	-1.75%	1.17%	0.05%	-0.29%	3.39%	0.82%	5.59%
1987	1.32%	-0.54%	0.67%	4.02%	0.80%	1.52%	2.90%	-1.69%	-0.16%	-2.08%	3.29%	4.26%	15.01%
1986	0.60%	3.11%	2.25%	1.33%	-1.48%	0.00%	2.48%	1.01%	-1.39%	-1.02%	0.83%	3.05%	11.17%
1985	0.99%	2.00%	-4.72%	-0.22%	3.10%	0.95%	3.96%	2.55%	2.90%	2.66%	3.09%	-0.14%	18.15%

was developed with the benefit of hindsight. The performance data disclosed in this document do not take into account taxes, brokerage commissions, advisory fees, or other fees, which would reduce the returns if they had been taken into account. Past performance is not necessarily indicative of future results and investing based on the S&P DTI may result in losses.

Tables A.8 and A.9 show the simulated monthly and annual combined live and pro forma returns for both the price return and the total return series, respectively.

It is noteworthy that the total return series did not have a negative annual return for the 22-year period, while the price return series had only two years with a negative return: 1988 with −1.51 percent and 2001 with −0.55 percent.

Table A.10 shows both price and total return performance and risk as measured by standard deviation for the S&P DTI compared with some key asset class benchmarks.

TABLE A.10 Return and Risk for Selected Exposures, 1985 to 2005

Returns	S&P DTI	S&P DTI TR	S&P 500 TR	Lehman Agg	CPI	S&P GSCI TR	SPCI TR
1-year	4.59%	7.55%	4.91%	2.43%	3.42%	25.55%	27.60%
3-year	6.79%	8.60%	14.39%	3.62%	2.85%	21.13%	18.90%
5-year	4.20%	6.42%	0.54%	5.87%	2.50%	9.83%	7.87%
10-year	6.00%	9.97%	9.07%	6.16%	2.52%	9.57%	7.45%
21-year	6.03%	11.30%	12.81%	8.52%	3.02%	10.80%	6.42%

Risk	S&P DTI	S&P DTI TR	S&P 500 TR	Lehman Agg	CPI	S&P GSCI TR	SPCI TR
1-year	7.22%	7.17%	7.92%	3.14%	1.90%	25.39%	18.61%
3-year	7.73%	7.69%	9.17%	4.12%	1.42%	23.85%	16.49%
5-year	6.75%	6.70%	14.82%	4.01%	1.27%	22.09%	16.76%
10-year	5.95%	5.98%	15.58%	3.70%	1.01%	21.50%	15.71%
21-year	6.00%	6.03%	15.19%	4.41%	0.89%	18.30%	12.57%

Sharpe Ratio @ 5%	S&P DTI	S&P DTI TR	S&P 500 TR	Lehman Agg	CPI	S&P GSCI TR	SPCI TR
1-year	−0.06	0.36	−0.01	−0.82	−0.83	0.81	1.21
3-year	0.23	0.47	1.02	−0.33	−1.52	0.68	0.84
5-year	−0.12	0.21	−0.30	0.22	−1.98	0.22	0.17
10-year	0.17	0.83	0.26	0.31	−2.45	0.21	0.16
21-year	0.17	1.04	0.51	0.80	−2.23	0.32	0.11

Return of the S&P DTI is directly related to the volatility of the underlying futures markets. Because inflation and futures volatility have been relatively low since 1985, the performance of both the price and total return pro forma indicators for the 22-year period is lower than stocks, albeit still positive. In relation to bonds, the price indicator has underperformed by 2.49 percentage points on an annualized basis, while the total return indicator outperformed by 2.78 percentage points annualized. However, both series have maintained a respectable spread over the consumer price index (CPI) over all time periods analyzed.

Figure A.2 shows the cumulative return of the indicators compared to equity and bond benchmarks, while Figure A.3 shows the indicators compared to CPI and commodity benchmarks.

The S&P DTI Measures Trends and Volatility

The S&P DTI is a long/short indicator methodology that measures price trends and volatility in the commodities and financial futures market. Because the indicator can represent either long or short positions, its return is more dependent on the trends in the futures markets rather than the direction. This is demonstrated by the fact that if coffee appreciated 300 percent over one year (from $1.00 per bushel to $4.00), the indicator would reflect this increase and the coffee component would be long. If coffee then declined 75 percent over the next year (from $4.00 per bushel to

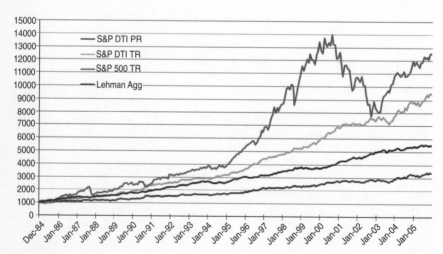

FIGURE A.2 Cumulative return of the S&P DTI compared to equity and bond benchmarks, 1985 to 2005.

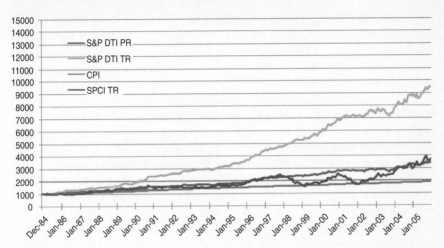

FIGURE A.3 Cumulative return of the S&P DTI compared to CPI for all urban consumers (not seasonally adjusted) and the S&P commodity index, 1985 to 2005.

$1.00 per bushel), the coffee component would be short. Therefore, the higher volatility or greater extent of the price change trend would reflect a higher return in the indicator than if coffee had moved from $1.00 to $1.25 to $1.00.

Why Has the S&P Diversified Trends Indicator Been Profitable on a Pro Forma Basis?

The key reasons why the pro forma indicator has been profitable can be explained by its structure and by the fact that commodities derive their returns differently than financial assets. Some explanations for performance behavior of the pro forma indicator include the following:

- High internal diversification
- Profit from rising and declining price trends
- Profit from futures markets' risk transfer processes

High Internal Diversification Since the 24 components are diverse and not affected by the same fundamentals, there is very little correlation among them. As one example, cotton has, practically speaking, no relationship with natural gas, live cattle, coffee, or the Swiss franc. Within a portfolio, internal correlations are often higher among equities because equities are generally affected by the same macroeconomic variables (i.e., interest rates and GDP). As a result, equities generally provide less diversification benefit as a composite.

Profit from Rising and Declining Price Trends   The ability of the indicator to represent either long or short positions allows it to capture profit, since the components generally behave in a cyclical manner. However, constant, especially month-to-month, directional changes in the components or sectors may cause the indicator performance to decline.

Profit from Futures Markets' Risk Transfer Processes   The bulk of returns could come simply from buying uptrending commodities at a discount and selling downtrending commodities at a premium. This *spread* characteristic is fundamental to the mechanics of futures markets (see discussion on backwardation and contango in Chapter 11). The methodology profits from rising (long position) and falling prices (short position) and price fluctuations of futures markets present profit opportunities to investors who are willing to bear risks of price fluctuations that the hedgers are not willing to bear.

THE ECONOMIC FUNCTION OF THE FUTURES MARKET

Futures contracts consist of agreements to buy or sell a controlled quantity and quality of an asset at a future date. The economic function of the futures market is to transfer the risk of price fluctuations between producers and consumers via a futures exchange. To facilitate this risk transfer, producers and consumers are generally willing to offer a discount or pay a premium to attract investors or speculators willing to accept this risk.

Because of supply/demand constraints and lead/lag times to production—commodity futures markets are far more cyclical than equities. This inherent difference suggests that an effective methodology can be long/short in nature, since both long and short positions can be beneficial in the market place.

The Risk Transfer Phenomenon

The S&P DTI benefits from the risk transfer mechanism in the futures market. Futures contract prices are determined by a process similar to that of a discount wholesaler. A wholesaler buys merchandise from a producer with the expectation of reselling it at a profit to a future consumer. In this process, generally, the futures contract price is in backwardation (discounted) to commodities in uptrends and in contango (premium) with commodities in downtrends.

In futures markets, a long hedge is taken when a market participant wishes to purchase an asset in the future while locking in a price today. On the one hand, the long hedger will purchase a futures contract to protect against the possible price increase of the commodity to be purchased in the future. On the other hand, a short hedge involves a short position in futures markets and is used by a hedger who owns an asset and who expects to sell it in the future. A short hedge can also be used when an asset is not owned yet, but will be owned in the future. The short hedger will sell a futures contract to hedge against the possible decline in the price of the contract held.

Speculators voluntarily assume the risk that a hedger avoids. They buy and sell futures contracts in the hope of making a profit between the sale and purchase price of a futures contract. They buy a futures contract and hope to sell it later at a higher price. In this case, the speculator is long. Speculators are short when they sell a commodity in the future for a price above the price at which they can purchase the commodity future at a lower price before the expected time of delivery. To illustrate the economic function of the risk transfer process, suppose a farmer makes the business decision to plant the equivalent of 500,000 bushels of corn based on its current price after an extensive appreciation. Yet, because the farmer will not be able to sell the corn for several months, a great deal of risk exists on this investment because the price of corn could fall dramatically over that time. The futures markets allow the farmer to transfer this risk to a speculator by selling 100 corn futures contracts short and locking in the price today to be received in the future.

Although the benefit to the farmer is obvious, the speculator benefits by being able to buy the farmer's corn at below market prices (this is generally referred to as *backwardation* or *discount*) in exchange for accepting the risk of a decline in corn prices before the speculator can sell the farmer's corn. This discount serves the same role as the premium that an insurance company receives in exchange for accepting a risk. This same relationship of transferring risk to speculators exists with consumers who want to lock in today's prices.

Attracting Capital

An important aspect of the futures market, as with all markets, is the constant need by producers and consumers to attract investors willing to accept the risk and provide liquidity. In this respect, by providing liquidity, speculators play a role similar to that played by specialists on exchanges with a *specialist system*. Correspondingly, on futures exchanges the specialist equivalent is called a *local* (i.e., a speculator) who provides liquidity, and, as a whole, receives a price advantage through the premiums and discounts of the futures traded. Generally, uptrending commodities trade at discounts and downtrending commodities trade at premiums. This reflects itself in a core return received by speculators risk in exchange for providing liquidity.

Futures Price in Backwardation (Discount)

Backwardation represents a price pattern in which a futures price is lower than a spot price. Normal backwardation occurs when the futures price is below the expected future spot price.

Let's assume that an oil producer wants to hedge future production. It can sell its current production at spot prices, but if it wants to hedge its future production and sell at a price that it thinks is high, the producer can only sell to a speculator who thinks (hopes) that he can sell the oil for more over time. The speculator has to buy his product (oil) at a discount to the expected future market price to secure a reasonable opportunity to potentially make a profit. The speculator needs this business (statistical) edge to make a consistent return over time.

The oil producer who wants to hedge future production is willing to pay the equivalent of business insurance fees by selling oil at a discount to a speculator. At a higher spot price, producers have a greater desire to lock in these high prices for their future production, while speculators demand a larger discount for their risk exposure because being long at higher prices incurs greater risk. If the futures contract is trading in contango where the spot price is lower than the expected future price, the speculator would expect the price to rise by more than the premium to obtain a profit, a lower probability event.

Backwardation is not an issue in financials because bonds and notes do not trade at a discount or a premium.

Futures Price in Contango (Premium)

Contango occurs when the futures price is above the spot price. The difference is the risk premium contained in futures prices, which represents the compensation to speculators for their risk of selling short and hoping to buy it back later at a lower price, even if the current price is unchanged.

Contango futures markets are generally a characteristic of downtrending markets. In this case, the producers are unwilling to lock in their future production at prices they believe are too low, while consumer-producers still need cost certainty for their own production.

Speculators, by contrast, will be willing to trade if they can get a premium for the risk taken. As consumers they have a desire to lock in low prices, and are willing to pay a premium to speculators willing to sell future production.

An example of a contango market was corn in 1999. With corn near a contract low of 193 on November 26, 1999, and approaching government price supports, corn producers refused to sell future production at anything but a premium because prices were very low. Therefore, March 2000 corn was 205, May 212, July 219, and so on.

However, Kellogg's wants to purchase corn for cornflakes because it needs product for its consumers. If farmers will not sell because they get paid the same price from the government anyway, Kellogg's must buy from speculators who demand a risk premium to be short. Thus, downtrending commodities take on a premium at some point, but this premium does not necessarily predict an uptrend.

The general tendency of commodities to trade at discounts in uptrends, or premiums in downtrends, has exceptions. Precious metals, for example, always trade at premiums, as they are *cost of carry assets*. This means that the holding of the metals always has an interest cost, and if the futures traded at a discount (to fair value), a holder of the metal would sell it and then buy the futures and thereby arbitrage the position—that is, sell the asset and deposit the proceeds in a interest-hearing instrument such as U.S. Treasury bills.

Also, if the premium is greater than fair value, an arbitrageur would borrow the capital, buy gold, and sell the future. Thereby, the premium on precious metal futures approximates short-term interest rates, less insurance, transportation, and storage costs.

THE S&P DTI AND INFLATION

Long Position Captures and Hedges Inflation Risk

Many investors consider futures markets as the ideal way to offset inflation risk in portfolios. The S&P DTI is long those futures contracts in markets with continuous rising prices and therefore tends to reflect the impact of those markets on the consumer price index (CPI) over long periods. Through the long exposure, the S&P DTI is long the risk transfer discount associated with rising future expected prices. This is equivalent to owning rising expected prices, or inflation. However, as inflation increases and causes yields to rise, prices of the financial contracts are more likely to fall and hence would be positioned as short in the indicator. As commodities rise and financials fall, the indicator reflects rising inflation.

Correlations between the S&P DTI and the CPI tend to be low in the short term. Partially, this may be due to the way that the CPI is calculated. It is data that are collected across 258 consumer products, collected monthly and published six weeks after month end. Additionally, the futures prices reflected in the S&P DTI, while directly impacting suppliers, are rarely passed fully on to their customers. Finally, the components of the indicator will not impact each and every one of the 258 consumer products found in the CPI—and in some cases, their impact may be in opposite directions, therefore potentially impacting short- and even medium-run correlations that will tend to be low in the short term.

However, the S&P DTI is an effective measure for inflationary and deflationary trends. Unlike the CPI, where some of the actual consumer products trade on a regulated exchange, the S&P DTI takes advantage of the listed commodity futures to own futures contracts whose prices are rising (i.e., owning inflation) and to sell futures whose prices are falling (i.e., selling deflation or profiting from deflation). Over the long run, the fact that the underlying components reflect many of the CPI's components, combined with the anticipated risk and return characteristics of the indicator, should allow the S&P DTI to be a relatively good, tradable proxy for inflation. Consequently, in very stable periods for the CPI (e.g., 1992–1994 and 2001–2003), the S&P DTI returns are also relatively low.

In summary, the S&P DTI's long portion could be a reflection of futures-based inflation over long periods of time, while the short position could be a better way to offset the impact of deflationary price trends on commodity measures and create a return that has historically been smooth and generally positive such as the CPI.

The Short Position Profits from Commodity and Financial Cyclicality

Since commodities and financials tend to behave in extended trends— falling as frequently as they rise—owning long-only futures would result in extended and significant declines in value. The S&P DTI, however, has tended to mitigate the long-only risk by shorting futures contracts that are in declining price trends.

This inherent potential structural advantage is most dramatically illustrated by examining the S&P DTI's performance when commodities decline. When commodity-tracking measures decline in price—generally in deflationary environments—the indicator tends to appreciate. This is because long-only commodity benchmarks usually measure the rise and fall of commodity prices only. The S&P DTI, by contrast, does not have this

i

TABLE A.11 Exponential Average Multiplier Schedule

Number of Months	Multiplier	Weight
7	1	2.23%
6	1.6	3.71%
5	2.56	5.94%
4	4.096	9.51%
3	6.5536	15.22%
2	10.48576	24.34%
1	16.777216	38.95%
Sum	43.072576	100.00%

structural handicap because it is able to short its components in down-trends, which reflect the producers' reason for hedging.

Exponential Average Multiplier Schedule

To create an exponential average for comparison, price inputs (percentage change from current and previous six PDDs) are weighted using a multiplier, using a base of 1.6 raised to $(0, \ldots , 6)$ to establish weights for each trailing month's input. See Table A.11 for the detailed view.

The weight given to the price seven months prior is 2.32 percent $(1/43.072576)$, and so on. Therefore, 78.5 percent of the indicator's moving average is weighted to the price movements of the last three months. This makes current price movements more important than those of the past, which is logical.

S&P DTI Calculation Algorithm

The daily values of the Standard & Poor's DTI (*SPDTI*) are:

$$SPDTI_t = \left(\frac{1 + WCh_t}{1 + WCh_{t-1}} \right) \times SPDTI_{t-1}$$

where

$t =$ time period, where $t = 0,1,2 \ldots$ and $t = 0$ is the initial time period;

$WCh_t =$ weighted year-to-date percentage change up to date t for *SPDTI*;

$WCh_{t-1} =$ weighted year-to-date percentage change up to date $t - 1$ for *SPDTI*.

Let i indicate the sector i in *SPDTI*.

$$WCh_t = \frac{\left(\sum\limits_{i=1}^{14} DWPS_{it}\right)}{DCA_t}$$

where
$DWPS_{it}$ = daily weighted percentage change of sector i at period t;
DCA_t = daily change adjustment at time t:
If Energy sector is flat:
DCA_t = 1—weight of energy sector
Otherwise:
DCA_t = 1.

For sectors that only have one component:

$$DWPS_{it} = SC_{it} \times SW_i \times ACP_t$$

where
SC_{it} = cumulative change of sector i on a roll-to-date basis;
SW_i = weight of sector i (initial weights);
ACP_t = the active contract position of sector i where it takes on values 1 (long), 0 (flat for energy only), and -1 (short).

For sectors that have more than one component:

$$DWPS = SC_{it} \times SW_i \times ACP_t$$

where

$$SC_{it} = \frac{1 + SWC_{it}}{1 + SWC_{i,rolldate}} - 1$$

SWC_{it} = the sum of weighted percentage changes of components in the sector:

$$SWC_{it} = \frac{\sum\limits_{c=1}^{C} w_c \times ACCP_{ct}}{SW_{i,where,c\in i}}$$

where
w_c = component (i.e., contract) weight;
SW_i = weight of sector i (initial weights);

TABLE A.12 Hypothetical Roll Date Calculation (Sector i)

Date	Roll Date	SWC (%)	SWC (Roll Date) (%)	SC (%)
$t - 1$		−3.79	−0.69	−3.11
t	y	−2.39	−0.69	−1.71
$t + 1$		−2.93	−2.39	−0.55
$t + 2$		−3.30	−2.39	−0.93
$t + 3$		−4.03	−2.39	−1.68
$t + 4$		−3.88	−2.39	−1.52

$ACCP_{ct}$ = active component (contract) cumulative percentage change (on a year-to-date basis);

$ACCP_{ct} = ((1 + ACCP_{ct-1}) \times (1 + ACDPC_{ct})) - 1;$

$ACDPC_{ct}$ = active component contract daily percentage change;

$SWC_{i,\text{rolldate}}$ = the value of SWC_i at the last roll date $= y$ before t. The value from $t + 1$ through the next roll date remains constant.

We can see from Table A.12 that SC_i depends on the roll date. The roll date at $t = y$ so $SWC_{i,\text{rolldate}}$ on date $t + 1$ takes on value of SWC_i on t and carry forward until the next roll date $= y$. SC_i on $t + 3 = (1 - 0.0403)/(1 - 0.0239) - 1 = -1.68$ percent.

The daily values of the Standard & Poor's DTI total return ($SPDTI\_TR$) are:

$$SPDTI\_TR = \left[\frac{SPDTI_t - SPDTI_0}{SPDTI_0} + \sum_{t=1}^{t} SPDTI\_TR\_DI_t \right] \times SPDTI_0 + SPDTI_0$$

where $SPDTI\_TR\_DI_t$ is the S&P DTI total return daily interest rate, which is equal to (daily three-month U.S. Treasury bill rate at $t = 0$ divided by 360) $\times$ (date t − date $t - 1$). Note that because there can be holidays or weekends, (date t − date $t - 1$) does not necessarily equal to 1. For example, the $SPDTI\_TR$ daily interest rate jumps from 0.003 percent (January 3, 2003) to 0.01 percent (January 6, 2003) because three days have elapsed; on January 6, 2003, $SPCTI\_TR$ daily interest rate $= 0.01\% = (1.215\%/360) \times 3$.

ACTIVE CONTRACT POSITION FOR SECTOR *i*

For each of the 14 sectors, the monthly percentage change is calculated using the closing price on the second to the last business of each month, identified as the position determination date (PDD). Let τ denote the time period by month associated with the PDD. The active contract position of sector i at $\tau + 1$ is:

$ACP_{i\tau+1} = 1$ if the cumulative monthly sector percentage return up to $\tau \geq$ exponential moving average of the cumulative monthly sector percentage return up to τ;

$$= -1 \quad \text{Otherwise}$$

$$= 0 \quad \text{If energy}$$

The exponential moving average of the cumulative monthly sector percentage return up to τ ($CMSR_\tau$) is:

$$\frac{CMSR_{\tau-6}+1.6CMSR_{\tau-5}+1.6^2CMSR_{\tau-4}+1.6^3CMSR_{\tau-3}+1.6^4CMSR_{\tau-2}+1.6^5CMSR_{\tau-1}+1.6^6CMSR_\tau}{43.07258}$$

where

$$\sum_{i=0}^{6} 1.6^i = 43.07258$$

and

$CMSR_\tau = [(1 + CMSR_{\tau-1}) \times (1 + \text{Monthly sector returns at } \tau) - 1]$.

S&P DTI Subindicator: Commodities—The S&P Commodity Trends Indicator

The S&P Commodity Trends Indicator (CTI) is an investable methodology that measures trends and volatility and seeks to benefit from trends (in either direction) in the commodity futures markets. Additionally, it measures the volatility of an aggregate of major commodity price movements. The S&P CTI is a composite of 16 commodity futures grouped into six sectors from around the world.

Generally, prices of these sectors and any underlying components are cyclical in nature. Each of the six sectors (with the exception of the energy sector) will be positioned either long or short, based on its price behavior relative to its moving average. This long/short aspect enables the S&P CTI to potentially capture profits in both up and down markets.

The S&P CTI can be used to capture inflation as many investors consider commodity futures markets useful to offset inflation risk in portfolios. In markets with rising prices, the S&P CTI is long in those futures contracts and therefore can reflect the impact of those markets on the consumer price index (CPI) over extended periods. The S&P CTI also has the potential to profit from futures cyclicality. Since commodities tend to behave in extended trends, simple long-only ownership of commodity futures could result in extended and significant drops in value. The S&P CTI mitigates the long-only risk by shorting futures contracts that show falling price trends.

The S&P CTI price return and total return series can be found under Bloomberg symbols SPTICDP and SPTICDT, respectively. The daily values of the S&P CTI are calculated in a manner similar to that of the S&P DTI.

How to Interpret Simulated Historical Results

U nderstanding past performance, whether real or simulated, can be an exacting process. The first thing that has to be determined is whether or not the performance has been optimized, data-mined, or curve fitted. Simulated performance which has been structured in such a way is generally useless, and should be used with caution; this is why I chose not to optimize or curve-fit the S&P Diversified Trends Indicator (S&P DTI) performance, and instead use the same moving average for all components.

Once you have determined the performance is useful and intellectually honest, the next step is to properly interpret them. It is crucial to understand that the importance of past performance for indexes and passive strategies is not in the nominal returns themselves. Instead, it is in the rate of increase or decrease of their performance, and their inter-relationship with other asset classes, measured within different economic periods. Similarly, the simulated returns of the S&P DTI act only as an example of the results which may have occurred (more or less) under past economic conditions versus the results of other asset classes.

When interpreting the results for the S&P DTI, it is best to keep certain historical events in mind. In the last 45 years, the United States has gone through three major macroeconomic phases:

1. **Rising inflation**, rising interest rates, and declining GDP growth from 1961–1981
2. **Declining inflation**, declining interest rates, and rising GDP growth from 1982–1999

3. **Disinflation**, depicted by the lowest short term interest rates in 55 years, the lowest CPI in 40 years, and declining GDP growth, (as well as a depression in equities from 2000–2002)

We also compared the 1929–1934 results of the long/short methodology (LSM) (see below) during the Depression, as a sample of what may have occurred during that important but rare economic period.

THE LSM AS A PROXY FOR THE S&P DTI

The historical simulated results used herein are for the S&P DTI from 1985 to the present, and the long/short methodology, which is a proxy for the S&P DTI, for any years prior to 1985. The LSM uses a similar (but not identical) basket of futures compared to that used in the S&P DTI. The only major difference is that in the LSM the individual components are equally weighted, and are not formed into sectors as in the S&P DTI. Also, there is a different basket of components to some degree in the LSM, as there were fewer futures contracts trading during past periods. However, the algorithm chosen to reflect trends in the LSM is exactly the same as that used in the S&P DTI.

For example, the results for the LSM during the Depression (1929–1934) were driven by only 7 commodity components (the only ones listed in the *Wall Street Journal* at the time), each with a weighting of 14.3 percent (100 percent divided by 7). By contrast, the results during the inflationary environment from 1973–1974 were driven by only 13 commodity components, each with a weighting of 7.7 percent (100 percent divided by 13). In addition, the LSM had no financial futures or energy exposure during such time periods, as in the S&P DTI today. The equal weighting was a more accurate proxy than a weighted strategy during the time period because no one could accurately guess the production levels on each commodity going back in time 30 to 45 years, or during the Depression. Attempting to weight the LSM components during these time periods would simply lead to a hypothetical estimate on top of a simulation.

In certain economic conditions the LSM return may have both understated and overstated the return the S&P DTI may have had, if it existed as is, in the 1970s. For example, this time period experienced sharp increases in energy prices. Without any energy exposure, the LSM returns may have understated what the S&P DTI returns would have been during the same time period. Today, the S&P DTI is weighted 18.75 percent to energy. Therefore, energy should have been a big contributor, rising 1004 percent from 1972 to 1979. On the other hand, this may have been offset by the fact the LSM results were driven by a less diversified but greater commodity exposure than the S&P DTI. Specifically, the 7.7 percent per commodity component of the LSM (equally weighted), may overstate the expected returns of the S&P DTI during this period, as commodities can appreciate *several hundred percent*. However, the S&P DTI has 50 percent financials, which in the 1970s, would almost certainly have been short in a rising inflationary environment while such sectors were falling, thus understating the returns of the S&P DTI, because nothing can decline more than 100 percent. Realistically, the financials might have declined anywhere from 25 percent to 50 percent during this period. This balance of offsets makes the LSM a good proxy for the simulated returns of this commodity allocation strategy, as it still would have profited greatly.

Even given the differences in the LSM and the S&P DTI in the above examples, the LSM is still a valid proxy for the S&P DTI. There is little question of whether the results *could* have occurred as this strategy was not data-mined or curve fitted. What cannot be determined is *how much capital* could have been executed, which is a subtle, underlying question in these and all simulations.

COMPARISON OF THE PERFORMANCE OF THE S&P DTI TO OTHER ASSET CLASSES MEASURED WITHIN DIFFERENT ECONOMIC PERIODS

During the rising inflation macroeconomic phase, the Great Society Programs of the 1960s, Vietnam, and the OPEC oil embargo caused the returns of the LSM to be very high (as all long commodity strategies appreciated greatly). Although the LSM was simulated, the returns are valid, as *all* commodity-like programs (long and short) showed similar levels of appreciation during this period.

It is critical to understand that when the LSM shows a simulated return of +13.48 percent in 1969, the nominal return number is not important in and of itself. The result could have been +12.00 percent or +30.00 percent. What is important is the fact that it was strongly positive while in 1969 the S&P 500 Index was −8.5 percent. You should also note that the LSM profit rate of change was greater than 1968 (which was 9.36 percent) while the S&P 500 return was 11.1 percent in 1968.

Another example would be the period between 1973 and 1974. Basically, *any* commodity index would have shown very high returns in 1973, with declining yet positive returns in 1974. The S&P Goldman Sachs Commodity Index (S&P GSCI) showed a simulated profit of 62.8 percent in 1973 and 28.7 percent in 1974. The S&P Commodity Index (SPCI) showed a simulated profit of 64.5 percent in '73, but only 4.1 percent in '74, while the LSM showed simulated returns during those same years of 87.4 percent and 42.3 percent respectively. Whether the 1973 returns were +87.42 percent, +50.00 percent or +100.00 percent is really not important, as long as they are largely positive, while stocks and bonds were negative over the 1973–1974 period (governments down in 1973, corporates down in 1974).

Similarly, for that same two year period, the compounded returns (losses) were −37.25 percent for the S&P 500 Index and −1.96 percent for corporate bonds, while the Consumer Price Index (CPI) was +22.06 percent during the same time frame. It is important to consider the following question: Were the LSM, S&P GSCI, and SPCI profits rising or falling compared to inflation (CPI), bonds, and the S&P 500 Index? The correlation of the 1-month, 1-, 3-, 5-, and 10-year comparisons, in Table B.1, are very telling.

Fundamentally, since 1961 the U.S. has been exchanging relatively high consistent inflation increases for continued GDP growth in its approach to monetary policy. From 1926 to 2006, the CPI rose at a 3.03 percent compounded rate; from 1961 to 2006, it was 4.3 percent; from 1985 to 2006, it was 3.0 percent; from 1997 to 2006, it was 2.43 percent; and from 2006 to 2006, it was 2.6 percent. Thus, stock/commodity and financial relationships have hedged one another, as the CPI and the S&P DTI are noncorrelated to stocks and bonds in most periods, while being negatively correlated in declining bond and equity markets. However, in the time period from 1929 to 1934, the Fed was not yet using Keynesian Economic Theory to manipulate interest rates, the money supply, or the economy. Therefore, at that time commodities were correlated to stocks and bonds. During this period, the profits in the LSM came from the extreme volatility via the long/short, trend-following structure.

In addition, *if* the environment in the United States changed to that of Japan today, which from 1989 to 2006 has had small, declining GDP growth

TABLE B.1   Correlation between S&P DTI/LSM, CPI, Stocks, and Bonds

	LSM/S&P DTI TR vs. CPI		SP500 vs. CPI		LT-BONDS vs. CPI
1-Month	12.91%	1-Month	−15.48%	1-Month	−11.74%
1-Year	51.36%	1-Year	−18.76%	1-Year	−28.86%
3-Year	60.21%	3-Year	−19.67%	3-Year	−32.93%
5-Year	65.89%	5-Year	−19.60%	5-Year	−29.47%
10-Year	88.86%	10-Year	−33.17%	10-Year	−37.89%

rates (even with very low interest rates), accompanied by low inflation, it is almost certain that stocks would decline. It would seem logical to assume the S&P DTI may also decline in value, as low inflation would mean choppy or stable commodity markets.

The worst, simulated 3-year (disinflationary) period was from 2001 to 2003. The S&P DTI price return was only 1.44 percent and the compounded total return was 3.67 percent during these years, when the inflation rate was only 1.93 percent and T-Bills were only paying 2.16 percent. Please keep in mind that generally the S&P DTI is positively correlated to the CPI and T-Bills. Therefore, if someone assumes a Japanese-like economic possibility, the simulated historical results would not reflect the future returns of the S&P DTI, as they would be lower than the UAV for the Price Return shown in Table B.2.

Notwithstanding this disinflationary scenario, the S&P DTI should reflect the previously mentioned performance during similar economic periods given similar fundamentals, just as the debt and equity markets would also reflect past economic periods, depending on what the fundamentals were. In the long-term a 3 percent inflationary period should produce a gross 6 percent Price Return for the S&P DTI. A lower CPI or higher inflation rate would adjust the S&P DTI returns lower or higher, as this relationship is fundamentally driven. A comparison of rolling 10-year periods between the CPI, the LSM/S&P DTI and the various equity and debt asset classes can be seen in Table B.3.

In Table B.4 you will see a broad comparison between the various asset classes during some of the time periods discussed in this appendix. Remember it is not simply the returns which are the basis of comparison, but also the rates of change from one year or one period to another.

Finally, in Figures B.1 through B.10, you can see some of the same data in graphical format. After all, they say a picture is worth a thousand words, so these ten charts are worth at least ten thousand!

Remember, since October 2001 S&P DTI methodology has demonstrated "real" positive results, and thereby, it is possible that future results could also be positive, more (during inflation) or less (during disinflation), depending on the economic environment.

TABLE B.2 UAV Performance for the LSM/S&P DTI

Year	$UAV LSM	Annual percent Change
1961	109	9.06
1962	122	12.09
1963	129	5.12
1964	152	18.52
1965	193	26.96
1966	216	11.79
1967	222	2.55
1968	242	9.36
1969	275	13.48
1970	306	11.07
1971	315	3.14
1972	377	19.71
1973	707	87.42
1974	1,006	42.29
1975	1,167	16.05
1976	1,471	26.01
1977	1,819	23.65
1978	1,726	−5.1
1979	2,098	21.55
1980	2,258	7.62
1981	2,898	28.36
1982	3,330	14.9
1983	3,550	6.62
1984	3,955	11.4
1985	4,343 S&P DTI	9.81
1986	4,545	4.65
1987	4,932	8.51
1988	4,857	−1.51
1989	5,253	8.15
1990	6,077	15.68
1991	6,346	4.43
1992	6,579	3.67
1993	6,716	2.09
1994	6,982	3.97
1995	7,547	8.09
1996	8,726	15.62
1997	8,867	1.61
1998	9,306	4.95
1999	9,869	6.05
2000	10,999	11.45
2001	10,939	−0.55
2002	11,098	1.46
2003	11,479	3.43
2004	12,921	12.56
2005	13,514	4.59
2006	13,706	1.42

Sources: LSM: Commodity Research Bureau (CRB) 1961–1984; S&P DTI: S&P White Paper 1985–2003; S&P DTI: S&P Website 2004–2006. Compiled by Enhanced Alpha Management, LP.

TABLE B.3 10-Year Rolling Period Returns (Gross Hypothetical Returns)[a]

Rolling Calendar Years

10 Yr's	LSM PR[b]	LSM TR[c]	CPI[d]	Ratio[e]	S&P 500	LT Gov't Bonds	T-Bills
61–70	11.82%	16.53%	2.92%	4.05 : 1	8.18%	**1.30%**	4.26%
62–71	11.19%	16.14%	3.19%	3.51 : 1	7.06%	2.47%	4.49%
63–72	11.93%	17.03%	3.42%	3.49 : 1	9.93%	2.35%	4.60%
64–73	18.59%	24.41%	4.12%	**4.51:1**	6.00%	2.11%	4.98%
65–74	20.78%	27.22%	5.20%	4.00 : 1	**1.24%**	2.20%	5.43%
66–75	19.70%	26.31%	5.71%	3.45 : 1	3.27%	3.03%	5.62%
67–76	21.14%	27.86%	5.86%	3.61 : 1	6.63%	4.26%	5.65%
68–77	23.43%	30.38%	6.24%	3.75 : 1	3.59%	5.20%	5.74%
69–78	21.69%	28.79%	6.67%	3.25 : 1	3.16%	5.10%	5.94%
70–79	22.53%	30.13%	7.37%	3.06 : 1	5.86%	5.52%	6.31%
71–80	22.14%	30.29%	8.05%	2.75 : 1	8.44%	3.90%	6.77%
72–81	**24.84%**	34.39%	8.62%	2.88 : 1	6.47%	2.81%	7.78%
73–82	24.33%	**34.67%**	**8.67%**	2.81 : 1	6.68%	5.76%	8.46%
74–83	17.51%	27.54%	8.16%	2.15 : 1	10.61%	5.95%	8.65%
75–84	14.67%	24.69%	7.34%	2.00 : 1	14.76%	7.03%	8.83%
76–85	14.04%	24.22%	7.01%	2.00 : 1	14.33%	8.99%	9.03%
77–86	11.94%	22.07%	6.63%	1.80 : 1	13.82%	9.70%	9.14%
78–87	10.49%	20.60%	6.39%	1.64 : 1	15.26%	9.47%	**9.17%**
79–88	10.90%	21.04%	5.93%	1.84 : 1	16.33%	10.62%	9.09%
80–89	9.61%	19.50%	5.09%	1.88 : 1	17.55%	12.62%	8.89%
81–90	10.41%	20.03%	4.49%	2.32 : 1	13.93%	13.75%	8.55%
82–91	8.15%	16.68%	3.91%	2.08 : 1	17.59%	**15.56%**	7.65%
83–92	7.05%	14.77%	3.81%	1.85 : 1	16.19%	12.58%	6.95%
84–93	6.58%	13.67%	3.71%	1.77 : 1	14.94%	14.41%	6.35%

White Paper Proforma

10 Yr's	S&P DTI PR	S&P DTI TR	CPI	PR:CPI Ratio	S&P 500	LT Gov't Bonds	T-Bills
85–94	5.85%	12.32%	3.58%	**1.63:1**	14.40%	11.86%	5.76%
86–95	5.68%	11.97%	3.46%	1.65 : 1	14.84%	11.92%	5.55%
87–96	6.74%	12.99%	3.68%	1.83 : 1	15.28%	9.39%	5.46%
88–97	6.04%	12.20%	3.41%	1.78 : 1	18.05%	11.32%	5.44%
89–98	6.72%	12.69%	3.12%	2.15 : 1	**19.19%**	11.66%	5.29%
89–99	6.51%	12.05%	2.93%	2.22 : 1	18.20%	8.79%	4.92%
90–00	6.11%	11.42%	2.66%	2.27 : 1	17.46%	10.26%	4.74%
91–01	5.60%	10.66%	2.51%	2.20 : 1	12.93%	8.73%	4.56%
92–02	5.37%	10.20%	2.46%	2.13 : 1	9.33%	9.67%	4.37%
93–03	5.51%	10.12%	2.37%	2.28 : 1	11.06%	8.01%	4.18%
94–04	6.35%	10.66%	2.43%	2.61 : 1	12.07%	9.78%	3.90%
96–05	6.00%	9.97%	2.53%	2.37 : 1	9.08%	7.60%	3.64%
97–06	**4.62%**	**8.43%**	**2.44%**	1.89 : 1	8.42%	7.83%	**3.60%**

Sources: Compiled by Enhanced Alpha Management, LP using data from the St. Louis Federal Reserve, CRB, and S&P DTI White Paper.

[a] PR = Price Return; TR = Total Return i.e with T-Bills; LSM has "equal" weightings of all futures contracts and are not formed into sectors. S&P DTI are weighted and the components are formed into sectors.

[b] 10 year compounded returns on LSM/S&P DTI Proforma; 1961–1984 LSM PR; 1985–2003 S&P DTI PR Proforma.

[c] LSM TR 1961—84 S&P DTI 85–03.

[d] 10 year returns on CPI.

[e] Ratio of LSM PR and S&P DTI PR returns to CPI.

TABLE B.4 Hypothetical Gross Returns of Passive Indexes versus LSM/S&P DTI[a,b]

	Passive Indexes History 81 Years 1926-2006	Growth with Rising Inflation 7 Years 1961-1968	Inflation Low Growth 12 Years 1969-1981	Poor Period for Equities 21 Years 1961-1981	Best Period for Equities 18 Years 1982-1999	Equities Last 10 Years 1996-2006	Best Years S&P 500 5 Years 1995-1999	Worst Years S&P 500 3 Years 2000-2002	Inception LSM/S&P DTI 46 Years 1961-2006	Inception S&P DTI 22 Years 1985-2006
S&P 500 Total Return (TR)	10.42%	11.01%	5.62%	7.64%	18.52%	8.42%	28.55%	−14.55%	10.72%	12.95%
S&P Capital Appreciation (CA)	5.99%	5.91%	1.28%	3.62%	14.80%	6.71%	26.18%	−15.71%	7.19%	10.21%
S&P Dividend	4.43%	5.10%	4.34%	4.02%	3.72%	1.71%	2.37%	1.16%	3.53%	2.74%
Small Cap Stocks	12.69%	24.69%	10.22%	15.52%	14.32%	13.48%	18.49%	0.87%	14.71%	13.43%
Long Term Corp. Bonds	5.89%	2.07%	3.76%	3.11%	12.17%	7.72%	8.35%	13.26%	7.46%	9.98%
Long Term Gov't Bonds	5.42%	0.84%	3.63%	2.56%	12.08%	7.83%	9.24%	14.07%	7.11%	10.22%
Long Term Gov't Bonds CA	0.04%	−3.49%	−4.34%	−4.01%	3.13%	2.12%	2.49%	7.82%	−0.19%	2.94%
Intermediate Gov't Bonds	5.28%	3.03%	6.42%	5.05%	9.86%	5.80%	6.95%	11.02%	7.04%	7.78%
T-Bills	3.72%	3.70%	7.33%	5.93%	6.23%	3.60%	5.12%	3.78%	5.60%	4.74%
Inflation	3.03%	2.21%	7.77%	5.62%	3.29%	2.44%	2.37%	2.43%	4.25%	3.00%
LSM/S&P DTI TR	N/A	15.79%	29.76%	24.25%	15.34%	8.43%	12.62%	9.10%	17.58%	11.04%
LSM/S&P DTI PR	N/A	11.70%	21.03%	17.39%	7.05%	4.62%	7.17%	5.15%	11.29%	5.81%

(continues)

TABLE B.4 (Continued)

Worst 10 Years for Stocks Since 1930s	1965-1974 S&P 500	Best for LSM	Fundamental Reason: Rising Inflation CPI
Compounded Total Return	1.24%	27.22%	Start: 1.19%
Compounded Capital Appreciation	<2.94%>	20.78%	End: 12.20%

Best 10 Years for Stocks Since 1950s	1989-1999 S&P 500	Very Positive for S&P DTI	Fundamental Reason: Disinflation + Growth CPI
Compounded Total Return	18.20%	12.59%	Start: 6.11%
Compounded Capital Appreciation	15.31%	6.48%	End: 2.68%

Worst 3 years for Stocks Since 1929-31	2000-2002 S&P 500	Profitable for S&P DTI	Fundamental Reason: Stock Deflation Bubble Popped for Internet/Telecom Stocks
			all stocks decline
Compounded Total Return	-14.55%	9.10%	CPI Start: 3.39%
Compounded Capital Appreciation	-15.71%	5.15%	End: 2.38%

Worst for S&P DTI	2001-2003 S&P 500	CPI	T-Bills	Fundamental Reason: Disinflation S&P DTI
Compounded Total Return	-4.05%	1.93%	2.16%	3.67%
Compounded Capital Appreciation	-5.56%			1.74%

Sources: St. Louis Federal Reserve, CRB, and S&P DTI White Paper. Compiled by Enhanced Alpha Management LP.

[a]Total Return or TR, as used herein throughout, includes the return earned on the underlying portfolio (i.e. U.S. Treasury bills) which is used as collateral to acquire the futures exposure. Price Return or PR, as used herein throughout, does not include the return earned on the underlying portfolio (i.e. U.S. Treasury bills) which is used as collateral to acquire the futures exposure.

[b]Data for the Standard & Poor's Diversified Trends Indicator (S&P DTI) for the period of 1985–2003 is from the Standard and Poor's White Paper and for the period of 2004 forward is from the Standard & Poor's website.

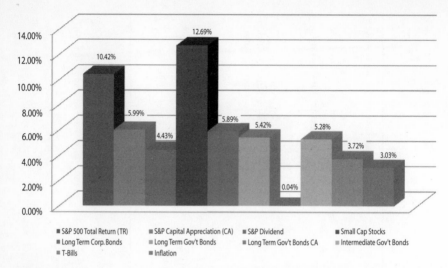

FIGURE B.1   Passive index history—1926–2006 simulated gross returns.
Source: Compiled by Enhanced Alpha Management LP.

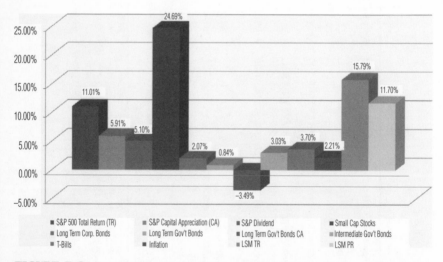

FIGURE B.2   Growth with rising inflation—1961–1968 simulated gross returns.
Source: Compiled by Enhanced Alpha Management LP.

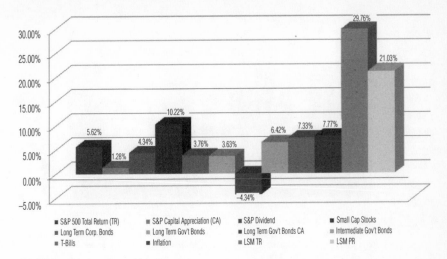

FIGURE B.3 Inflation—1969–1981 simulated statistical information.
Source: Compiled by Enhanced Alpha Management LP.

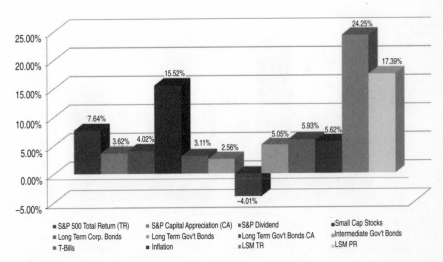

FIGURE B.4 Poor period for equities—1961–1981 simulated statistical information.
Source: Compiled by Enhanced Alpha Management LP.

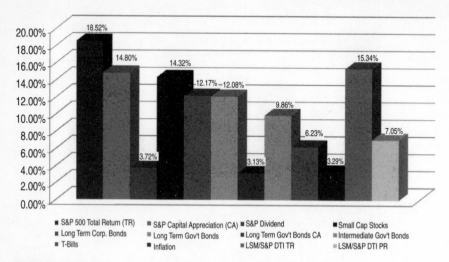

FIGURE B.5 Best period for equities—1982–1999 hypothetical gross returns.
Source: Compiled by Enhanced Alpha Management LP.

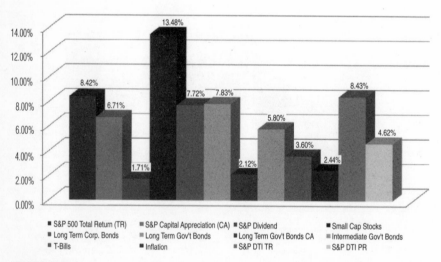

FIGURE B.6 Equities in the last 10 years—1997–2006 simulated statistical information.
Source: Compiled by Enhanced Alpha Management LP.

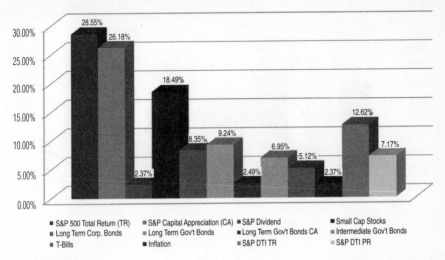

FIGURE B.7 Best years for the S&P 500—1995-1999 simulated statistical information.
Source: Compiled by Enhanced Alpha Management LP.

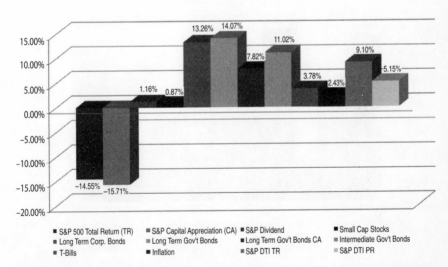

FIGURE B.8 Worst years for the S&P 500—2000-2002 simulated statistical information.
Source: Compiled by Enhanced Alpha Management LP.

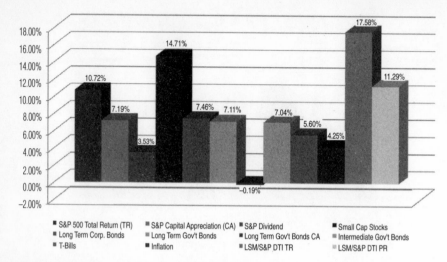

FIGURE B.9 Inception—1961–2006 hypothetical gross returns.
Source: Compiled by Enhanced Alpha Management LP.

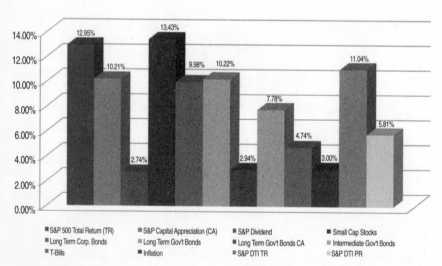

FIGURE B.10 Inception   of   S&P   DTI—1985–2006   simulated   statistical
information.
Source: Compiled by Enhanced Alpha Management LP.

APPENDIX C

Correlation
Statistics

TABLE C.1 Correlation Statistics with S&P GSCI & SPCI[a,b]

	Annual Returns				**Standard Deviation of 12 returns within each year**			
	DTI	**Long-Only**	**S&P GSCI**	**SPCI**	**DTI**	**Long-Only**	**S&P GSCI**	**SPCI**
1970	11.1%	5.8%	7.8%	1.3%	7.0%	7.6%	9.2%	13.3%
1971	3.1%	7.5%	15.8%	−9.8%	7.3%	8.8%	7.3%	6.1%
1972	19.7%	31.8%	36.6%	28.3%	9.7%	13.1%	10.0%	10.1%
1973	87.4%	109.3%	62.8%	64.5%	27.0%	30.2%	30.7%	32.1%
1974	42.3%	26.5%	28.7%	4.1%	13.6%	33.7%	34.7%	34.2%
1975	16.0%	−6.9%	−22.0%	−18.4%	15.6%	22.6%	25.5%	21.2%
1976	26.0%	16.0%	−16.3%	−0.5%	10.1%	11.5%	16.7%	14.5%
1977	23.6%	7.0%	4.6%	−1.6%	6.8%	11.7%	13.6%	13.5%
1978	−5.1%	14.7%	22.3%	16.8%	10.4%	12.5%	15.9%	14.3%
1979	21.5%	20.3%	20.6%	51.6%	7.0%	11.5%	17.2%	17.2%
1980	7.6%	−3.4%	−1.4%	−4.6%	9.8%	15.9%	21.0%	26.9%
1981	28.4%	−27.7%	−33.4%	−29.4%	9.5%	11.1%	10.8%	10.2%
1982	14.9%	−11.2%	−0.1%	−5.6%	6.9%	7.7%	10.9%	9.2%
1983	6.6%	7.7%	6.4%	13.4%	8.5%	8.8%	8.8%	12.8%
1984	11.4%	−19.0%	−8.5%	−16.5%	8.7%	11.4%	10.3%	15.0%
1985	9.8%	14.5%	1.9%	−2.0%	7.9%	8.4%	11.4%	9.5%
1986	4.7%	5.0%	−4.0%	−14.9%	5.4%	13.2%	15.7%	9.1%
1987	8.5%	15.9%	16.6%	16.9%	7.1%	6.2%	13.5%	9.9%
1988	−1.5%	6.8%	19.5%	8.2%	5.8%	7.9%	11.2%	11.6%
1989	8.1%	4.4%	27.3%	−9.0%	6.4%	5.8%	11.7%	7.8%
1990	15.7%	11.4%	19.5%	−4.7%	8.6%	9.5%	29.6%	9.3%

(continues)

191

TABLE C.1 *(Continued)*

	Annual Returns				Standard Deviation of 12 returns within each year			
	DTI	Long-Only	S&P GSCI	SPCI	DTI	Long-Only	S&P GSCI	SPCI
1991	4.4%	−2.3%	−11.2%	−9.7%	4.9%	6.7%	14.6%	8.8%
1992	3.7%	1.0%	0.8%	−1.0%	4.9%	5.5%	5.8%	4.4%
1993	2.1%	1.4%	−15.0%	0.6%	4.0%	4.2%	7.4%	5.7%
1994	4.0%	7.7%	0.8%	13.4%	4.5%	4.5%	12.5%	6.6%
1995	8.1%	8.7%	13.8%	5.0%	4.1%	4.7%	10.8%	10.1%
1996	15.6%	6.9%	27.2%	0.4%	4.8%	4.0%	12.1%	7.8%
1997	1.6%	−5.2%	−18.4%	−4.9%	4.3%	6.1%	15.8%	10.2%
1998	5.0%	−13.0%	−38.8%	−20.1%	3.4%	9.2%	17.7%	13.4%
1999	6.0%	6.5%	34.4%	13.1%	5.6%	9.3%	20.7%	15.7%
2000	11.4%	10.1%	41.1%	36.0%	4.9%	8.3%	22.2%	16.3%
2001	−0.5%	−13.6%	−34.3%	−33.1%	4.2%	6.7%	14.0%	13.1%
2002	1.5%	21.8%	29.9%	37.8%	5.6%	6.6%	17.9%	16.5%
2003	3.4%	17.7%	19.5%	12.3%	7.7%	8.4%	24.7%	16.0%
2004	12.6%	13.6%	15.7%	7.9%	8.0%	7.2%	21.4%	13.5%
2005	4.6%	6.1%	21.6%	33.2%	6.9%	7.4%	24.3%	18.3%
2006	1.4%	0.9%	−19.1%	−2.9%	5.5%	8.3%	20.7%	20.3%

37 years

Cumu	4882%	982%	482%	184%
ROR	11.1%	6.6%	4.9%	2.9%
Volatility	9.5%	12.6%	18.4%	15.9% (annualized standard deviation of monthly results)

Source: This fact sheet was compiled by EAM, LLC based on information believed to be correct, but is subject to revision and adjustment.

[a]This fact sheet contains Simulated Gross Returns which are no indication of future performance. It is for informational purposes only, should not be construed as an investment advice, and does not constitute an offer to buy or sell any investment product or vehicle.

[b]"GSCI" is the "excess return" Goldman Sachs Commodity Index; "SPCI " is the Standard & Poors Commodity Index. Return is the S&P DTI from 1985 forward and the LSM (described below) prior. "Long-Only" is similarly constructed, with the limitation that all positions in the S&P DTI and LSM are forced to always be long.

The methodology for the S&P DTI prior to 2004 is the "classical" method, where trades are effected on the last trading day of each month. Since January 1, 2004, the "Official" S&P DTI is executed on a random day chosen by S&P. The "Return" results were determined using both the "classical" and "official" methods. The "Long Only" results were determined using the classical method for the entire period.

The "LSM" (Long Short Methodology) is a proxy for the S&P DTI used for the period 1961–1984. The LSM uses a similar (but not identical) basket of futures as compared to the S&P DTI. Individual components in the LSM are equally weighted and are not formed into sectors as in the S&P DTI. Also, the LSM basket of components is different to some degree as there were less futures contracts trading during that period.

TABLE C.2 Equity Index Correlation Statistics[a]

	Annual Returns - price return only				Standard Deviation of 12 returns within each year			
	DJ Transports	DJ Utilities	ValueLine G	S&P Index Only	DJ Transports	DJ Utilities	ValueLine G	S&P Index Only
1970	−3.0%	9.1%	−20.6%	0.1%	31.3%	21.9%	24.8%	19.3%
1971	42.1%	−3.4%	9.0%	10.8%	24.5%	11.1%	18.2%	12.9%
1972	−6.8%	1.5%	1.0%	15.6%	15.7%	10.1%	10.8%	5.9%
1973	−13.6%	−25.2%	−35.5%	−17.4%	25.7%	14.8%	23.7%	13.7%
1974	−26.9%	−23.1%	−33.5%	−29.7%	26.6%	23.6%	22.3%	23.1%
1975	20.4%	21.7%	44.4%	31.5%	14.6%	22.4%	28.4%	17.0%
1976	37.3%	29.6%	32.2%	19.1%	17.0%	12.2%	19.8%	13.5%
1977	−8.4%	2.7%	0.5%	−11.5%	11.7%	9.5%	10.0%	9.0%
1978	−4.9%	−11.7%	4.3%	1.1%	20.8%	10.5%	22.0%	15.8%
1979	22.2%	8.5%	24.4%	12.3%	18.1%	13.6%	17.9%	12.9%
1980	57.7%	7.3%	18.3%	25.8%	30.5%	15.3%	21.1%	17.3%
1981	−4.5%	−4.7%	−4.4%	−9.7%	19.5%	13.4%	14.8%	12.2%
1982	17.9%	9.6%	15.3%	14.8%	26.4%	14.4%	19.0%	18.3%
1983	33.1%	10.4%	22.3%	17.3%	12.3%	8.9%	11.8%	9.4%
1984	−6.5%	13.2%	−8.4%	1.4%	17.5%	10.4%	15.1%	13.4%
1985	27.0%	17.0%	20.7%	26.3%	19.0%	13.3%	13.4%	11.5%
1986	14.0%	17.8%	5.0%	14.6%	17.0%	17.6%	15.1%	17.0%
1987	−7.3%	−14.9%	−10.6%	2.0%	33.4%	15.3%	32.6%	29.3%
1988	28.5%	6.4%	15.4%	12.4%	15.4%	12.8%	11.5%	9.8%
1989	22.6%	26.2%	11.2%	27.3%	30.2%	9.9%	10.5%	12.0%
1990	−22.7%	−10.8%	−24.3%	−6.6%	25.4%	13.1%	20.2%	17.4%
1991	49.2%	7.8%	27.2%	26.3%	26.6%	10.3%	14.8%	15.1%
1992	6.7%	−2.3%	7.0%	4.5%	13.7%	10.9%	9.0%	7.1%
1993	21.6%	3.7%	10.7%	7.1%	8.5%	11.2%	7.0%	5.7%
1994	−17.4%	−20.8%	−6.0%	−1.5%	15.0%	13.1%	10.0%	10.2%
1995	36.1%	24.2%	19.3%	34.1%	12.5%	11.0%	7.1%	4.9%
1996	13.9%	3.2%	13.4%	20.3%	13.6%	13.1%	10.1%	10.4%
1997	44.4%	17.4%	21.1%	31.0%	15.5%	10.6%	12.4%	15.2%
1998	−3.3%	14.4%	−3.8%	26.7%	22.2%	13.7%	23.1%	20.6%
1999	−5.5%	−9.3%	−1.4%	19.5%	17.6%	14.4%	13.3%	12.6%
2000	−1.0%	45.5%	−8.7%	−10.1%	28.1%	22.3%	15.0%	16.4%
2001	−10.4%	−28.7%	−6.1%	−13.0%	29.3%	17.5%	24.0%	19.0%
2002	−12.5%	−26.8%	−28.6%	−23.4%	19.1%	22.5%	23.9%	19.7%
2003	30.2%	24.0%	37.4%	26.4%	19.4%	16.6%	15.4%	10.9%
2004	26.3%	25.5%	11.5%	9.0%	13.1%	7.0%	11.8%	6.9%
2005	10.5%	20.9%	2.0%	3.0%	16.9%	11.8%	12.0%	7.5%
2006	8.7%	12.8%	11.0%	13.6%	15.8%	10.0%	10.0%	5.5%

(continues)

TABLE C.2 *(Continued)*

| 37 years | | | | Does not include dividends |

Cumu	2478%	309%	251%	1441%
ROR	9.2%	3.9%	3.4%	7.7%
Volatility	21.7%	15.2%	18.2%	15.2% (annualized standard deviation of monthly results)

Regression Statistics

Correlation of Annual Returns

	DJ Transports	DJ Utilities	ValueLine G	S&P Index Only
DJ Transports	1.00	0.58	0.81	0.75
DJ Utilities		1.00	0.61	0.61
ValueLine G			1.00	0.82
S&P Index Only				1.00

Correlation of STDs

	DJ Transports	DJ Utilities	ValueLine G	S&P Index Only
DJ Transports	1.00	0.43	0.65	0.74
DJ Utilities		1.00	0.61	0.63
ValueLine G			1.00	0.87
S&P Index Only				1.00

Correlation of each index's returns ot its volatility

DJ Transports	DJ Utilities	ValueLine G	S&P Index Only
−0.15	−0.17	−0.30	−0.28

Source: This fact sheet was compiled by EAM, LLC based on information believed to be correct but is subject to revision and adjustment.
[a]This fact sheet contains gross returns which are no indication of future performance. It is for informational purposes only, should not be construed as an investment advice, and does not constitute an offer to buy or sell any investment product or vehicle.

About the Author

Victor Sperandeo is a professional trader and money manager with over 40 years experience in the stock, bond, futures, commodities, and currency markets. He has traded independently for, among others, George Soros, Leon Cooperman, and BT Alex Brown. He is well known for his ability to make money in declining financial markets, and to accurately predict their arrival.

Mr. Sperandeo was featured in the best-selling *The New Market Wizards* and *Super Traders*, has been profiled in *Barron's*, *The Wall Street Journal*, and *Stocks & Commodities*. He has appeared on CNBC, CNN, Fox, and other networks. Mr. Sperandeo has authored two books detailing his philosophy: *Trader Vic—Methods of a Wall Street Master* and *Trader Vic II—Principles of Professional Speculation* (both published by John Wiley & Sons), in addition to co-authoring, with Alvaro Almeidi, *Crashmaker—A Federal Affaire*, a philosophical novel about Wall Street.

Currently, Mr. Sperandeo manages several commodity pools and creates derivative products based on his concepts. He has received two patents in the United States, two in the Bahamas, and one in Australia on financial products using long/short futures structures or indicators and indexes in conjunction with leverage, which add alpha while simultaneously reducing risk. He created the Diversified Trends Index™, which is an evolution of these strategies. It is a rules-based, investable trading methodology incorporating a diversified group of highly liquid, exchange-traded commodities and financial futures contracts, reflecting market expectations of near-term and future price movements. The concept was exclusively licensed to Standard & Poor's as the S&P Diversified Trends Indicator in December 2002. It is now constructed, calculated, and maintained by Standard & Poor's.

Index